"Americans who read this outstanding history of the financial crisis will know, by the end, exactly who created the meltdown of 2008 and how they did it. At times *Reckless Endangerment* unfolds like a hideous mirror image of the classic war movie *Midway*. . . . In Ms. Morgenson and Mr. Rosner's book, a bipartisan parade of famous Washington movers-and-shakers appear in cameos to do some disservice (now largely forgotten) to taxpayers. . . . Perhaps the most amazing part of this tale is that so many of those responsible for the disaster remain in power. [An] excellent story."
—James Freeman, *The Wall Street Journal*

"Most explanations of the financial calamity have been indecipherable to people not fluent in the language of 'credit default swaps' and 'collateralized debt obligations.' The calamity has lacked human faces. No more. Put on asbestos mittens and pick up *Reckless Endangerment,* the scalding new book by Gretchen Morgenson, a *New York Times* columnist, and Joshua Rosner, a housing-finance expert. . . . *Reckless Endangerment* is a study of contemporary Washington, where showing 'compassion' with other people's money pays off in the currency of political power, and currency."   —George F. Will, *The Washington Post*

"The authors are at their best demonstrating how the revolving door between Wall Street and Washington facilitated the charade. . . . Although the rest of America has paid dearly, we seem more recklessly endangered than ever."
—Robert B. Reich, *The New York Times Book Review*

"This book is unmatched in its depth and invaluable to anyone interested in the causes and lessons of the financial crisis."
—Charles Ferguson,
Academy Award–winning director of *Inside Job*

"A chilling account of the reckless disregard for ethical or civilized values at the heart of our financial system."
—Simon Johnson, coauthor of *13 Bankers: The Wall Street Takeover and the Next Financial Meltdown*

"Gretchen Morgenson is a national treasure. . . . In stunning detail, Morgenson exposes the truth behind the worst financial calamity of modern times, weaving a tale that is as mesmerizing as it is horrifying."
—Kurt Eichenwald, *New York Times* bestselling author of *Conspiracy of Fools* and *The Informant*

"Ms. Morgenson and Mr. Rosner have done what is uncommon: produce a book that is substantive but also readable, even entertaining. The result is a Washington 'whodunit' story—the authors report not only what happened, but who did what. . . . Books often are called 'must-read.' But *Reckless Endangerment* really is a 'must-read' for anyone who wants to understand the crash of 2008 and why more government-created economic crises are likely in the future."
—Doug Bandow, *The Washington Times*

"[Morgenson and Rosner] provide the best account yet of how this system went off the rails. . . . *Reckless Endangerment* may be the umpteenth book on the crisis, but it sheds new light on its causes."
—*The Economist*

"Gretchen Morgenson, a *New York Times* business reporter and columnist, is never one to pull her punches—and certainly not in her new book, *Reckless Endangerment*. . . . Throughout the financial crisis, Morgenson has persistently ferreted out instances of wrongdoing in the mortgage market. . . . The authors' arguments are powerful."
—William Cohan, *Financial Times* (UK)

"An engaging and insightful analysis of the subject . . . Morgenson and Rosner are great at filling in the details. . . . One of the more readable and thought-provoking takes on the financial crisis from which the nation is still trying to extricate itself."

—Claude R. Marx, *The Boston Globe*

"A worthy addition to the genre . . . Drawing on their deep expertise, the authors ably trace the legal and regulatory changes that stoked the unsustainable housing boom. . . . Illuminates several small decisions that later had huge, unintended consequences. . . . A particular strength of this book is the number of doubters the authors unearthed. . . . The reader has a sickening sense of missed opportunity as these prophets are ignored or, worse, vilified, by those in a position to halt the mania."

—Pam Luecke, *The New York Times*

"A great revisionist history . . . *Reckless Endangerment* utterly deflates the perceived history of the 2008 crash."

—Mona Charen, *National Review*

ALSO BY GRETCHEN MORGENSON

The Capitalist's Bible

The New Rules of Personal Investing
(with Floyd Norris)

The New York Times Dictionary of Money and Investing
(with Campbell Harvey)

RECKLE$$
ENDANGERMENT

HOW OUTSIZED AMBITION, GREED, AND CORRUPTION CREATED THE WORST FINANCIAL CRISIS OF OUR TIME

GRETCHEN MORGENSON

AND

JOSHUA ROSNER

St. Martin's Griffin
New York

www.stmartins.com

Designed by Meryl Sussman Levavi

The Library of Congress has cataloged the Henry Holt edition as follows:

Morgenson, Gretchen.
   Reckless endangerment : how outsized ambition, greed, and corruption led to economic
armageddon / Gretchen Morgenson, Joshua Rosner.—1st ed.
      p. cm.
   Includes index.
   ISBN 978-0-8050-9120-5 (hardback)
   1. Subprime mortgage loans—United States—History—21st century.   2. Fannie
Mae—History—21st century.   3. Financial crises—United States—History—21st
century. 4. Global Financial Crisis, 2008–2009.   I. Rosner, Joshua.   II. Title.
   HG2040.5.U5M58 2011
   332.7'20973—dc22

                                                                      2010047594

ISBN 978-1-250-00879-4 (trade paperback)

First published in hardcover by Times Books, an imprint of Henry Holt and Company

First St. Martin's Griffin Edition: June 2012

10 9 8 7 6 5 4 3 2 1

To Paul and Conor: God's gifts to me.

—G.M.

⇌

*This book is dedicated to my mother and to the memory of my
father, who taught me that our civic obligations are our highest
calling. It is also dedicated to my son, Noah, my greatest joy and
a constant reminder of why those obligations matter.*

—J.R.

CAST OF CHARACTERS

FANNIE MAE AND FRIENDS

JAMES A. JOHNSON, chief executive officer, Fannie Mae, 1991–1998, director, Goldman Sachs; former director, KB Home; former chairman of The Brookings Institution and The Kennedy Center for the Performing Arts

FRANKLIN DELANO RAINES, former director, Office of Management and Budget; chief executive officer, Fannie Mae, 1999–2005

DAVID O. MAXWELL, chief executive officer, Fannie Mae, 1981–1991

WILLIAM JEFFERSON CLINTON, forty-second president of the United States

BARNEY FRANK, Democratic congressman from Massachusetts

ROBERT ZOELLICK, executive vice president, Fannie Mae, 1993–1997

THOMAS DONILON, head of government affairs, Fannie Mae, 1999–2005

LARRY SUMMERS, deputy secretary, United States Treasury, 1995–1999. Secretary of the Treasury, 1999–2001

ROBERT RUBIN, Secretary of the United States Treasury, 1995–1999

RICHARD HOLBROOKE, cofounder with James Johnson of Public Strategies, consulting firm

LELAND BRENDSEL, former chief executive, Freddie Mac, 1987–2003

TIMOTHY HOWARD, chief financial officer, Fannie Mae, 1990–2005

THOMAS NIDES, executive vice president, human resources, Fannie Mae, 1998–2001

HERB MOSES, community affairs official, Fannie Mae, 1991–1998, and former partner of Barney Frank

R. GLENN HUBBARD, Columbia Graduate School of Business

PETER ORSZAG, senior economist, Council of Economic Advisors, 1995–1996

BRUCE VENTO, Democratic representative from Minnesota, 1977–2000

ROBERT BENNETT, Republican senator from Utah, 1993–2010

KIT BOND, Republican senator from Missouri, 1987–2003

STEPHEN FRIEDMAN, former director, Fannie Mae, and former chief executive, Goldman Sachs

MAXINE WATERS, Democratic representative from California

DOUBTERS AND THOSE WHO PUSHED BACK

DEAN BAKER, codirector, Center for Economic & Policy Research

ANNE CANFIELD, lobbyist for community banks and author of *The GSE Report*

MARVIN PHAUP, former director, Financial Studies/Budget Process group, Congressional Budget Office

JUNE O'NEILL, director, Congressional Budget Office, 1995–1999

WALKER TODD, former chief counsel at Federal Reserve Bank of Cleveland

RICHARD S. CARNELL, assistant secretary for financial institutions, United States Treasury

EDWARD DEMARCO, director, office of Financial Institutions Policy, Treasury Department, 1993–2003

WILLIAM LIGHTFOOT, former D.C. Council member

ARMANDO FALCON, director, Office of Federal Housing Enterprise Oversight, 1995–2005

ROY E. BARNES, governor of Georgia, 1999–2003, and predatory lending adversary

WILLIAM J. BRENNAN JR., former director, Home Defense Program, Atlanta Legal Aid

JANET AHMAD, president, Homeowners for Better Building, San Antonio

MARC COHODES, former money manager, Marin County, California

SUBPRIME LENDERS AND THEIR ENABLERS

ANGELO MOZILO, cofounder and former chief executive, Countrywide Financial

WRIGHT H. ANDREWS JR., subprime lending lobbyist

WALTER FALK, founder, Metropolitan Mortgage of Miami

DAVID SILIPIGNO, founder, National Finance Company

J. TERRELL BROWN, former chief executive, United Companies Financial

SCOTT HARTMAN, former chairman, NovaStar

W. LANCE ANDERSON, former chief executive, NovaStar

BRUCE KARATZ, former chief executive, KB Home

HENRY CISNEROS, secretary, Housing & Urban Development, 1993–1997

MURRAY ZOOTA, former chief executive, Fremont Investment & Loan

DAVID MCINTYRE, former chief executive, Fremont Corporation

LOUIS RAMPINO, former chief executive, Fremont General

FECKLESS REGULATORS

TIMOTHY F. GEITHNER, president, Federal Reserve Bank of New York, 2003–2008

ROGER FERGUSON, vice-chairman of the Federal Reserve, 1999–2006

ANDREW CUOMO, secretary, Housing & Urban Development, 1997–2001

ROBERT PEACH and JOHN MCCARTHY, researchers at the Federal Reserve Bank of New York

ALAN GREENSPAN, chairman, Federal Reserve Board, 1987–2006

FREDERIC MISHKIN, governor, Federal Reserve Board, 2006–2008

INTRODUCTION

This is not the first book to be written about the epic financial crisis of 2008 and neither will it be the last. But Josh and I believe that *Reckless Endangerment* is different from the others in two important ways. It identifies powerful people whose involvement in the debacle has not yet been chronicled and it connects key incidents that have seemed heretofore unrelated.

As a veteran business reporter and columnist for the *New York Times*, I've covered my share of big and juicy financial scandals over the years. For more than a decade as an established financial and policy analyst, Josh has seen just about every trick there is.

But none of the scandals and financial improprieties we experienced before felt nearly as momentous or mystifying as the events that culminated in this most recent economic storm. That's why we felt that this calamity, and the conduct that brought it on, needed to be thoroughly investigated, detailed, and explained.

The disaster was so great—its impact so far-reaching—that we knew we were not the only ones who wanted to understand how such a thing could happen in America in the new millennium.

Even now, more than four years after the cracks in the financial foundation could no longer be ignored, people remain bewildered about the causes of the steepest economic downturn since the Great Depression. And they wonder why we are still mired in it.

Then there is the maddening aftermath—watching hundreds of billions of taxpayer dollars get funneled to rescue some of the very institutions that drove the country into the ditch.

The American people realize they've been robbed. They're just not sure by whom.

Reckless Endangerment is an economic whodunit, on an international scale. But instead of a dead body as evidence, we have trillions of dollars in investments lost around the world, millions of Americans jettisoned from their homes and fourteen million U.S. workers without jobs. Such is the nature of this particular crime.

Recognizing that a disaster this large could not have occurred overnight, Josh and I set out to detail who did it, how, and why. We found that this was a crisis that crept up, building almost imperceptibly over the past two decades. More disturbing, it was the result of actions taken by people at the height of power in both the public and the private sectors, people who continue, even now, to hold sway in the corridors of Washington and Wall Street.

Reckless Endangerment is a story of what happens when unfettered risk taking, with an eye to huge personal paydays, gains the upper hand in corporate executive suites and on Wall Street trading floors. It is a story of the consequences of regulators who are captured by the institutions they are charged with regulating. And it is a story of what happens when Washington decides, in its infinite wisdom, that every living, breathing citizen should own a home.

Josh and I felt compelled to write this book because we are angry that the American economy was almost wrecked by a crowd of self-interested, politically influential, and arrogant people who have not been held accountable for their actions. We also believe that it is important to credit the courageous and civically minded people who tried to warn of the impending crisis but who were run over or ignored by their celebrated adversaries.

Familiar as we are with the ways of Wall Street, neither Josh nor I was surprised that the large investment firms played such a prominent role in the debacle. But we are disturbed that so many who contributed to the mess are still in positions of power or have risen to even higher ranks. And while some architects of the crisis may no longer command center stage, they remain respected members of the business or regulatory community. The failure to hold central figures accountable for their actions sets a dangerous precedent. A system where perpetrators of such a crime are allowed to slip quietly from the scene is just plain wrong.

In the end, analyzing the financial crisis, its origins and its framers, requires identifying powerful participants who would rather not be named. It requires identifying events that seemed meaningless when they occurred but had unintended consequences that have turned out to be integral to the outcome. It requires an unrelenting search for the facts, an ability to speak truth to power.

Investigating the origins of the financial crisis means shedding light on exceedingly dark corners in Washington and on Wall Street. Hidden in these shadows are people, places, and incidents that can help us understand the nature of this disaster so that we can keep anything like it from happening again.

PROLOGUE

More Americans should own their own homes, for reasons that are economic and tangible, and reasons that are emotional and intangible, but go to the heart of what it means to harbor, to nourish, to expand the American Dream.

—WILLIAM JEFFERSON CLINTON,
forty-second president of the United States,
November 1994

The president of the United States was preaching to the choir when he made that proclamation in 1994, just two years into his first term. Facing an enthusiastic crowd at the National Association of Realtors' annual meeting in Washington, D.C., Clinton launched the National Partners in Homeownership, a private-public cooperative with one goal: raising the numbers of homeowners across America.

Determined to reverse what some in Washington saw as a troubling decline of homeownership during the previous decade, Clinton urged private enterprise to join with public agencies to ensure that by the year 2000, some 70 percent of the populace would own their own homes.

An owner in every home. It was the prosperous, 1990s version of the Depression-era "A Chicken in Every Pot."

With homeownership standing at around 64 percent, Clinton's program was ambitious. But it was hardly groundbreaking. The

U.S. government had often used housing to achieve its public policy goals. Abraham Lincoln's Homestead Act of 1862 gave away public land in the nation's western precincts to individuals committed to developing it. And even earlier, during the Revolutionary War, government land grants were a popular way for an impoverished America to pay soldiers who fought the British.

Throughout the American experience, a respect, indeed a reverence, for homeownership has been central. The Constitution, as first written, limited the right to vote to white males who owned property, for example. Many colonists came to America because their prospects of becoming landowners were far better in the New World than they were in seventeenth- and eighteenth-century Europe.

Still, Clinton's homeownership plan differed from its predecessors. The strategy was not a reaction to an economic calamity, as was the case during the Great Depression. Back then, the government created the Home Owners' Loan Corporation, which acquired and refinanced one million delinquent mortgages between 1933 and 1936.

On the contrary, the homeownership strategy of 1994 came about as the economy was rebounding from the recession of 1990 and '91 and about to enter a long period of enviable growth. It also followed an extended era of prosperity for consumer-oriented banks during most of the 1980s when these institutions began extending credit to consumers in a more "democratic" manner for the first time.

Rather than pursue its homeownership program alone, as it had done in earlier efforts, the government enlisted help in 1995 from a wide swath of American industry. Banks, home builders, securities firms, Realtors—all were asked to pull together in a partnership made up of 65 top national organizations and 131 smaller groups.

The partnership would achieve its goals by "making homeownership more affordable, expanding creative financing, simplifying the home buying process, reducing transaction costs, changing conventional methods of design and building less expensive houses, among other means."

Amid the hoopla surrounding the partnership announcement, little attention was paid to its unique and most troubling aspect: It was unheard of for regulators to team up this closely with those they were charged with policing.

And nothing was mentioned about the strategy's ultimate consequence—the distortion of the definition of homeownership—gutting its role as the mechanism for most families to fund their retirement years or pass on wealth to their children or grandchildren.

Instead, in just a few short years, all of the venerable rules governing the relationship between borrower and lender went out the window, starting with the elimination of the requirements that a borrower put down a substantial amount of cash in a property, verify his income, and demonstrate an ability to service his debts.

With baby boomers entering their peak earning years and the number of two-income families on the rise, banks selling Americans on champagne hopes and caviar dreams were about to become the most significant engine of economic growth in the nation. After Congress changed the tax code in 1986, eliminating the deductibility of interest payments on all consumer debt except those charged on home mortgages, the stage was set for housing to become Americans' most favored asset.

Of course, banks and other private-sector participants in the partnership stood to gain significantly from an increase in homeownership. But nothing as crass as profits came up at the Partners in Homeownership launch. Instead, the focus was on the "deeply-rooted and almost universally held belief that homeownership provides crucial benefits that merit continued public support." These included job creation, financial security (when an individual buys a home that rises in value), and more stable neighborhoods (people don't trash places they own).

In other words, homeownership for all was a win/win/win.

A 1995 briefing from the Department of Housing and Urban Development did concede that the validity of the homeownership claims "is so widely accepted that economists and social scientists have seldom tested them." But that note of caution was lost amid bold assertions of homeownership's benefits.

"When we boost the number of homeowners in our country," Clinton said in a 1995 speech, "we strengthen our economy, create jobs, build up the middle class, and build better citizens."

Clinton's prediction about the middle class was perhaps the biggest myth of all. Rather than building it up, the Partners in Homeownership wound up decimating the middle class. It left Americans in this large economic group groaning under a mountain of debt and withdrawing cash from their homes as a way to offset stagnant incomes.

It took a little more than a decade after the partnership's launch for its devastating impact to be felt. By 2008, the American economy was in tatters, jobs were disappearing, and the nation's middle class was imperiled by free-falling home prices and hard-hit retirement accounts. Perhaps most shocking, homeownership was no longer the route to a secure spot in middle-class America. For millions of families, especially those in the lower economic segments of the population, borrowing to buy a home had put them squarely on the road to personal and financial ruin.

Fueled by dubious industry practices supported by many in Congress and unchecked by most of the regulators charged with oversight of the lending process, the homeownership drive helped to plunge the nation into the worst economic crisis since the Great Depression.

Truly this was an unprecedented partnership.

But what few have recognized is how the partners in the Clinton program embraced a corrupt corporate model that was also created to promote homeownership. This was the model devised by Fannie Mae, the huge and powerful government-sponsored mortgage finance company set up in 1938 to make it easier for borrowers to buy homes in Depression-ravaged America. Indeed, by the early 1990s, well before the government's partnership drive began, Fannie Mae had perfected the art of manipulating lawmakers, eviscerating its regulators, and enriching its executives. All in the name of expanding homeownership.

Under the direction of James A. Johnson, Fannie Mae's calculating and politically connected chief executive, the company capitalized on its government ties, building itself into the largest and most powerful financial institution in the world. In 2008, however, the colossus would fail, requiring hundreds of billions in taxpayer backing to keep it afloat. Fannie Mae became the quintessential example of a company whose risk taking allowed its executives to amass great wealth. But when those gambles went awry, the taxpayers had to foot the bill.

This failure was many years in the making. Beginning in the early 1990s, Johnson's position atop Fannie Mae gave him an extraordinary place astride Washington and Wall Street. His job as chief executive of the company presented him with an extremely powerful policy tool to direct the nation's housing strategy. In his hands, however, that tool became a cudgel. With it, he threatened his enemies and regulators while rewarding his supporters. And, of course, there was the fortune he accrued.

Perhaps even more important, Johnson's tactics were watched closely and subsequently imitated by others in the private sector, interested in creating their own power and profit machines. Fannie Mae led the way in relaxing loan underwriting standards, for example, a shift that was quickly followed by private lenders. Johnson's company also automated the lending process so that loan decisions could be made in minutes and were based heavily on a borrower's credit history, rather than on a more comprehensive financial profile as had been the case in the past.

Eliminating the traditional due diligence conducted by lenders soon became the playbook for financial executives across the country. Wall Street, always ready to play the role of enabler, provided the money for these dubious loans, profiting mightily. Without the Wall Street firms giving billions of dollars to reckless lenders, hundreds of billions of bad loans would never have been made.

Finally, Fannie Mae's aggressive lobbying and its methods for

neutering regulators and opponents were also copied by much of
the financial industry. Regulators across the country were either
beaten back or lulled into complacency by the banks they were
supposed to police.

How Clinton's calamitous Homeownership Strategy was born,
nurtured, and finally came to blow up the American economy is
the story of greed and good intentions, corporate corruption and
government support. It is also a story of pretty lies told by politicians, company executives, bankers, regulators, and borrowers.

And yet, there were those who questioned the merits of the
homeownership drive and tried to alert regulators and policymakers to its unintended consequences.

A handful of analysts and investors, for example, tried to warn
of the rising tide of mortgage swindlers; they were met with a deaf-
ening silence. Consumer lawyers, seeing the poisonous nature of
many home loans, tried to outlaw them. But they were beaten back
by an army of lenders and their lobbyists. Some brave souls in academia argued that renting a home was, for many, better than owning. They were refuted by government studies using manipulated
figures or flawed analysis to conclude that homeownership was a
desired goal for all.

Even the credit-rating agencies, supposedly neutral assayers
of risks in mortgage securities, quelled attempts to rein in predatory lending.

All the critics were either willfully ignored or silenced by well-
funded, self-interested, and sometimes vicious opposition. Their
voices were drowned out by the homeownership trust, a vertically
integrated, public-private housing machine whose members were
driven either by ideology or the vast profits that rising homeownership would provide.

The consortium was too big and too powerful for anyone to take
on. Its reach extended from the mortgage broker on Main Street to
the Wall Street traders and finally to the hallowed halls of Congress. It was unstoppable.

Because housing finance was heavily regulated, government participation was vital to the homeownership push. And Washington played not one but three starring roles in creating the financial crisis of 2008. First, it unleashed the mortgage mania by helping to relax basic rules of lending that had been in place for decades. Then its policymakers looked the other way as the mortgage binge enriched a few and imperiled many. Even after the disaster hit and the trillion-dollar bailouts began, Congress and administration officials did little to repair the damaged system and ensure that such a travesty could not happen again.

This was a reckless endangerment of the entire nation by people at the highest levels of Washington and corporate America.

Barney Frank, the powerful Massachusetts Democrat and ardent supporter of Fannie Mae, summed it up perfectly back in March 2005. He had just delivered a luncheon speech on housing at the Four Seasons Hotel in Georgetown.

Walking up from the lower-level conference room where he had addressed the Institute of International Bankers, Frank was asked whether he had considered the possible downsides to the homeownership drive. Was he afraid, for instance, that easy lending programs could wind up luring many of his constituents into homes they could not ultimately afford? Was he concerned that, after the groundbreaking and ribbon-cutting ceremonies were forgotten, the same people he had put into homes would be knocking on his door, complaining of being trapped in properties and facing financial ruin?

Frank brushed off the questioner. "We'll deal with that problem if it happens," he barked.

CHAPTER ONE

*I'm not big on losing. Somebody may have mentioned
that to you.*

—JAMES A. JOHNSON,
chief executive officer, Fannie Mae

It was a cool and partly cloudy day in May 2002, when Augsburg College seniors gathered in their downtown Minneapolis campus to collect the undergraduate degrees they had worked so hard to earn. Before them stood James Arthur Johnson, a major donor to the college and a Minnesota boy, made good. A man who had climbed to the top of two cutthroat worlds—corporate America and the Washington power scene—Johnson had been invited to provide guidance and advice to the class of 2002. He was returning to his roots that day in Minneapolis—Johnson's mother, Adeline, a schoolteacher, had been an "Auggie" graduate seventy-one years earlier.

Invoking Adeline, his father, Alfred, and his Norwegian emigrant grandparents, Johnson urged the graduates to pursue their careers with integrity and honesty. Just months after a rogue energy company called Enron had hurtled into bankruptcy, faith in corporate America and the nation's markets had been shaken.

Avuncular, professorial, and attractive, Johnson delivered a reassuring message: "Good ethics are good business."

It was the kind of advice to be expected from a man who just three years earlier had presided over Fannie Mae, one of the world's largest and most prestigious financial institutions. Johnson had then gone on to serve on the boards of five large and well-known public companies, including the mighty investment bank, Goldman Sachs. "What we want from friends—honesty and integrity, energy and optimism, commitment to family and community, hard work and high ethical standards—are the same qualities we need from American business," he told the graduates.

But as he wound up his speech, the fifty-nine-year-old Johnson struck a wistful tone. Just before George Bernard Shaw died, Johnson said, the playwright had been asked to name a famous deceased man—artist, statesman, philosopher, or writer—whom he missed the most.

Johnson recounted Shaw's reply: "The man I miss most is the man I could have been."

It was a surprising, almost regretful comment from a man who had it all—wealth, power, prestige, and access to men and women at the highest levels of government. Johnson was not only the former chief executive of Fannie Mae, the quasi-government mortgage finance giant; he had also run the Kennedy Center for the Performing Arts in Washington and the Brookings Institution, an influential D.C.-based liberal think tank. Even as he addressed the graduates, he was vice-chairman of a blue-chip private equity firm, Perseus Capital.

A regular in Washington's halls of power, Johnson had also been a top adviser to Walter Mondale, when he was vice president of the United States. John Kerry, the 2004 Democratic presidential nominee, had also relied on Johnson for guidance.

Just one of Johnson's achievements, by almost anybody's reckoning, would have placed him in the top echelons of success.

And yet, for all of his accomplishments, Johnson's ultimate aspirations in Washington remained unmet that May. "The man I could have been" was a likely nod to his longtime desire to become

Treasury secretary of the United States, people who know him say.

But that appointment never came. Nor is it likely to. In the wake of the mortgage crisis of 2008, Johnson's legacy has become decidedly darker. Sure, he retired as vice-chairman of Fannie Mae in 1999, almost a decade before the financial debacle took hold. But Johnson's command-and-control management of the mortgage finance giant and his hardball tactics to ensure Fannie Mae's dominance amid increasing calls for oversight are crucial to understanding the origins of the worst financial debacle since the Great Depression.

Little known outside the Beltway, Johnson was the financial industry's leader in buying off Congress, manipulating regulators, and neutralizing critics, former colleagues say. His strategy of promoting Fannie Mae and protecting its lucrative government association, largely through intense lobbying, immense campaign contributions, and other assistance given to members of Congress, would be mimicked years later by companies such as Countrywide Financial, an aggressive subprime mortgage lender, Goldman Sachs, Citigroup, and others.

Perhaps more crucial, Johnson's manipulation of his company's regulators provided a blueprint for the financial industry, showing them how to control their controllers and produce the outcome they desired: lax regulation and freedom from any restraints that might hamper their risk taking and curb their personal wealth creation.

Under Johnson, Fannie Mae led the way in encouraging loose lending practices among the banks whose loans the company bought. A Pied Piper of the financial sector, Johnson led both the private and public sectors down a path that led directly to the credit crisis of 2008. It took more than a decade to assemble the machinery needed to create the housing mania. But it took only a year or two for the juggernaut to collapse in a heap, destroying millions of jobs and retirement accounts, and devastating borrowers.

After years of crisis coverage in the media, multiple government investigations, and numerous books on the topic, Johnson's role in the mortgage maelstrom has escaped scrutiny. Remarkably, his reputation as a mover and shaker in both business and government remains largely intact, even after the September 2008 taxpayer takeover of an insolvent Fannie Mae, at a cost of hundreds of billions of dollars.

And while others on Wall Street and in the mortgage lending industry have been damaged by the crisis, Johnson is still viewed as a D.C. power broker, respected corporate director, and philanthropist. He enjoys a luxurious life, splitting time between homes in such glamorous locales as Ketchum, Idaho; Palm Desert, California; and a penthouse apartment atop the Ritz-Carlton in Washington, D.C.'s Georgetown neighborhood.

Johnson continues to hobnob with highly placed friends in government and industry—indeed, before Barack Obama was elected president of the United States, Johnson hosted a party to honor the candidate at his $5.6 million Washington apartment.

Some of Johnson's past associations did come back to haunt him in the summer of 2008, however. Obama had asked Johnson to help sift through possible vice presidential candidates but just weeks after he began the search, details emerged of sweetheart mortgage deals Johnson had received from Countrywide Financial, the nation's largest purveyor of toxic subprime loans during the lending boom. Johnson was forced to resign quickly from the Obama team.

But Johnson's involvement in the mortgage crisis goes far beyond receiving low-cost loans from Countrywide and its chief executive, Angelo Mozilo. Former colleagues say that Johnson, during his years running Fannie Mae, was the original, if anonymous, architect of what became the disastrous homeownership strategy promulgated by William Jefferson Clinton in 1994. Johnson, after becoming chief executive of Fannie Mae in 1991 and under the auspices of promoting homeownership, partnered with home builders, lenders, consumer groups, and friends in Congress to transform Fannie Mae into the largest and most influential financial institution in the world.

"Clinton was clearly coordinating with him—they had the

same goals at the same time," said Edward Pinto, former chief credit officer at Fannie Mae, who is a consultant. With other high-level Democrats on his side, Johnson beat back all attempts to rein in Fannie Mae's operations or growth plans.

Although Johnson left Fannie Mae's executive suite in 1999, his stewardship of the company not only opened the door to the mortgage meltdown, it virtually guaranteed it, former colleagues said.

Johnson's many peers in the financial and homebuilding industries watched closely as he remade the government-created and -sponsored Fannie Mae from a political lapdog of housing policy into an aggressive, highly politicized attack dog. In the meantime, he created enormous wealth for himself and his executives even as the company took on outsized risks.

Fannie also funneled huge campaign contributions to supporters in Congress. Between 1989 and 2009, according to the Center for Responsive Politics, Fannie Mae spent roughly $100 million on lobbying and political contributions.

Johnson's most crucial win was making sure that Congress was the company's boss, not the Office of Federal Housing Enterprise Oversight (OFHEO), a regulator created in 1992 to watch over the company. With Congress as his de facto overseer and with millions of dollars to hand out to lawmakers, Johnson could be confident his company would always receive the support it sought on Capitol Hill.

"Fannie has this grandmotherly image," a congressional aide told a writer for *The International Economy* magazine in 1999. But when it came to opponents, "they'll castrate you, decapitate you, tie you up, and throw you in the Potomac. They're absolutely ruthless."

As Daniel Mudd, a former Fannie Mae executive, wrote in an e-mail after Johnson's departure from the company: "The old political reality was that we always won, we took no prisoners, and we faced little organized political opposition."

⇔

Fannie Mae, which was originally known as the Federal National Mortgage Association, was not always ruthless and all-powerful.

Like many financial institutions, it had a near-death experience in the 1980s when interest rates rocketed into the high teens. Technically insolvent in the early part of the decade because its mortgage portfolio carried interest rates well below prevailing levels, the mortgage finance company was delivered from the brink by an executive named David O. Maxwell.

The U.S. government had created Fannie Mae in 1938 to buy mortgages from banks that loaned money to homebuyers. Fannie Mae did not lend directly to borrowers, but by buying mortgages from banks the company reduced consumer reliance on mortgages that were short-term in nature, hard to refinance, and issued by fly-by-night lenders. It was a Depression-era creation designed to ease financing costs for borrowers still recovering from the economic devastation of the 1930s.

In 1968, President Lyndon B. Johnson changed the company from an agency of the government into a partially private entity that issued common stock to public investors. With the costs of the Vietnam War escalating, the president's idea was to get the company's liabilities off the government's balance sheet. It still had close ties to the government and perquisites that other finance companies could only dream of, but by the 1980s, Fannie Mae was a financial colossus that had to please both shareholders and the government. Its shares were first offered to the public in 1989.

Before becoming the head of Fannie Mae in 1981, Maxwell had a career that spanned private industry and public service. He had been president of a mortgage insurance company and then in 1970 became general counsel at the Department of Housing and Urban Development, the federal agency that oversaw the Federal Housing Administration loan programs and also served as part-time regulator to Fannie Mae and its sibling, Freddie Mac.

Maxwell was a brilliant manager and a natural leader, according to those who worked under him. "He was a Brahmin," one former employee said. Unlike Johnson, the man he chose to be his successor, Maxwell was a businessman, not a politician.

While Fannie Mae was faltering, James A. Johnson was

overseeing the 1984 presidential campaign of Walter Mondale, a fellow Minnesotan who had been vice president under Jimmy Carter.

Johnson was born on Christmas Eve in 1942 to Alfred and Adeline Rasmussen Johnson, residents of Benson, Minnesota, a town of four thousand. Democratic politics was the mainstay in the house—Alfred Johnson was Speaker of the House in Minnesota during the 1950s. Adeline was a schoolteacher.

Johnson's upbringing was typical of a 1950s Scandinavian family. Words were few and displays of affection even fewer. In an interview with the *Washington Post*, he described life at home with his parents and older sister, Marilyn.

"There was no touching, no kissing, no 'I-love-yous,'" he said. "On the other hand, there could not have been a warmer, more protective, more supportive unspoken environment. If you go to the maximum of what you get through the unspoken, that's where we were. If you go to the furthest you can get in not touching and not speaking, I think we were there."

Johnson was interested in politics early on, working on campaigns locally even before he could vote. As a sophomore at the University of Minnesota, he won election for student body president; after graduation, he moved to Princeton, where he received a master's degree in public policy at the Woodrow Wilson School in 1968. He joined the antiwar movement and avoided serving in Vietnam on the strength of a student deferment. He worked on Senator Eugene McCarthy's campaign in 1968, and in 1972 he volunteered for George McGovern.

In 1969, Johnson attended a strategy session convened by antiwar activists in Martha's Vineyard. He roomed with William Jefferson Clinton, then an unknown twenty-two-year-old Georgetown University graduate.

When he wasn't campaigning, he worked at the Minneapolis department store, Dayton Hudson, and taught at Princeton.

Johnson, a tall and trim man who favors horn-rimmed glasses, met Mondale through his father, who knew him from Minnesota politics. Mondale recalled the meeting in a 2008 interview with

MinnPost.com. "As I remember it," Mondale said, "he came by to visit. He was bright and interested and so I hired him."

He became his aide-de-camp both when Mondale was a senator and later when he became vice president under Jimmy Carter in 1977.

After losing the 1980 election as the vice presidential candidate, Mondale decided to run for the presidency in 1984, hoping to unseat the popular Ronald Reagan by making him appear to be disengaged. Mondale chose Johnson, only forty years old at the time, to be his campaign chairman. Johnson's campaign machinery was highly centralized, with decisions made by a small circle of trusted officials. Prominent Democrats described the campaign as insular, arrogant, and "uncomfortable with outsiders." The *New York Times* quoted an influential party official this way: "There has been a real effort to keep out individuals who threaten that structure."

Such a setup was vintage Johnson. During the presidential race, advice from party leaders was not requested by the Mondale campaign, and ignored if it came. A highly polished operation that worked more like a hushed corporate boardroom than a frenetic presidential contest, the campaign was a closed shop, in the words of a midlevel aide. "Only a very few people know what's going on and why, and there's a sense of exclusivity, almost secrecy, that's potentially very damaging," the official said.

Those trying to plumb Johnson's inner reaches found it to be "a lot like the Minnesota pastime of ice fishing." The man was all politics all the time. During the Mondale campaign, the candidate's family and friends put together a book of recipes for supporters. All the staffers provided their favorites, according to Mondale's recollections recounted in MinnPost.com.

"In his recipe, Jim said you put a hot dog in steaming water, put the hot dog in a bun, open a can of Coke and turn on the 6 o'clock news," Mondale recalled.

There was no doubt about Johnson's ambitions. A political junkie, he had been "preparing himself for 15 years to be White House chief of staff," according to one staffer.

It was not meant to be, alas. Mondale never caught on with

voters. The bland and buttoned-down Midwesterner lost the election in a landslide, winning only one state—his home territory of
Minnesota.

After the defeat, Johnson returned to the Washington-based
political consulting firm he had started with Richard Holbrooke,
an investment banker who was a former assistant secretary of
state for Asia. In 1985 the firm—Public Strategies—was bought
by Shearson Lehman Brothers, a Wall Street investment bank.
Both Johnson and Holbrooke became managing directors at the
firm and remained in Washington.

Around this time, Johnson met David Maxwell, the Fannie Mae
head, at a dinner party in Washington. It was a fateful introduction
that would not only bring immense wealth and power to Johnson
but would also pave the way for the housing bubble years later.

Although their meeting was strictly social, Maxwell saw Johnson as someone who might help him protect Fannie Mae. The
political winds were shifting, thanks to the conservative, small-
government approach of the Reagan administration, and Fannie
Mae, a company with lucrative federal ties, was at risk.

Fannie Mae was now a private company with shareholders but
it was also a quasi-government enterprise with a raft of lush perquisites associated with its federal ties. The biggest benefit of its
government association was the impression held by investors that
Fannie was backed by the full faith and credit of the United States,
a view that translated to far cheaper borrowing costs, fully one
half of one percentage point for the company.

Now there was talk of making Fannie Mae a fully private company, removing its government benefits. In addition to the lower
borrowing costs, these benefits included a $2.5 billion line of
credit at the U.S. Treasury, an exemption from paying state and
local taxes, and freedom from filing financial statements with the
Securities and Exchange Commission.

Eliminating these perks would make Fannie Mae far less profitable and turn its business model upside down, Maxwell knew. Perhaps Johnson, an investment banker with Washington sensibilities,
could provide guidance on how to fend off the privatization crew.

"We needed some analytical work done at Fannie Mae to help chart our future course," Maxwell said of his meeting with Johnson in an interview with the *Post*. "There was a lot of pressure from the Reagan administration to give up our federal ties and privatize the company. People like [Reagan budget director] David Stockman were very determined. We just wanted to take a look at exactly what this might mean and whether it was possible to do it."

Shearson Lehman was hired to conduct the privatization analysis and Johnson oversaw the task. The report they produced in 1989 concluded that privatization was not feasible. "To put it another way," Maxwell said, "at this point in time it was a pretty ridiculous proposition."

Ridiculous or no, the threat continued to hang over the company. A slew of losses at savings and loans across the country that had also threatened Fannie's solvency earlier in the decade, and the ensuing $500 billion in taxpayer funds to clean up the mess, focused Congress on the possibility that bad loans might also be lurking on the books at Fannie Mae and Freddie Mac. In 1989, lawmakers ordered a study of both government-sponsored enterprises.

While this analysis was going on, Maxwell began preparing for his retirement. In 1990, he recruited Johnson to be vice-chairman of Fannie Mae and a member of its board. It was a clear sign that Johnson would succeed Maxwell at the helm of Fannie Mae.

"David Maxwell had built a very good company and ran it well," recalled one of his lieutenants. "Maxwell recognized that there were risks. But in Johnson, he picked the wrong heir apparent."

During the transition from Maxwell to Johnson, a young man who was looking to start his career recalled lunching with Fannie Mae's new chief executive at the Metropolitan Club in Washington. Johnson's laserlike focus on how he planned to monetize the company's government ties was remarkable, he said. There was little talk of Fannie Mae's social purpose; it was all about how much money he would make if he came to work at the company.

As soon as Johnson took over Fannie Mae he began to demonstrate his mastery of political patronage and populist spin. Hoping to tamp down a controversy that erupted after the disclosure of Maxwell's $27 million retirement package, real money in 1991, Fannie Mae announced that Maxwell had agreed to contribute his final bonus payment of $5.5 million to the Fannie Mae Foundation. It, in turn, would dispense the $5.5 million to low-income housing projects.

When Johnson took over, the tone at the top of Fannie Mae began to change. This was partly because the political spotlight was trained on the company, insiders say, and partly because the new chief executive was such a political animal. Maxwell had run the company as a sleepy utility that facilitated mortgage lending, as its charter required. But under Johnson, Fannie's primary goal changed to protecting—at all costs—the company's government ties and the riches that sprang from them.

Protecting the company's federal sponsorship was all the more crucial, insiders say, because Johnson intended to expand Fannie's portfolio and balance sheet significantly. Along the way, he and his lieutenants would be able to enrich themselves on the government's dime.

Fannie Mae was on sound financial footing when Maxwell retired in January 1991, in spite of the massive losses the company had suffered in the savings and loan crisis. Maxwell told a *Post* reporter "it would take an event of such cataclysmic proportions as to result in a change of our form of government to put this company under."

The cataclysm was, in fact, just fifteen years away.

⇌

When James Johnson took over Fannie Mae, no one in the government had taken the time to quantify precisely how much the federal charter was worth to the company. But those inside Fannie's Colonial Williamsburg–like headquarters in Washington knew its value was significant. Because the company was perceived to be at least implicitly backed by the government, Fannie Mae could raise money from investors who were willing to buy its debt at lower yields than they would accept from fully private and riskier companies. That the government would step in to save Fannie if it ever got into trouble was the prevailing assumption, and investors were happy to accept lower interest rates on the company's debt because of it.

Fannie Mae routinely claimed that it passed along every penny of its cost savings to homebuyers in the form of lower mortgage rates. This allowed the company to argue that any change in its status would result in higher housing costs for everyday Americans.

It wore the claim like a coat of armor, protecting itself from critics' slings and arrows. Only later would it emerge that the company kept billions of dollars—at least one third of the government subsidy—for itself each year. This money it dispensed to its executives, shareholders, and friends in Congress.

That the company was siphoning off billions of dollars every year was unknown outside its Wisconsin Avenue headquarters in 1991. But inside Fannie Mae, in his capacious office with its working fireplace, Johnson knew he had to work hard to protect the subsidy if he was to enjoy the power and wealth that the top job at the company promised. After all, when Maxwell had retired from Fannie, he walked away with a retirement package worth more than $20 million. A princely sum in the early 1990s, it was not bad for quasi-government work.

Johnson also recognized that if he wanted to make the company larger and more profitable, and reap the personal benefits its growth would provide, Fannie Mae's special privileges had to be maintained. To reach its full profit potential, the company needed to grow its portfolio of mortgage securities, but Johnson knew that some in government, the meddlesome privatization crowd, would be wary of a bulked-up Fannie Mae. Unlike fully private companies that increased their operations on the strength of consumer demand and private financing, Johnson was aware that if he were to grow Fannie Mae's revenues and earnings, he had to have the government on his side.

Fannie Mae was already something of a political species, of course. Always concerned with the company's image, Johnson drove his employees to ensure that the company regularly ranked high on the dubious "best of" lists published by various consumer magazines. These included *Fortune's* "Best Companies to Work For in America" and "Best Companies for Minorities," *Working Mother's* Best Companies list, and the *American Benefactor's* "America's Most Generous Companies."

But generating this soft spin was not nearly enough to protect the company, and Johnson himself, from the kind of political ill winds that could rise up out of nowhere in Washington. The rumblings about privatization posed a more significant threat than Fannie Mae had experienced before.

One of those who outlined this threat was Thomas H. Stanton, a professor at Johns Hopkins University, who wrote an article arguing for privatization in the magazine *The Financier* in May 1995. In "Government-Sponsored Enterprises and Changing Markets: The Need for an Exit Strategy," Stanton contended that the government should remove these companies' perquisites sooner rather than later.

"Pressures for the status quo, often backed by powerful political constituencies, can deter the government from acting until it is very late," he wrote, presciently.

To protect against this threat, Johnson turned to the political action committee (PAC) the company had set up years before. Unique among federally created organizations, Fannie Mae's PAC made generous contributions to lawmakers.

Under Johnson, it became bigger and brassier than ever.

"Johnson knew he had to keep the golden goose laying the golden eggs," another former executive said. "Once he walked in the door, Fannie Mae became a political machine."

⇌

As Fannie Mae was ramping up its political efforts, the regulator charged with its oversight was fighting for its life. The Department of Housing and Urban Development, created as a cabinet-level agency in 1965, was supposed to promote homeownership and eliminate housing discrimination.

HUD was a second-tier agency visited regularly by scandals. Its officials spent a good deal of time justifying their existence to Republicans eager to shut the inefficient agency down. These assaults had only grown during the Reagan presidency.

HUD was not much of a watchdog. Its oversight of Fannie and Freddie was a part-time arrangement—only a handful of people at the agency dealt with matters involving the companies, and they juggled other duties as well.

But in the aftermath of the savings and loan crisis, the days of part-time regulators for Fannie appeared to be numbered. After paying out millions to clean up failed savings and loans, Congress was considering legislation to protect taxpayers from potential losses at Fannie and its smaller cohort, Freddie Mac.

Founded in 1970, Freddie Mac was created by an act of Congress to provide competition for Fannie Mae in housing finance. Like Fannie, Freddie was a hybrid institution—a public company with shareholders but one that also enjoyed government perquisites.

There were several ways to protect taxpayers from possible harm where Fannie and Freddie were concerned. First was to create a new overseer for the companies. In addition, Congress wanted the institutions to increase the money they held in reserve to cover possible losses. Increased capital requirements, as they are called, act as a safety measure, a cushion to soften the effect of loans purchased by the company that went bad. But such a cushion also means lower earnings for financial institutions because the money they set aside cannot be used to buy mortgages or other interest-bearing assets.

Confronting the reality that his company might soon be dealing with a much more energetic regulator and significantly higher capital requirements, Johnson went to war on two fronts.

One attack was to be conducted very much in public. The program to advance homeownership was a quintessential "white-hat" issue, in Washington parlance. Johnson's launch of a high-level public relations campaign to turn renters into homeowners would put a friendly face on Fannie Mae, an enigmatic entity that was neither bank nor mortgage lender and not quite a government agency either.

Johnson's other battlefront, designed to protect the company's government benefits, would occur behind the scenes, in the halls of Congress. The sunny public relations campaign about how Fannie Mae helped homeowners would provide cover for the company's backroom dealings, through which it subdued critics and showered money and favors on supporters.

Among Johnson's first public initiatives was a $10 billion commitment by the company in 1991 to provide financing for lower-income borrowers. Called the "Open Doors to Affordable Housing," it was one of many Fannie Mae programs designed to blunt criticism of Johnson's aggressive growth plans. The idea, according to former company employees, was to finance so much low-income housing that Fannie Mae's government perquisites could never be taken away.

As Congress mulled over the company's future, Fannie Mae began making significant grants, hundreds of thousands of dollars each, to consumer and community groups favoring increases in low-income housing. The groups, such as the Association of Community Organizations for Reform Now, or ACORN, had been agitating for tighter regulations on Fannie Mae. But after receiving the grants, ACORN and most of the other groups changed their tunes.

"The timing of the grants is self-evident," Congressman James Leach, a Republican from Iowa, told the *New York Times*. "This is the most important legislation since the inception of Fannie and Freddie and they pulled out all the stops to make sure potential critics were silenced."

Even as Fannie Mae trumpeted its "Open Doors" program and spread money around low-income communities, Johnson was working to ensure that the new regulations being created by Congress would be weak and malleable.

First was the problem of a new regulator. An assertive over-seer could throw a monkey wrench into Johnson's plans to increase Fannie's profits by growing its portfolio of mortgage investments and entering other businesses. He needed to ensure that his regulator would be unable to thwart those plans, that it would be captive to the institution it was supposed to police.

Capital requirements were another potential disaster. Setting aside greater reserves meant lower earnings for his company, anathema to any chief executive hoping to please demanding investors.

But beyond his need to keep shareholders happy, Johnson had an even more compelling reason to keep Fannie's earnings on the rise: his own paycheck.

For years, Fannie Mae's compensation structure had been a conservative one, with executive pay linked to a wide range of performance measures. These metrics included how well the company managed its costs each year and what its return on assets was, a calculation of how much the company made on the loans it held on its books.

But after Johnson took over the company, Fannie Mae's executive pay structure changed. Compensation became tied almost solely to earnings growth.

Beginning in 1992, for example, earnings-per-share growth and "strategic" goals were the only measures used to determine incentive pay for Fannie executives. Salaries were never that large at Fannie, its former executives said, but stock grants and bonuses could make its executives wealthy indeed.

The shifts in Fannie Mae's pay structure had a clear, measurable effect. During Johnson's years at the company—between 1993 and 2000—the percent of total after-tax profits devoted to annual incentive pay for Fannie's executives rocketed from 0.46 percent to 0.79 percent. In actual numbers, the incentive pay handed to Fannie executives more than quadrupled, rising from $8.5 million to $35.2 million.

But in the early 1990s, it was clear that Fannie's new executive pay structure would be severely threatened by new and more onerous capital requirements on the horizon. Earnings per share would likely fall, hurting the potential for pay bonanzas. Johnson had to get involved in the writing of the 1992 law.

Brazen it was. And unusual. Manipulating the legislative process was an entirely new strategy for a corporate executive, according to a former government official who worked with Johnson. "He was the designer of the culture of obstinance," this official said. "Take on your regulator. Go to the Hill. Use your muscle."

⇌

It had taken three years for Congress to enact the Federal Housing Enterprises Financial Safety and Soundness Act of 1992, and it had many moving parts. Its chief aim was to protect taxpayers from potential losses if Fannie or Freddie got into trouble with mortgages they financed or held. Nobody wanted a repeat of the shocking savings and loan crisis where corrupt lenders enriched themselves at the taxpayers' expense.

The largest change in the law was the creation of two separate overseers for the companies. A new and supposedly independent regulator within the Department of Housing and Urban Development, called the Office of Federal Housing Enterprise Oversight, was tasked with overseeing the operations of Fannie and Freddie with an eye for safety and soundness.

Meanwhile, HUD had the often conflicting task of ensuring that the companies fulfilled their mission of promoting homeownership. It was proposed that OFHEO, like other financial regulators, be funded by fees charged to the regulated institutions, in this case Fannie and Freddie. This proposal was never implemented.

Among OFHEO's tasks, under the new law, was calculating and enforcing minimum capital requirements for Fannie and Freddie, as well as conducting examinations of the companies' operations. The law also required that OFHEO come up with a so-called stress test that would create worst-case scenarios for the companies, and then calculate how much capital and cash flows the companies would need to survive them.

The stress test was supposed to include situations where interest rates gyrated as they had during the 1980s when Fannie Mae teetered on the edge of solvency. Both the new capital requirements and OFHEO's stress test were to be finalized by December 1, 1994.

But the law had another key element that would, more than any other single act, lead to the disastrous home lending practices of the 2000s. The Federal Housing Enterprises Financial Safety and Soundness Act actually encouraged unsafe and unsound activities at both Fannie and Freddie by assigning them a new affordable housing mission.

Under the law, the companies had to use their mortgage purchases to help provide housing to those across the nation who had previously been unable to afford a home. While historically Fannie and Freddie supported housing by buying safe mortgages when other sources of capital for borrowers dried up, now the companies' focus on soundness was diluted by the requirement that they serve the housing needs of "low-income and underserved families."

The act required Fannie and Freddie to meet three separate housing goals through their mortgage purchases. First were those related to low- and moderate-income housing; then came so-called special affordable housing goals, and, finally, those associated with inner cities, rural areas, and other underserved areas.

Initially, the law specified that 30 percent of the housing units financed by the companies must go to low- and moderate-income families; another 30 percent would go to housing located in inner cities.

Congress did not come up with these requirements on its own. It asked for help from community activist groups like ACORN, which had helped lawmakers draw up the affordable housing goals for Fannie and Freddie. Henry B. Gonzalez, the Texas Democrat who headed the House Banking Committee and its subcommittee on housing and community development, had invited ACORN, Fannie's new ally, to help legislators define the goals when they were devising the new legislation covering Fannie and Freddie.

Meeting these targets required that the companies take an easier approach to what they considered acceptable underwriting standards from banks whose loans they would buy. Safety and soundness, the supposed goals of the legislation, took a backseat to politically driven housing goals.

Down-payment requirements were the first to go. Traditionally, banks had required that borrowers put 20 percent of the property price down to secure a mortgage loan, but the 1992 act encouraged Fannie and Freddie to buy mortgages where borrowers put down a nominal amount—5 percent or less—of the total loan amount. Never mind that the risks associated with these loans were far greater; history showed that the more money, or equity, borrowers had in their homes, the less likely they would be to default on their mortgages.

With lower down payments blessed by the 1992 legislation, Fannie and Freddie were suddenly far more likely to buy riskier loans from banks. And if those loans helped the companies meet their affordable housing targets, well, all the better.

While Johnson and his crew knew the risks among such loans were far higher, they also recognized that meeting affordable housing goals would give Fannie Mae enormous political cover for its growth plans. If it wanted to move into new and more lucrative businesses, such as mortgage insurance, for example, the company could always argue that without new business lines, it could not meet its housing goals.

"Affordable housing was the price they would have to pay to keep their benefits," recalled one industry official who was on hand during the legislative process.

While input on the legislation was provided by both Fannie Mae and Freddie Mac, Fannie approached the project much more aggressively. Leland Brendsel, the chief executive of Freddie Mac, was not a politician, former colleagues say and, unlike Johnson, he did not have friends on the Hill. "Leland didn't run with this crowd," said a former Fannie Mae executive. "He may have had some lobbyists working in different places but Leland listened to his lobbyists for direction. Johnson gave his lobbyists direction."

When the administration began prescribing broad outlines of the government-sponsored enterprises regulation, Fannie Mae was right there, guiding the officials tasked with the project. And

when the legislation moved to Capitol Hill, Fannie exploited relationships it had forged over the years there to make sure that the
Safety and Soundness Act would not be hazardous to the company's expansion plans.

Laws governing the appointment of Fannie and Freddie's board
allowed the president to choose five directors for each firm, and
Johnson recognized the power this gave him. Fannie hired an
army of lobbyists, and increased the use of its politically chosen
directors to help it blanket the Capitol. The company even paid
lobbyists to agree not to lobby against it.

Coupling power politics with populist support through shrewd
moves like a $5.5 million donation to create the National Center for
Lead-Free Housing, Johnson was able to work closely with those
writing the legislation that would create a new regulator for the
company, a former high-level Fannie executive said.

In September 1992, for example, Texas congressman Gonzalez withdrew the new regulatory bill from the House floor as it
was about to be debated. Gonzalez did so "to allow more time for
Fannie Mae to pursue changes in the bill," a staffer told the *New
York Times*. Those changes involved capital requirements; Johnson believed the bill, as written, gave too much discretion to regulators on the matter of such requirements and he had voiced his
alarm over it.

Johnson got his way.

The executive's interference meant Fannie got two bites of the
apple and was able to manipulate the terms of the debate from
beginning to end, said Jonathan G. S. Koppell, a former OFHEO
employee who is a professor at Yale University's School of Management. "In each part of the Act, the government sponsored enterprises were able to dilute or obfuscate the objectives," Koppell
wrote in a 2003 book, *The Politics of Quasi-Government*. "Fannie
Mae was able to design its regulation. The government sponsored
enterprises control their own controllers."

With Fannie Mae as a key architect of the legislation, it is no
surprise that the company extracted huge benefits from it. Fannie's
biggest win involved capital requirements, which were set at levels

far below those of other lenders—2.5 percent versus the 10 percent demanded of banks. This sliver of a capital cushion was appropriate, Johnson argued, because losses on Fannie Mae's mortgages had been a fraction of those experienced by other lenders and other banks held higher-risk assets.

But the company's past experience with losses was almost certainly not going to be repeated going forward, given the new low-income housing requirements mandated by Congress. Fannie was embracing a new world of riskier loans that would benefit Johnson, his protectors in Congress, and his paycheck. Those who stood to lose, because of the microscopic capital requirements that left Fannie unequipped to deal with its losses—taxpayers.

A financial executive who tried to get Congress to raise Fannie's capital requirements said: "If the company is run rationally and carefully it represented a governor on the rest of the industry. If they were rational, then everyone else was forced to be rational. If they had to have more capital, that would have been good for everybody. We were quite active in lobbying for that legislation but we never had a chance."

Meanwhile, Fannie also got what it wanted in a regulator—a ninety-eight-pound weakling. While the Government Accountability Office had recommended in a 1991 report that Fannie be placed under a tougher and more established regulator, the company persuaded legislators to keep HUD as its overseer. The company preferred the regulator it knew could be controlled. Never an aggressive or especially effective overseer, HUD was far preferable to an unknown and possibly more assertive agency, in Johnson's eyes.

HUD was weak, but Fannie Mae also needed to make sure that the agency would never grow more muscular. So Johnson and his army of persuaders argued that OFHEO, the cop on the beat inside HUD, should be forced to ask Congress for approval over any new regulations, even those related to capital requirements, that the overseer wanted to implement. In addition, Fannie suggested that, unlike bank regulators, OFHEO be forced to submit to annual appropriations reviews before lawmakers. The overseer would have to beg for money to operate.

Not only were these crucial hurdles for the regulator to leap over, they also allowed Fannie to shift the power of oversight to congressional subcommittees, run by members who could be easily swayed by the company's lobbying efforts and campaign contributions. Once his company's oversight was in the hands of Congress, Johnson knew that he could work behind the scenes to derail any restrictions on the company's activities that OFHEO might suggest.

The long arm of Fannie Mae was often felt by other financial executives who traveled to Washington to meet with lawmakers. As one recalled, "I used to go to Washington and lobby on issues we thought were wrong. I would go to Jim Leach, Chuck Schumer, and half an hour or an hour later they would have a visit from Fannie Mae. How the hell did they know I was there?"

If lobbying money and campaign contributions didn't do the trick, Johnson had another high card to play. Simply tell lawmakers that proposed rules disliked by Fannie would prevent the company from meeting its affordable housing goals. Any congressman or -woman who objected would instantly be labeled anti-housing, elitist, or an enemy of the American dream.

Fannie Mae's influence over the legislation may have been unusual, but not many in Congress found it objectionable. Two who did were James Jarrell Pickle, a Democratic congressman from Texas who had served on the powerful Ways and Means Committee, and Willis David Gradison Jr., a Republican congressman from Ohio.

"The time has come to protect the public purse, not Fannie Mae's profits," they wrote in a prescient letter to their colleagues in 1992. "Fannie Mae should not possess a veto over the form of its own supervision. The primary concern of Congress in drafting this legislation should be to protect the taxpayer by requiring all G.S.E.'s to be capitalized adequately. Public policy on such a serious issue should not be stalled, perhaps permanently, by lobbying efforts that put the private interest of a single enterprise above the broader public interest."

Articulate though they were, these objections were overridden by Fannie's many friends on the Hill. The safety and soundness legislation that the company had been so instrumental in devising passed both the House and the Senate resoundingly. By the end of 1992, it had become law.

It soon became clear that Fannie Mae had scored a major win with the passage of the legislation. Even those on Wall Street took note of Johnson's feat. Jonathan Gray, an analyst at Sanford C. Bernstein and Company, a respected research firm in New York, characterized Johnson's role in formulating the legislation as the executive's finest moment. It "really created Fannie Mae as a growth stock," he said.

That feat would translate to immense paydays for Johnson and his high-level cronies. Indeed, over his nine years at the company, he took out roughly $100 million in pay.

Those who criticized Fannie Mae got nowhere with their arguments. As Johnson had told the *New York Times* a few months earlier: "One of the points I generally make to people in the administration and people on Capitol Hill is that in the context of there being so few clear public-policy successes, you should rejoice in Fannie Mae and Freddie Mac rather than fight them. This is a very unique idea that Congress and the Presidency put in place that works beautifully."

CHAPTER TWO

The regulatory issues in the 1990s will not be limited to safety and soundness, but will increasingly emphasize fairness: whether or not banks are fulfilling the needs of their communities.

—LAWRENCE B. LINDSEY, member, Board of
Governors of the Federal Reserve System,
addressing the California Bankers Association,
May 11, 1992

While Congress wrestled with new regulations for Fannie Mae and Freddie Mac, researchers at the Federal Reserve Bank of Boston, one of the more powerful regional banks in the United States' Federal Reserve System, were hard at work analyzing thousands of mortgages. Their goal: to determine whether lenders were discriminating against minority borrowers.

Discrimination in lending practices had been a target of lawmakers since the civil rights era swept across America in the 1960s. But in 1977 the focus on the problem intensified when Congress passed the Community Reinvestment Act, a law requiring banks to lend broadly across their areas. The legislation was designed to eliminate so-called redlining practices, where banks refused to make loans in poor neighborhoods.

Two years earlier, the Home Mortgage Disclosure Act of 1975 had required lenders to supply the government with details of their loans and the people who applied for them. Armed with this data, the government rated banks' compliance with the Community Reinvestment Act, handing out scores based upon the institutions' adherence to the law.

Still, years after the law had been enacted, accusations of discrimination by banks against minority borrowers—especially blacks and Hispanics—continued. Banks contended that they were willing lenders and color-blind in their operations; why would they pass up the profits that such loans would generate? And yet, activist consumer groups such as ACORN, the Association of Community Organizations for Reform Now, maintained that discrimination was rampant.

Too often, though, the bias claims were based upon anecdotal evidence, a handful of cases in a few low-income neighborhoods. This all changed in 1991, when the Home Mortgage Disclosure Act began requiring information about the race of a prospective borrower to be included on every application.

That year, ACORN used the new data to study loans made by twenty banks in ten cities across the nation. It found that in every city, minority applicants were between 1.6 and 3.4 times more likely to be rejected for loans than whites.

"In cities across the country, ACORN members have seen their communities devastated by banks' systematic refusal to make loans in low-income neighborhoods and to people of color," the organization said.

At about the same time, Boston Fed researchers, led by Alicia H. Munnell, the institution's research director, were digging into the HMDA figures. They hoped to determine once and for all whether home-mortgage discrimination was indeed a major problem.

In October 1992, "Mortgage Lending in Boston: Interpreting HMDA Data" was published by the Boston Fed. Its authors were Munnell, Lynn E. Browne, James McEneaney, and Geoffrey M. B. Tootell. Although the title was dull and the writing dry, its conclusions were explosive. The study was immediately hailed as a landmark in research on lending discrimination.

Racial bias by mortgage lenders, Munnell and her colleagues

wrote, not only existed, it was pervasive. The HMDA data showed that black and Hispanic loan applicants were far more likely to be rejected by banks than were whites. The rejection ratio for minorities was 2.8 to 1 compared with white applicants.

The findings lit up the media, confirming many people's suspicions about banks' lending practices. The fact that the study emerged from an institution as credible and supposedly apolitical as the Boston Fed made its conclusions all the more damning.

Federal regulators heaped praise on the study. Calling its analysis "definitive," an official at the Office of the Comptroller of the Currency, the overseer for large national banks, said that it "changes the landscape."

The president of the Boston Fed, Richard F. Syron,* said the study "comports completely with common sense." Then he added, "I don't think you need a lot more studies like this." Munnell herself even weighed in, telling a reporter for the *Wall Street Journal* that her work "eliminates all the other possible factors that could be influencing decisions" made by banks relating to mortgages.

To those inside Fannie Mae, the Boston Fed analysis was another threat to its political power. If banks were discriminating against minority borrowers, then Fannie Mae and Freddie Mac, the buyers of those mortgages, were by extension aiding and abetting the questionable practices.

"It was one of our biggest problems," a former executive said. "A lot of our congressional protectors had political relationships with the black community and needed a 90 percent vote, so that was a big blow. After that report, the activist groups just kept piling on us."

James Johnson saw the opportunity for Fannie Mae in this potential problem: Lending to minorities could help his company's expansion efforts as well as its image. He was soon fanning the flames lit by the Fed's report. "We see evidence that there are a

---

*Syron would later run Freddie Mac, proving to be an example of the revolving door between regulators and the entities they oversaw. Syron was chief executive of Freddie when it was threatened by insolvency and taken over by the government in 2008.

significant number of prospective home buyers in this country whose only barrier to achieving their dream of home ownership is not their economic status, but their racial status," he wrote in the *Wall Street Journal* in late November 1992.

One "outreach effort" was the creation in October 1992 of the Housing Impact Advisory Council, a thirty-five-member group that would advise Fannie on how the company could meet the affordable housing goals set out by Congress in the new legislation.

Knowing how important it was to keep potential adversaries, especially low-income housing groups, close to Fannie Mae, Johnson invited top-level executives at nonprofits like ACORN, the National Council of La Raza (an entity devoted to the Hispanic community), and the National Low Income Housing Coalition in Washington to join his council. Of course, bankers and mortgage lenders were also asked to join the council, as were executives from the National Association of Real Estate Brokers. But almost half of the advisory council's initial members came from housing advocacy groups.

Not only did they get a seat at Fannie's council table, these housing advocacy groups also received grants from the company.

In addition to setting up the advisory council, Fannie Mae offered to begin buying new types of mortgages to expand its affordable housing reach. This allowed the company to grow its operations, and its earnings, while positioning itself as a do-gooder.

With this action, Johnson created the centerpiece of what would, by the fall of 1994, become William Jefferson Clinton's National Partners in Homeownership. The partnership's strategy served Johnson's goal by "making homeownership more affordable, expanding creative financing, simplifying the home buying process, reducing transaction costs, changing conventional methods of design and building less expensive houses, among other means."

A brand-new initiative from the company was "FannieNeighbors," a program "to increase homeownership and promote revitalization in minority and low- and moderate-income urban areas across America. Single-family homes that fall within specially designated low- and moderate-income and/or minority census tracts, or areas designated by housing finance agencies as targeted areas for neighborhood revitalization, are eligible for community lending underwriting flexibilities."

As Johnson would later proudly point out, Fannie Mae spent $7 billion between 1994 and 1997 on "underwriting experiments."

Underwriting flexibilities. New products. Expanding outreach efforts. All were code words for loosening underwriting standards and lending to people whose incomes, assets, or abilities to pay fell far below the traditional homeowner spectrum. No longer would Fannie Mae stick to its practice of ensuring that borrowers could meet their obligations and, therefore, that the loans it purchased carried relatively low risk. These standards had for decades acted as a kind of governor on lax lending among banks interested in selling loans to Fannie. But amid cries of racial discrimination, risk-averse practices were jettisoned.

There was only one problem. The methods used by the Boston Fed researchers to prepare their report were flawed, according to a throng of critics in and out of academia who questioned the paper's findings the following year. Its claims of bias were by no means proved, these people contended.

The analysis did not consider whether an applicant met a lender's credit guidelines, one researcher noted, while others pointed out that the type of model used by the Boston Fed oversimplified the complex mortgage lending process.

Given these weaknesses, it was impossible to conclude that banks routinely rejected minority borrowers or that their decisions were driven by anything other than sound lending decisions.

Forbes magazine was among the few media outlets to question the study's findings. For an article published on January 3, 1993, staffers Peter Brimelow and Leslie Spencer interviewed Munnell, who revealed yet another problem with the analysis. Munnell told *Forbes* that in preparing the study, Fed researchers looked at default rates across census tracts and found that minorities do not tend to fail more often on their loans than whites.

"What we found was, there was no relationship between the racial composition of the tract and the default rate," Munnell told *Forbes*. "So it wasn't true that tracts with large minority populations had higher default rates."

Such a finding should have been a signal to the researchers that their discrimination findings were off base, *Forbes* contended. After all, if bias were at work in minority neighborhoods, default rates in those areas would have been lower than among white areas, indicating that bankers were refusing loans to legitimate minority borrowers.

Munnell agreed that discrimination against blacks should show up in lower, not equal, default rates. "You need that as a confirming piece of evidence," Munnell told the *Forbes* reporters. "And we don't have it."

But the magazine's criticisms did nothing to cool the frenzy surrounding the report's "evidence" of bias in banking. Only years later did Munnell's peers in academia begin publishing papers attacking the Boston Fed's findings. In 1996, for example, an economist at the Cleveland Federal Reserve Bank, Stanley D. Longhofer, wrote that if the question is whether widespread discrimination exists in the home-mortgage market, "Ultimately, the answer must be 'we don't know.'"

⇌

The regulatory response to the Boston Fed study was immediate. Bankers received a new message from their overseers: Discrimination against minorities hoping to become homeowners must be eliminated.

Just six months after its questionable report was published, the Boston Fed put out a twenty-eight page guide for banks called "Closing the Gap, a Guide to Equal Opportunity Lending." It was a blueprint for banks showing them how to relax their lending practices to eliminate discrimination. "Special care should be taken to ensure that standards are appropriate to the economic culture of urban, lower-income, and nontraditional consumers," the guide said.

What did this mean in practice? Dispensing with tried-and-true lending rules. As Franklin D. Raines, Johnson's successor as chairman of Fannie Mae, said later, "We have to keep bending financial markets to serve the families buying the homes you build."

First to go was a reliance on credit history, an age-old method for measuring borrower risk. "Lack of credit history should not be seen as a negative factor," the recommendations said. "In reviewing past credit problems, lenders should be willing to consider extenuating circumstances." Neither should relatively high expenses among low-income borrowers disqualify them from receiving loans. "Special consideration could be given to applicants with relatively high obligation ratios who have demonstrated an ability to cover high housing expenses in the past," the guide said.

Changes should also be made in down-payment requirements, the guide pointed out. Because poor borrowers are less able to save for their housing needs, banks should be open to the use of monetary gifts from others as a way for these people to satisfy down-payment requirements. Among those who might donate to such causes, the Boston Fed said, were relatives, municipal agencies, or nonprofit groups. Mortgages using down-payment programs from municipal agencies and nonprofits would later demonstrate among the highest default rates.

"Cash-on-hand could also be an acceptable means of payment if borrowers can document its source and demonstrate that they normally pay their bills in cash," the publication pronounced.

The Boston Fed went on to advise lenders that to facilitate minority lending, they should track the more unusual aspects of such loans and make exceptions to their normal standards. "Loan production staff may find that their experience with minority applicants indicates that the institution's stated loan policy should be modified to incorporate some of the allowable compensating factors," the guide urged.

Banks that did not abide by these suggestions should take heed: "Management should also review HMDA data regularly, monitoring the volume, location, and composition of loan applications received, and the disposition of those applications," the guidelines noted. "If the number of applications received from minorities seems disproportionately low, the cause should be determined. If denial rates are relatively high for minority applicants, management should be able to explain the disparity."

For loan officers who might be worried about the risks of default in such mortgages, the Fed's guidelines provided a wonderful out. "Institutions that sell loans to the secondary market should be fully aware of the efforts of Fannie Mae and Freddie Mac to modify their guidelines to address the needs of borrowers who are lower-income, live in urban areas, or do not have extensive credit histories."

In other words, a banker confronted with these new relaxed requirements could off-load any risky loans to the government-sponsored enterprises responsible for financing home mortgages for millions of Americans. For institutions concerned about having to hold onto questionable loans and possibly generate losses in them, the fact that they could sell them to Fannie or Freddie meant one beautiful thing: Any downside could be handed off to the government.

Under Johnson's leadership, Fannie was especially supportive of this downward slide in lending standards. "This was the beginning of the company deciding to put itself in the crosshairs of lowering underwriting standards," said a former Fannie executive. "They started doing that with new products in 1993 and this began to characterize everything they were."

Because Fannie was the leader in housing finance, its actions set the tone for private-sector lenders across the nation. "They were omnivores," the former executive said. "The further they moved out on the risk curve, the more they pushed the market to follow. Johnson viewed this as his strategy of protecting the franchise at all costs."

While some of those who dealt with Fannie thought that the company was forced to lower its standards by the prevailing political winds, some who worked inside the company contend that Johnson worked closely with the community groups to argue for relaxed lending. After all, lower underwriting standards meant Fannie could grow its portfolio and, of course, its earnings.

Increasing the portfolio, and the fees and revenues associated with that, was a major Johnson goal, one that his company expressed openly to lenders in an early 1992 letter. "We will pursue every avenue," Fannie said. "Mortgage lenders, community groups, builders and developers, housing finance agencies, mortgage insurers, and federal, state, and local governments—to find partners that will help us fulfill our corporate objective of providing viable financial products and services that will increase the availability and affordability of housing for low-, moderate-, and middle-income Americans."

In late 2010, the degradation of mortgage lending and its disastrous effects, especially on minorities whom predatory lenders had targeted, had become obvious to all. In an interview, Munnell said that she never intended her 1992 study to result in relaxed lending practices for minorities. She said that she left the Boston Fed two months after her study was published and had nothing to do with its guidelines.

Now a professor at Boston College, Munnell said that her 1992 findings had not meant that bankers were biased against minorities, but rather that they were biased toward people like themselves. "Bankers worked with people with whom they felt comfortable and they didn't do that for people who seemed different from them," Munnell said. "It was not that they were doing bad things to black people, they were doing nice things for white people so when you look at it statistically, race becomes a factor.

We were never arguing that you should give loans to people who don't qualify."

Still, that was the result.

⇌

At the same time that the Boston Fed was making a fool of itself on the subject of home-mortgage discrimination, a lawyer and researcher at the Cleveland Fed was making a nuisance of himself with his superiors in Washington.

That lawyer was Walker F. Todd, an assistant general counsel and research officer at the Federal Reserve Bank of Cleveland. Todd had been examining the intricacies of a 1991 law known as Federal Deposit Insurance Corporation Improvement Act, or FDICIA (pronounced "fidisha").

Yet another response to the savings and loan crisis of the late 1980s, FDICIA was designed to limit the taxpayer's exposure to failing financial institutions. It required the Federal Deposit Insurance Corporation, the entity that insured deposits at commercial banks and paid depositors if their institutions failed, to take prompt corrective action when a bank got into trouble. The law also required that the FDIC resolve failing institutions at the least possible cost to the government.

Both of these elements represented significant improvements to previous rules and protected taxpayers from future losses produced by troubled banks.

But in scrutinizing FDICIA, Todd had uncovered an obscure amendment to the law that dramatically expanded the federal safety net, increasing the likelihood of taxpayer bailouts in the future. While previously only commercial banks who were members of the Federal Reserve System could request emergency financial support from the central bank in times of crisis, the amendment to FDICIA increased the availability of Fed assistance to include investment banks and insurance companies.

The amendment had not attracted much attention before or after the bill was passed. Todd discovered that the change had been quietly inserted late in the legislative process by Christopher Dodd, the Connecticut senator whose constituents include most of the nation's large insurance companies.* During a debate about the bill on the Senate floor, Dodd said that his provision would give "the Federal Reserve greater flexibility to respond in instances in which the overall financial system threatens to collapse. My provision allows the Fed more power to provide liquidity, by enabling it to make fully secured loans to securities firms in instances similar to the 1987 stock market crash."

Lawmakers asked if the Fed had a point of view on the amendment. The Fed took no exception to it, they were told.

Todd, an expert on bank failures and dubious lending practices, was among the few who recognized the significance of the amendment at the time. "This amendment was introduced suddenly in the Senate markup, with no hearings, no prior notice," he recalled in an interview almost twenty years later. "It was antithetical to the spirit of FDICIA, which was to retrench emergency lending."

In a 1993 article about the change published by the Federal Reserve Bank of Cleveland Economic Review and entitled "FDICIA's Emergency Liquidity Provisions," Todd identified the change and its potential impact. "Although nonbanks still have strong incentives to run their firms prudently, their managers now have potential access to another funding source during financial crises," he wrote. "Whether this potential access alters nonbanks' business decisions—so as to make their calling upon that funding source more likely—remains to be seen."

"Moral hazard" is the term used by economists to describe what Todd was talking about. If access to emergency capital made bank managers less likely to exercise caution, as they would if they could not expect help when experiencing losses, then that would be a moral hazard—it would encourage risk taking among

---

*Years later, H. Rodgin Cohen, a lawyer to Goldman Sachs, American International Group, Bear Stearns, Lehman Brothers, Merrill Lynch, Fannie Mae, and JPMorgan Chase (to name a few), said he drafted the amendment on behalf of his financial services company clients.

banks because their executives knew they could be bailed out if they got into trouble.

Todd's uncertainty about whether nonbanks would take on more risk would be erased some fifteen years later when the Fed rescued the world's largest insurance company, the American International Group, providing $180 billion in taxpayer assistance. Despite claims by government officials that taxpayers profited from rescues of GM, AIG, and Citigroup, the expansion of the federal safety net that began with a little-noticed amendment to FDICIA would wind up costing taxpayers hundreds of billions of dollars.

But Todd received no praise from his colleagues at the Federal Reserve Board in Washington for his groundbreaking research. In fact, they worked feverishly to prevent its publication. When those efforts were unsuccessful, Fed officials in Washington rewarded Todd with a reprimand in his personnel file.

Twenty years later, working as a senior research fellow at the American Institute for Economic Research, Todd was still perplexed by the episode. He could only conclude, he said, that Washington wanted no discussion of the expanding safety net and its costly implications for taxpayers.

⇌

Even as Congress was writing legislation to allow investment banks and insurance companies to tap the Federal Reserve in times of crisis, the Federal Reserve Bank of New York, the most powerful of the twelve regional banks that make up the nation's central bank system, was reducing its oversight of the Wall Street firms it did business with. Known as primary dealers, these firms were used by the government to help manage its auctions of U.S. Treasury securities. The dealer firms also acted as the Fed's eyes and ears on Wall Street, supplying information about goings-on in the financial world.

In January 1992, the Fed ended a program called dealer surveillance that it had long used to audit and inspect these Wall

Street firms. The Fed had decided to close one of the windows it had onto the workings of the Street.

A press release issued by the New York Fed said that its long-standing surveillance arrangement needed to be changed "to address certain shortcomings." The program had helped to create a widespread misperception that the Fed regulated the primary dealer firms. So it decided to shutter the unit altogether. "This change reiterated the point that the bank does not have—nor did it ever have—regulatory authority over the primary dealers," the Fed said in its release.

From this moment on, the Fed would no longer be able to conduct its own due diligence on dealer firms. Now it would have to rely on audits and reports filed by the firms but that were verified by other regulators, such as the Securities and Exchange Commission or the Office of the Comptroller of the Currency, a division of the Treasury that oversaw large national banks. It was, to some Fed officials, a dangerous delegation of an important duty that had given the central bank access to crucial information about the soundness of the Wall Street firms it was dealing with.

Like the amendment to FDICIA uncovered by Walker Todd, the Fed's decision to close down dealer surveillance went largely unnoticed. But to some inside the organization, it was a clear indication that the days of a tough regulatory approach at the Fed were over.

Supervision and regulation, as the bank overseers' unit is called, had for years been a tight ship run by William Taylor, an independent thinker with a bulldog personality. A top adviser to Alan Greenspan, the chairman of the Federal Reserve Board, Taylor was an aggressive supervisor who "had no political sponsors, nor did he seek any," according to Paul Volcker, the chairman of the Federal Reserve Board in the 1980s and, for a decade, Taylor's boss.

Taylor was a tough-guy regulator. He had, for example, forced Citibank to stop paying its stock dividend in October 1991 when the bank was staggering under a mountain of bad loans. Taylor knew that eliminating its dividend was necessary for Citibank to shore up its capital; the bank's management resisted the idea because it would cause shareholders to flee and Citi's stock to plummet.

As head of "supe and reg," Taylor's primary goal was to ensure the safety and soundness of the nation's banking system. To him that meant Citibank had to improve its capital position by the most expedient method possible. If that meant axing its dividend, so be it.

But in the midst of Citi's crisis, Taylor left the Federal Reserve to become chairman of the FDIC. It was the autumn of 1991; by the following August, Taylor was dead at the age of fifty-three.

"The regulatory ethos at the Fed died with Bill Taylor," a former colleague said. "After Taylor left, and especially after he died, Alan Greenspan, the Fed chairman, was never really engaged in bank regulation. In 1992 or '93, the Senate asked Greenspan: 'With Taylor gone who is in charge of regulatory policy at the Board?' The answer surprised the Senate staff when it came back in writing because Chairman Greenspan said he had delegated the task to E. Gerald Corrigan, the president of the New York Fed."

This was news. For the first time the Board was not managing its own supervisory policy, the former Fed official said. Instead, it was delegating that important duty to the New York Fed, an organization that operated hand in glove with the banks it was supposed to regulate.

The New York Fed is a private corporation with a board comprised primarily of top executives of the banks it oversees in its region, and its president is chosen by those board members. As such, they are unlikely to choose a president they think will be especially tough on them.

Suddenly, supervision of the nation's banks was being overseen by an organization viewed by many as a captive to the entities it regulated. It was a power shift that would, years later, prove to be disastrous for the American people.

Bill Taylor's death also coincided with another shift at the Fed in Washington. In the early 1990s, the regulatory view was that capital requirements at the nation's banks should be strict. The savings and loan crisis and Citibank's woes had struck fear in many regulators' hearts. But over the next decade, the Fed would side with the major banks on capital requirements, pushing harder for looser rules and regulations.

CHAPTER THREE

Company downsizings, stagnating incomes, death, disability, rolling recessions, divorce—we want to bridge folks through financial hard times and lend based on their credit future, not their past.

—J. TERRELL BROWN, chief executive, United
Companies Financial, subprime lender, quoted in
Time magazine, October 1996

The drive by Jim Johnson, the Fed, and others to expand home-ownership to lower-income Americans was more radical than many of them wanted to admit. Indeed, a completely new approach to lending would be necessary if policymakers wanted the ranks of homeowners to grow beyond current levels.

All the old rules about what made a prospective borrower a good risk—based upon past repayment practices—would have to go by the boards. Looking to what a borrower could become—his credit future—had so much more potential. "The power of 'Yes!'" was what Washington Mutual, a big subprime lender, would later call its lax lending during the great mortgage bubble of the late 2000s.

But in the early and mid-1990s, "The Power of No" held sway in the traditional banking world. To entrepreneurs like J. Terrell Brown, head of United Companies Financial, traditional bankers were the abominable No-men, stick-in-the-muds who refused to see that times had changed. The 1950s-era *Leave It to Beaver* household where Dad worked and Mom stayed home to mind the kids was giving way to a world of two-income families and latch-key children. Lenders that failed to respond to these changes by being open to more atypical borrowers would be left behind.

Happily for the housers, as the homeownership brigade was known, Wall Street's creative minds were on the case. Teaming up with Brown and a handful of other upstart financial companies, Wall Street bankers helped devise newfangled mortgage products and services to expand the pool of potential borrowers. The innovation not only made borrowing easier, it brought increased profits to the companies that embraced it.

Underwriting loans, a bank's bread and butter, had long been a burdensome task. Loan officers collected information from credit bureaus, amassed data on applicants' job histories and financial holdings, and, perhaps most important, looked a potential borrower in the eye to decide if the loan was a risk worth taking for the next thirty years.

It was hard for renters, living from paycheck to paycheck, to build credit histories that were extensive and clean enough to be taken seriously by a mortgage lender. Among people who didn't have a history of paying credit-card bills, being approved for a mortgage was unlikely in the late 1980s and early 1990s.

Although there was no industry standard for what separated a good borrower from a bad one, banks used benchmarks to judge a consumer's financial position and ability to pay off a loan. One measure compared the amount of debt the borrower carried versus his or her income. Anything over 36 percent was deemed too onerous.

Another metric compared the size of the loan to the worth of the property that would secure it—known as the loan-to-value ratio. Normally a bank would only lend 80 percent of a property's appraised value.

Finally, there was the credit history of the borrower to consider.

Using these benchmarks, banks graded potential borrowers.

Like a side of beef, the best prospects were considered "prime" or "A." Those with blemishes on their credit histories or numerous job changes over a short period were "B&C" customers. Lenders later renamed this category "subprime" because "B&C" sounded vaguely insulting to borrowers in these ranks.

Many of those in the B&C category had never had relationships with traditional banks. They relied instead upon unregulated and costly check-cashing services or payday lenders, entities that provided loans to tide borrowers over until they received their paychecks. Such services charged astronomical interest rates and were only a step above loan sharks.

Still, low-income consumers preferred their loan sharks to the intimidation that the local branch banker represented. Walking into a bank to ask for a loan meant submitting to a lengthy and invasive process involving endless questions about finances. Getting approved on a home mortgage seemed so difficult for those who were unfamiliar with the financial world that it was simply not worth attempting. With weak or no credit histories and little to no savings to put toward a down payment, borrowers figured they were shut out of homeownership.

Although banks were careful to make only those loans to people they felt certain would be "money good," in Wall Street parlance, or able to repay their loans, these institutions did not always hold on to the mortgages they made. If the bank made a loan that it thought Fannie Mae, Freddie Mac, or the government's Federal Housing Administration programs would buy, then the bank could sell it to one of those entities and free up that money to make another loan. Fannie and Freddie would then turn around and bundle thousands of these loans into mortgage-backed securities that income-seeking investors would buy.

But if the bank could not convince Fannie or Freddie to buy a loan, it had to hold on to it and hope the borrower would pay it off. Banks did not create pools of loans and sell them to investors like Fannie and Freddie did. They either sold them to the government or kept them.

All this changed, however, in June 1993 when United Companies Financial, a publicly traded mortgage lender based in Baton Rouge, Louisiana, cobbled together its first mortgage pool. The company, founded in 1946, had been originating loans, bundling them into pools of mortgages, and selling them to affiliates and government agencies for almost a decade. But the $165 million worth of mortgages that it bundled into a security in the summer of '93 was the first ever to be sold to investors under the United Companies name.

The pool, part of a series or "shelf" of securities under which United could raise up to $1 billion from investors, received an investment grade rating of AAA, the highest possible, from all three ratings agencies. With this imprimatur from Moody's, Standard & Poor's, and Fitch Ratings, investors felt comfortable buying the deal.

This AAA rating was crucial. Analyzing one mortgage to try to predict its performance was hard enough. Assessing the risks in a security that contained thousands of loans was beyond complex. If the ratings agencies were convinced that the securities were good enough to assign them a triple-A rating, then most investors were happy to go along.

Little fanfare accompanied the United Companies residential mortgage-backed securities offering that June. Nobody on Wall Street rang a bell to memorialize the moment. But the issuance of its first mortgage pool represented the dawning of a new age, one in which mortgage-backed securities issued by private lenders would compete with those sold by Fannie and Freddie. By 2003, ten years after the United Companies issue, mortgage securities worth $467 billion were sold to investors.

No one recognized it at the time, but the financial world's equivalent of an arms race had begun. Rather than producing nuclear weapons, though, this race would generate millions of worthless loans, leaving investors with hundreds of billions in losses. As often occurs in the financial world, a good idea was soon transformed into a monstrosity by Wall Street.

⇌

Officials at Fannie Mae and Freddie Mac certainly took notice of the United Companies deal. Neither agency had ever had competition from the private sector when they went into the market to sell their mortgage pools. But the success of the United Companies Financial deal meant investors interested in the risks and returns of the mortgage market had a new option.

Two months after it sold its first private-label securitization to investors, United Companies returned to the market with another $130 million in mortgage-backed securities. In a little over sixty days, this obscure company had shifted almost $300 million of mortgage risks from its own books to those of investors. The following year, United Companies increased the size of its securities "shelf" to $3 billion.

The United Companies deals might have been a one-hit wonder had it not received a big assist from Duff & Phelps, a financial services firm that assessed risks in securities and rated them accordingly. In an August 1993 study entitled "Special Report on the Securitization of B&C Quality Loans," Duff & Phelps made a novel and counterintuitive argument about the risks inherent in such loans. While many investors viewed lower-quality loans made to sketchy borrowers as high-risk, one important aspect of these obligations made them somewhat less risky in actual practice, the Duff & Phelps analysts argued. Indeed, risk-averse investors might actually gain from buying securities made up of these loans.

Like any investment, fixed-income securities posed multiple risks to investors who bought them. The most obvious was credit risk—the potential that the loan would not be repaid. Another was interest-rate risk—if prevailing rates rose, then the market value of a loan paying a lower rate would decline.

A third risk, and one that was harder to predict, involved the early repayment of the loan. Because an investor wanted to keep receiving the stream of income on the loan he or she had purchased for as long as possible, getting repaid before the loan matured was a big risk associated with mortgage investing. This was known as prepayment risk.

Such was the risk that Duff & Phelps argued was reduced

among loans made to sketchy borrowers. Because the loan approval process required of these borrowers was so much more onerous, the firm maintained, they would be far less likely to be able to refinance their loans if interest rates dropped. Getting a new loan might be a cinch for stellar customers, Duff & Phelps noted, but B&C borrowers had a harder time refinancing. Therefore, the risk that these mortgages would be repaid early was vastly reduced.

Investors would benefit twice, therefore. First, the income streams were larger because riskier borrowers were forced to pay higher interest rates on their obligations. Second, because these borrowers were locked in, prepayment risk was diminished.

This argument was made more compelling by the fact that at this particular moment prepayment risk was a serious threat. With interest rates declining in the early 1990s and competition for better-quality mortgage loans rising, locking borrowers into higher rates was an attractive investment concept. It meant that the higher income stream prized by investors would keep on paying far longer than was typical among better loans.

It came as no surprise, therefore, that investors began to embrace this less competitive, more fractured market. They loved its richer margins and appreciated B&C loans' reduced sensitivity to interest-rate moves. In 1994, some $40 billion in subprime loans was made. Just five years later, annual issuance of subprime mortgages would rise to $160 billion.

At the time of its 1993 report, Duff & Phelps seemed simply to be making a persuasive investment thesis. But by allaying investor fears about the risks inherent in lower-quality loans, Duff & Phelps helped open the floodgates of subprime lending. Millions of investors were on the prowl for interest income—insurance companies and pension funds, for example, had billions to invest in fixed-income securities. Pointing out the appeal of such loans to these and other investors helped unleash a boom that would be the downfall not only of the mortgage market but also of the entire mortgage securitization process.

In 1993, though, investors were just beginning to whet their appetites for riskier mortgage loans. Nevertheless, their rising interest in these loans encouraged Wall Street banks and other investors to provide mortgage lenders with capital to make them.

Just as manufacturers of tires, dishwashers, and other goods need warehouses and funding to build up inventory until they can sell it, so do lenders. And with increasing support for loans from rating agencies like Duff & Phelps and the investors who heeded them, lenders suddenly found it far easier to establish warehouse lines of credit. Money soon flowed in from investment banks and other investors eager to make money on the warehouse lines and ensure a steady stream of mortgages to package and sell to investors. The larger the volume of loans originated by a lender, and the more quickly they could sell those loans to investors, the larger the "warehouse line" the lender was likely to receive.

Quantity, not quality, was rewarded by the firms providing the warehouse lines. And because those institutions buying the loans had to take the losses if they went bad, the bankers making the loans had less incentive to ensure the borrowers were "money good."

Fannie Mae, always on the alert for competitors out to eat its lunch, closely watched the activities of United Companies and other newcomers to the mortgage securitization business. And in the early fall of 1993, Fannie and Freddie Mac joined with PNC Bank of Pittsburgh, Sears Mortgage, and Mortgage Guaranty Insurance Corporation to launch a pilot-underwriting program that would redefine lending practices in the "conforming market," the term used for loans that could be purchased by Fannie and Freddie.

The new program had a prosaic name—it was known as "Alternative Qualifying"—but it challenged many conventional lending rules. For example, "AQ" did away with long-standing traditions requiring that a borrower's monthly housing payment not exceed 28 percent of his or her income and that his or her debt did not exceed 36 percent of income. Instead, the program said that if an applicant had previously demonstrated some ability to manage very high payments as a percent of their income, perhaps in the form of rent, then that should be considered favorably.

It was all reminiscent of the guidelines put out by the Boston Fed earlier in the year, after publication of its problematic mortgage discrimination study. "Closing the Gap," the Boston Fed's rules for nondiscriminatory lending, directed banks to "consider extenuating circumstances" of atypical borrowers.

But while the Fed's suggestions were just that, the new Fannie and Freddie program institutionalized the endorsement of untested underwriting criteria. By allowing greater flexibility in the loans they would consider for purchase, these historically conservative firms offered B&C lenders like United Companies Financial the chance to expand their own lending and receive what seemed to be the U.S. government's "Good Housekeeping Seal of Approval" on loans they made and sold to Fannie or Freddie.

Although risky borrowers were supposed to make larger down payments when they bought a home or have more equity in their property before they could refinance, the "AQ" program was the first in a series of steps to ease lending practices and expand loan volumes. The years of profits and peril that would be known as "Subprime 1.0" were about to begin.

Within months, advertisements detailing new opportunities for borrowers began appearing in newspapers and on radio. It wasn't quite the anything-goes lending spree that would characterize the mid-2000s where all you needed was a pulse to get a loan, but it was on the way there.

Watching the growth in securitization of B&C loans by United Financial and other upstarts, Fannie Mae grew worried about rising competition. Fannie Mae was not allowed to own a mortgage underwriter, so it had to rely on the kindness of third parties to produce the loans that the company would buy. Johnson needed to ensure that such lenders would continue to send the lion's share of their loans to Fannie Mae.

An obvious solution to this problem involved cultivating a

company that Fannie Mae already had a relationship with: Countrywide Financial.

A mortgage lender launched in 1969 by two entrepreneurs named David Loeb and Angelo R. Mozilo, Countrywide Financial was, by the mid-1990s, a formidable mortgage machine generating billions of dollars in loans a year. Johnson's goal was to ensure that Countrywide sold as many of these loans as possible to Fannie Mae rather than its rival, Freddie Mac.

Countrywide's ties to Fannie went back to the days when David Maxwell ran the company. During his time as head of a mortgage insurance company in Los Angeles, Maxwell had written a letter of recommendation for Countrywide when it was just getting on its feet.

To strengthen its ties with the growing Countrywide, Johnson went about courting Mozilo. Johnson "became a student of Angelo," according to *Mortgage Strategy*, an industry publication, and set about learning the executive's likes, dislikes, and routine.

A crude and hotheaded butcher's son from the Bronx, Mozilo was the polar opposite of the cool and calculating Johnson. A perennially tanned man who drove flashy cars, Mozilo wore his ambitions on his French-cuffed and monogrammed sleeve.

The two men did share a love of golf, however. Whenever Johnson headed out West for business, he'd make a point of setting up a golf game with Mozilo. Johnson showcased Mozilo at corporate retreats for Fannie Mae's executives and sales force and took time out to be interviewed for "The Countrywide Story," a television program that aired in 1997 as part of a series on Californian entrepreneurs.

Mozilo returned some of these favors. He allowed Johnson frequent flights on Countrywide's corporate jet and provided Johnson with cut-rate loans on the many properties the Fannie Mae chief owned.* These included Johnson's multimillion-dollar

---

*These sweetheart loans would come back to haunt Johnson in 2008 when he was asked to vet vice presidential candidates for President-elect Barack Obama. Johnson was forced to resign from his position when the nature of these loans was disclosed.

homes in Ketchum, Idaho; Washington, D.C.; and Palm Desert, California.

His "friendship" with Johnson, Mozilo well knew, was driven by money. He had once characterized Johnson to reporters at *Mortgage Strategy* as so slick that "he could cut off your balls and you'd still be wearing your pants."

Recognizing that Johnson needed him more than he needed Johnson, Mozilo forced Fannie to discount the fees it charged to guarantee the company's loans it sold to investors. Fannie's guarantee fees were typically 0.23 percent of a loan's amount. They were also a nonnegotiable item.

But under the terms of Countrywide's special deal, reported in the *Wall Street Journal*, Fannie charged the company only 0.13 percent of the loan amount. To keep its side of the bargain, Countrywide agreed to provide enormous volume to Fannie Mae and refused altogether to deal with Freddie Mac.

It was a deeply symbiotic relationship and central to the public-private partnership at the heart of the homeownership push. Fannie got the volume it needed to balloon its portfolio and profits, and Countrywide fattened its earnings by paying reduced fees to Fannie Mae. Soon Countrywide was Fannie Mae's single largest provider of home loans.

In the mid-1990s, Countrywide was still making the types of standardized loans Fannie Mae favored. Elsewhere in the market, more liberalized lending programs were springing up. For example, Arbor National Mortgage, a lender based in Uniondale, New York, was offering to refinance customers' homes through its "50/50 Homeflex" program. Borrowers could be approved even if their debt payments ate up half their monthly incomes.

And by early 1994, Option One Mortgage, a company that would become a major player in the mortgage mania of the mid-2000s, was approving loans for borrowers whose debt-to-income levels went as high as 60 percent.

Soon, mortgage lenders that had stuck to the upper tiers of borrowers were setting up subsidiaries devoted to B&C loans. The industry had come to understand borrowers better, its representatives explained. Those whose loans would have been rejected in the past were being given a second chance.

Many of these lenders made their new business sound almost altruistic. "These (borrowers) are often people who've had credit problems that were beyond their own control," Larry R. Swedrowe, vice-chairman of Prudential Mortgage, told a reporter for the *Los Angeles Times* in a July 1994 interview. The company, one of the more conservative lenders in the business, had begun approving borrowers for loans even if they had been late with their mortgage payments in three of the previous twelve months.

Business was business, after all. Because these borrowers were willing to pay a fatter interest rate than higher-quality customers, "they represent a very sound business opportunity," Mr. Swedrowe acknowledged.

When interest rates began rising in 1994, slowing the wave of refinancing among prime borrowers, subprime lending gained even more traction as lenders saw that lower-quality borrowers could pick up some of the slack in the diminished prime loan arena. The fact that subprime loans could be significantly more profitable was icing on the cake.

⇌

The final piece of the puzzle fell into place in March 1994. Equifax Inc., one of the emerging leaders in credit scoring, introduced a system specifically tailored to assess the mortgage risk posed by a loan applicant. The system used information about a prospective borrower, applied different weightings to the data, and then predicted whether he or she would be likely to pay off the loan. It was novel and seen by the financial industry as a shiny new toy.

Such systems had already been used to analyze applications made by consumers opening credit-card accounts or borrowing to buy a car. But using a scoring system to try to predict the performance of a far more complex mortgage loan was something new.

Officials at Equifax said they believed that with their model, predicting credit risk in a mortgage application was relatively easy. Because applicants for mortgages typically had a better risk profile as well as a lengthy history of paying their obligations, they would not be difficult to assess. The changes transforming the old and conservative world of mortgage financing were ignored by Equifax.

Models like those used by Equifax had already begun to find a real foothold with smaller mortgage brokers and lenders. While it once had taken hours to process a loan application, credit check and approval lenders using desktop scoring models developed by firms like Fair Isaac Corporation (FICO) ramped up their production to fifty or so loans a day.

These new approaches embraced by a historically risk-averse industry sounded too good to be true to some. But to the entrepreneurs in the lending market, the models were a natural progression from a staid and buttoned-down business based on personal interactions to a technologically advanced, faster-paced operation that put a premium on speed of execution. The investment banks, who profited by filling the lenders' deal pipelines, and the investors, who reaped higher yields on mortgage securities issued by new lenders, welcomed the changes in lending practices.

Perhaps most surprising was the regulatory response to the relaxed lending rules. Financial regulators either stood by as the old rules designed to promote sound lending were scuttled or, like the Boston Fed, actually encouraged their demise.

An early change came from the Department of Housing and Urban Development, the regulator that Fannie Mae had worked so hard to weaken. In 1995 it relaxed rules involving appraisals, eliminating the requirement that those assessing the value of a property before a borrower took out a mortgage on it were independent from other companies involved in the process. Under a new rule designed to streamline regulations, HUD said that lenders could hire their own appraisers, setting up the potential for inflated valuations.

That is precisely what happened. The inflation game, which would help propel home prices into the stratosphere, began almost immediately.

Unfortunately for United Companies, the pioneer of these game-changing practices, its moment of fame was fleeting. Like many early players in subprime mortgages, the company fell victim to the financial downturn that began as a currency crisis in 1998. The following year, United filed for bankruptcy, closing its two hundred offices and selling off its mortgage servicing and whole loan portfolio to Bear Stearns's EMC Mortgage. Few would remember, years later, that United Companies had been the first mover in private-label mortgage securities.

CHAPTER FOUR

Fannie Mae's recent announcement of $1 trillion in targeted financing by the end of the decade, representing over $140 billion of net new financing, is an extraordinary commitment. The leadership demonstrated by Fannie Mae and its chairman Jim Johnson in envisioning this commitment must be applauded.

—HENRY CISNEROS, secretary, the Department of
Housing and Urban Development,
September 13, 1994

As United Companies Financial and other upstart lenders readied themselves for a borrowing binge, James Johnson pondered ways to shield Fannie Mae from the critics he knew lurked around every corner. How could he innoculate his company from those who viewed its growth plans with alarm, the naysayers who argued that the bigger Fannie Mae got, the more likely the taxpayer would have to bail it out someday?

The answer to this question was, as usual, money. Truckloads of it.

In March 1994, Johnson announced Fannie Mae's Trillion Dollar Commitment, a program that earmarked $1 trillion to be spent on affordable housing between 1994 and 2000.

The money would finance "more than 10 million homes for low-income families, minorities and new immigrants, families who live in central cities and other underserved communities, and people with special housing needs," the company said. Setting aside these funds meant that "Fannie Mae will transform the nation's housing finance system by working with other industry partners to eliminate the barriers to homeownership, and promote a ready supply of affordable rental housing."

One trillion dollars. Even for a man with plans as big as Johnson's, the figure was audacious.

But it had to be, as those inside the company knew, if Johnson was going to secure the protection Fannie Mae needed. The plan, former Fannie executives say, was to commit so much money to low-income housing—"for families and communities most in need," as the company liked to say—that no one would dare to criticize its other activities.

"This was the beginning of the use of the word 'trillion' in housing," marveled Edward Pinto, a former Fannie executive. "When Johnson announced the $1 trillion commitment, it told Washington that the company could do even more than they already were doing. It was pouring gasoline on the fire."

Fannie Mae boasted that its trillion-dollar commitment contained "11 very significant initiatives that address every dimension of the housing finance system."

The first priority was to bring a new flexibility to the loan underwriting process. Fannie Mae promised to use $5 billion worth of loans by the end of the decade to test new technology-fueled underwriting methods; it would also set up toll-free "flexibility hotlines," and comprehensive training programs, reference materials, and tools. A new automated underwriting system to ease the loan application process was being developed as well.

As always, Fannie's plan was watched closely by banks and other lenders across the country. Indeed, just over ten years later, Countrywide Financial, the subprime lender overseen by Mozilo, Johnson's old friend, launched its own trillion-dollar commitment, known as "We House America."

Mozilo said his plan embodied Countrywide's "long-standing commitment to lead the mortgage industry in closing the homeownership gap for minority and lower-income families and communities." Never mind that closing this gap meant trapping millions of unsuspecting people, many of them minorities, in high-cost loans they could ill afford.

A trillion dollars was a lot more in 1995 than it was a decade later. Still, Johnson's plan to throw all that money at the housing market to neutralize Fannie Mae's sophisticated critics in Washington did nothing to meet another challenge he confronted. How could he make Fannie Mae, a mortgage finance company whose operations few understood, into a company that was known for helping people realize the American dream of homeownership?

Fannie Mae was a creature of Washington, D.C., and this, Johnson knew, did not help its image. He had to win the hearts of everyday people on Main Street if he were to bullet-proof his company, and his lucrative position atop it.

So, after a cross-country trip in 1993, Johnson came up with the idea that Fannie Mae needed a local presence in communities nationwide. Boots on the ground was what his company required.

Thus were born the Fannie Mae Partnership Offices. Devised by Johnson, the partnership offices put Fannie Mae executives in place across America; soon the company was opening storefronts in cities and towns where it could partner with local officials to promote homeownership and, by association, its role as a good-deed doer. The partnership offices and their large financial commitments were soon garnering upbeat headlines in local newspapers, promoting Fannie's soft side to everyday people.

Even more important, though, the partnership offices cemented the company's relationships with members of Congress. By supporting housing initiatives that lawmakers could take credit for in their home districts, Fannie provided publicity for the very congressmen and -women whom it relied on for help and protection in Washington. With Fannie Mae's new regulator, OFHEO, in the midst of devising new and possibly punishing capital requirements for the company, support in Congress was more crucial than ever.

The partnership offices were vintage Johnson, a decisive response to a challenge. "The test between a strong and a weak organization is not whether you have problems—you always have problems—but how quickly you identify those problems," he had told an interviewer from the *New York Times* way back during the Mondale for President campaign. "How quickly you solve them and how quickly you change when you're on the wrong course."

The company launched its effort with twelve partnership offices, or POs in company parlance. Initial cities included Boston; Miami; Baltimore; Cleveland; Portland, Oregon; and Los Angeles. By the end of 1994, the company had twelve offices up and running across the nation.

Robert B. Zoellick, then the general counsel at Fannie Mae, described it this way: "For a relatively small investment, Fannie Mae will be recognized as a force for good in each of those cities or states. And by doing so, will have . . . more networks of support."

Boston's was one of the first offices to be opened and in October 1994, Johnson was there, trumpeting Fannie Mae's commitment of $1.5 billion in affordable home financing for twenty thousand local families. At his side during the photo op was Ted Kennedy, the Massachusetts senator who also happened to be engaged in a pitched battle for his Senate seat. His Republican challenger, Mitt Romney, was causing Kennedy so much trouble that he had to take out a second mortgage on his Virginia home to cover campaign costs.

Kennedy wound up prevailing over Romney that November, winning 58 percent of the vote. The Fannie Mae ribbon-cutting ceremony may not have won the election for Kennedy, but it certainly hadn't hurt him.

Democrats like Kennedy were not the only beneficiaries of Fannie Mae's partnership offices. Republicans, who believed in smaller government and fewer agencies, were potential threats requiring special care and feeding by the company. So when Johnson traveled to Atlanta to launch the new office there in February 1995, he made sure to invite some powerful Republicans to join him at the podium.

Once again, the focus for the Atlanta partnership office would be on creating mortgage products for first-time homebuyers and low- and moderate-income consumers, Johnson said. "Our commitment is to make homeownership in the greater Atlanta area more accessible than ever before. We think that the best way to do that is to work as closely as possible with the people of the city and the surrounding counties in their neighborhoods, and with local community groups, mortgage lenders, nonprofit housing organizations, and the city and county governments."

There to celebrate the Fannie Mae commitment was none other than Newt Gingrich, the Georgia Republican who was Speaker of the House of Representatives and a big proponent of reducing government's size.

"Fannie Mae is an excellent example of a former government institution fulfilling its mandate while functioning in the market economy," Gingrich crowed, not quite accurately, for there was nothing "former" about Fannie Mae's government status. "Fannie Mae has had a regional presence in Atlanta for over 40 years and the announcement of a partnership office demonstrates its continued commitment to affordable housing in the Atlanta metropolitan area."

Another powerful Republican was on hand in another city in 1996, when Fannie Mae opened a partnership office in Kansas City, straddling Missouri and Kansas. As Johnson announced his company's plan to deliver $650 million to promote homeownership and rental financing in the area, Christopher S. Bond, a Republican senator from Missouri, stood beside him at the city hall photo op. "Fannie Mae is committed to making the nation's mortgage finance system work better for the people of Kansas City," Bond said. "I look forward to seeing thousands of families rewarded with new housing opportunities through this partnership."*

But the partnership offices did more than simply provide ribbon-cutting celebrations for members of Congress and local

---

*Campaign records from this period show that contributions totaling $15,700 from officials at Fannie Mae put the company at number 19 on Bond's top corporate donor list between 1993 and 1998. Bond would return these and other favors in 2004 when he urged the inspector general of HUD to investigate the company's overseer, OFHEO. A draft of his letter urging the investigation was found on a computer at Fannie Mae two weeks before it was sent to HUD.

elected officials. They also supplied jobs for relatives and former staffers of elected officials.

When Fannie Mae opened a partnership office in Utah in 1999, for example, it was headed by Tim Stewart, a former legislative aide to Robert Bennett, the Republican senator. Bennett's son Rob was also hired to work in the office. Up north in South Dakota, Bob Simpson, a former aide to Senator Tom Daschle, ran Fannie Mae's local office.

A former executive working closely with Johnson when the partnership offices came about recalled fears by some inside the company that the strategy would require Fannie Mae to back money-losing projects to satisfy local politicians. "When we started these partnership offices we were all afraid of what it meant—that we were going to politicize all our underwriting decisions," he said.

As it turned out, however, the benefits of what was essentially a Fannie Mae patronage scheme far outweighed the potential for ill-conceived property developments. "The partnership offices gave us an enormous advantage when Congress was debating further regulations," the former executive continued. "We were able to call on our lenders and upon all our partners in the cities where we had these offices and say you have to weigh in. Write to Congress."

Fannie Mae's partnership offices were also mimicked later on by the federal government when it set out to promote homeownership by combining the private sector and public entities.

The projects undertaken by the POs always involved a close collaboration between homebuilders, Realtors, banks, housing agencies, local advocacy groups, and even corporations, such as retail chains, that would seem to have nothing to do with housing. At the launch of the Kansas City office, for example, Larry Small, Fannie's president and chief operating officer, described all those he had invited into the company's big housing tent.

"Over the next few months," Small said, "we will work with city representatives, mortgage lenders, nonprofit housing organizations, real estate professionals, and other housing leaders to craft a comprehensive investment plan designed to help meet the specific housing needs of Kansas City home buyers and renters."

Among those whom Fannie Mae enlisted in its Kansas City effort was Colleen Hernandez, executive director of the Kansas City Neighborhood Alliance, who was asked to join the company's National Advisory Council.*

Richard Moore, president of Commerce Mortgage Corp., a local company, was another Kansas City friend of Fannie—he sat on the company's Southwestern Regional Advisory Board. David Stanley, chief executive of Payless Cashways, a regional supermarket chain, was on the board of the Local Initiative Support Coalition, a nationwide nonprofit that regularly partnered with Fannie Mae.

The partnership offices bolstered a company effort begun by Johnson in 1992 that was designed to broaden the reach of Fannie Mae to include a wide array of public and private partners. This was the Housing Impact Advisory Council, a forum sponsored by Fannie Mae that convened more than sixty people interested in increasing the availability of affordable mortgage financing. Council members included civic leaders and those running state housing authorities, financial executives, developers, and real estate professionals. Each served a two-year term.

The council met three times a year with Fannie Mae's senior management "to discuss issues affecting products for low- and moderate-income home buyers and renters."

Under Johnson's direction, Fannie Mae duplicated this public-private partnership effort in every major urban area. Enlisting the aid of bankers, builders, Realtors, and advocacy groups nationwide, all of whom stood to benefit from an increase in homeownership, Fannie Mae soon had an army of foot soldiers at the ready to thwart any opponents.

"I wanted to have everybody and anybody who cared about housing working in partnership with us," Johnson told a reporter from the *Washington Post*.

---

*Hernandez would later receive a plum position on the board of the Fannie Mae Foundation, the company's charitable giving unit that dispensed millions of dollars in grants to favored groups each year.

The company did not hesitate to marshal these troops when it felt threatened. And that is just what it did in 1995 when one of the company's lucrative perquisites, related to its quasi-government status, came under fire.

Under its charter, Fannie was exempt from paying income taxes to the District of Columbia, where it is headquartered. With the city's budget deficit ballooning, some local officials, such as D.C. council member William P. Lightfoot, suggested that Fannie Mae, an enormously profitable company, start paying local income taxes. One year of taxes, according to an estimate based on Fannie Mae's profits, would bring $300 million to the District, eliminating the entire D.C. budget deficit.

But making such tax payments would also diminish Fannie Mae's earnings and those of its executives. So the company sprang into action, calling in chits from community organizers in the District with whom it had worked in the past.

One was Lloyd Smith, head of the Marshall Heights Community Development Organization, a group devoted to helping residents of a blighted area in Washington, D.C.'s 7th Ward. A neighborhood that was 97 percent black and where one third of its children were living in poverty, the 7th Ward needed all the help it could get.

Well before Fannie Mae's tax fight began, Smith's organization had received affordable housing funds from the company. So when it asked Smith for help in battling the tax issue, he was happy to oblige. He told the *Washington Post* that he telephoned council members and wrote to them, urging that the idea of levying a local income tax on Fannie be junked.

Fannie Mae had provided affordable housing and scholarships to local high school students, Smith argued. If the company was forced to pay income taxes, it might leave the district and take its programs with it.

Other community leaders joined forces with Smith, at the urging of two Fannie Mae lobbyists, Fred Cooke and David Wilmot. A tidal wave of letters arguing against the tax swamped the offices of

D.C. council members. Cooke, whose wife worked at Fannie Mae, met with each member of the city council, requesting that they give up on the proposal.

Barbara Lett Simmons, a local talk show host and former D.C. school board member, also got in on the act. She invited students from 7th Ward schools to appear on her radio and cable television programs to describe assistance they had received from Fannie Mae. "I started having people on my show to help get the word out," she told the *Washington Post*. "We have got to support our friends." Simmons's husband, Pat, sat on the board of the Fannie Mae Foundation, the company's charitable giving organization.

During the summer of 1995, Representative Pete Stark, a California Democrat, tried to schedule a hearing of the House District Committee on the Washington, D.C., budget problems. He had drafted a legislative proposal that would allow the District to tax Fannie Mae, but when it came time to find witnesses willing to support his plan, everyone he contacted ran for cover.

"The committee staff attempted to get a lot of witnesses to testify about this issue of Fannie Mae," Broderick Johnson, the staffer who worked on the hearing, told a reporter from the *Washington Post*. "Many of them quite frankly told us that they could not do it because of philanthropic relationships they have with Fannie Mae."

In the face of this pressure, the tax idea died. The $300 million in potential taxes that Fannie Mae might have been forced to pay each year remained safe and sound in its own coffers.

In November 1995, Fannie Mae increased its funding to Smith's Marshall Heights organization, pledging $650,000 in grants and loans to the community. Some of the money was earmarked for new housing construction. "This will enable us to double our production of affordable housing of various types for Ward 7 residents," Smith said upon receiving the check from Fannie Mae in a public ceremony.

Lightfoot, the council member who had tried to get Fannie to pay taxes to the District, recalled the fight years later. "I knew I was taking on the behemoth, but it seemed only fair that they should pay a tax to the government that allowed them to operate, generating such profits," Mr. Lightfoot said. "Their argument was they donated millions of dollars a year in charitable work to D.C. and that that should be counted in lieu of taxes."

Mr. Lightfoot and two other local representatives traveled to Texas to make their case before shareholders and directors attending Fannie Mae's annual stockholders' meeting. "They allowed us to stand up and make our arguments and there was no response and we left," he recalled. "It was like talking to the wall but the wall did let us talk to it."

It would take another decade before HUD, Fannie's "mission regulator," would investigate the use of Fannie's fifty-five partnership offices and conclude that their activities "were not confined to affordable housing initiatives, rather, a central purpose of the Partnership Offices was to engage in activities that were primarily designed to obtain access to or influence members of Congress."

Taxpayers still don't know how much money was involved in the influence peddling done through these offices because HUD refused to release the full report. But, back in 1995, there were many happy beneficiaries of the Fannie Mae hustle.

⇌

It appears that Fannie Mae was highly creative when it came to "encouraging" its higher-level executives to donate to political campaigns.

A major recipient of Fannie Mae's largesse, albeit indirectly, was Barney Frank, the combative Democrat from Massachusetts. He was a member, and later the chairman, of the House Financial Services Committee, one of the most powerful on the Hill, charged with oversight of "all components of the nation's housing and financial services sectors." The committee also watched over regulators such as HUD, the Federal Reserve, and the Federal Deposit Insurance Corporation.

Fannie Mae was one of the committee's top priorities. As such, its members were targeted by the company for special treatment if they were supporters or punishment if they were not.

Frank was a perpetual protector of Fannie, and those in his orbit were rewarded by the company.

In 1991, for example, Fannie Mae hired Herb Moses, Frank's partner who was a recent graduate of the Amos Tuck School of Business at Dartmouth. Frank praised Moses's qualifications in a conversation with Gerald R. McMurray, the company's vice president for housing initiatives who had for decades been staff director of the House Banking Committee's subcommittee on housing and community development. "Herb had been an economist with the Department of Agriculture and he went and got an M.B.A. from the Tuck School and was interested in a job," Frank said. "I talked to Jerry McMurray and said: 'Herb's a very good economist and has a business degree.'"

Almost immediately, Moses was being interviewed by an array of executives at Fannie Mae. A former company executive who first met Moses as he went through the interview process at the company believed Johnson was behind hiring Moses.

"Barney wanted him to have a job at Fannie Mae so the word was Johnson wanted him hired," the executive recalled. "He was just getting out of school and we all sort of bid for him. Ultimately, we chose him to be in our targeted community affairs group, the people who were looking for ways to increase our footprint."

Moses stayed at Fannie Mae for seven years. His title was assistant director for product initiatives and two of his projects involved relaxing Fannie Mae's restrictions on home improvement loans and small farm mortgages.

In late 2010, Frank was asked whether Fannie's hiring of Moses had put him in a conflicted position as a legislator voting on matters relating to the company. "I don't think it influenced me at all," he said. "I was not totally engaged with Fannie Mae and Freddie Mac."

But the record shows Frank exercising a deep and abiding interest in defending the companies in 1991 as Congress considered crafting legislation that would ensure their safety and soundness in the future. In a May 1991 hearing of the House Banking sub-committee on housing and community development, Robert D. Reischauer, director of the Congressional Budget Office, made a reasoned recommendation: "Making sure that Fannie and Freddie are entities that are independent, that have some visibility, that have safety and soundness as their prime objective, I think, is a way to ensure that the taxpayer is protected at those times when the klieg lights go off."

This triggered so fierce and unrelenting a cross-examination of Reischauer by Frank that Henry B. Gonzalez, the subcommittee chairman, had to admonish the congressman to let the witness answer.

Frank fumed that concerns about safety and soundness of Fannie and Freddie were overdone. "The focus on safety and soundness to the exclusion of any concern about their mission suggests to me that what we're going to get is a result where safety and soundness become, not the primary but the exclusive focus at the sacrifice of our ability to do housing," he said.

In 2010, however, after concerns about the companies' safety and soundness had been proven justified, Frank said: "I really have no recollection of that '92 Act."

Fannie Mae also made sizable contributions on more than one occasion and awarded its "Fannie Mae Maxwell Award of Excellence" at least twice to a Boston nonprofit group cofounded by Elsie Frank, the congressman's mother.* A newsletter issued by the Committee to End Elder Homelessness thanked Frank for "working behind the scenes to open many doors for us to help achieve our goal."

In fact, at a June 2002 Senate hearing, the co-chair of the Commission on Affordable Housing and Health Facility Needs for Seniors in the 21st Century, who was also a cofounder of the Elsie Frank nonprofit, thanked Barney Frank for appointing

---

*In May 1994, the company gave a $25,000 grant to the Committee to End Elder Homelessness for its creation of Bishop Street House for low-income women. In 2001, Fannie Mae awarded another grant, this time in the amount of $50,000, to the organization.

her to the Commission post. At the same hearing she praised Fannie Mae.

Whenever concerns were raised about Fannie growing too large and potentially perilous to the taxpayers, Frank would defend the company vociferously. During a House Financial Services hearing in 2003, Frank and the company's other favored members of Congress maintained that the company and Freddie Mac presented no potential harm to taxpayers. "The more people, in my judgment, exaggerate a threat of safety and soundness, the more people conjure up the possibility of serious financial losses to the Treasury, which I do not see," Frank said. "I think we see entities that are fundamentally sound financially."

⇌

One of the most powerful instruments Johnson used in his protection strategy was the Fannie Mae Foundation, a charitable organization founded in 1979. Under Johnson, however, the foundation became a powerhouse in charitable giving that targeted organizations associated with favored politicians or located in their areas.

The foundation took off after 1995, when Johnson put $350 million of Fannie Mae shares into it. As the company's stock rose, so did the amount of money the entity had to dispense. By 1998, the Fannie Mae Foundation was handing out $20 million a year.

A big portion of foundation money went to advertisements about Fannie Mae and its advocacy of homeownership. In 1998, for example, the foundation spent $38.6 million on advertising. This was money that would otherwise come from Fannie Mae's operations. As a result, tapping the nonprofit entity to cover ad expenses helped boost the company's earnings and its executives' pay.

In 1996, Fannie Mae took its strategy to the presidential primaries, inserting itself into the Iowa and New Hampshire contests with full-page ads and mailers damning the proposal for a flat income tax. A key plank of candidate Steve Forbes's platform, a flat tax would have eliminated all individual deductions in exchange for lowering the overall tax rate from the mid-30s to 19 percent.

While most individual deductions had been eliminated in the Tax Reform Act of 1986, the mortgage interest deduction remained a sacred cow. By proselytizing for the flat tax, and by gaining traction with the plan, Forbes became public enemy number one for Fannie Mae.

In an audacious move to sway voters, the foundation placed numerous ads in the *Manchester Union-Leader*, the most powerful newspaper in New Hampshire. Using simple drawings, the ads depicted the flat tax as a home wrecker equal to tornadoes, fires, and other natural disasters.

It is unclear, of course, whether the campaign had an effect. But Forbes, who had placed third in the Iowa caucuses, had been riding high in the polls before the New Hampshire primary. On Election Day, however, he won only 12.2 percent of the vote, winning fourth place.

The ads enraged some lawmakers, including Russ Feingold, a Wisconsin Democrat, and John McCain, a Republican from Arizona. "Is it appropriate for a government sponsored enterprise to be involved in activities that may influence the outcome of a federal election?" the senators asked in a joint letter to Fannie and Freddie. Both companies responded by saying the ads had not been designed to manipulate voters.

Fannie Mae's nonprofit foundation also gave the company numerous opportunities to reach out and touch a member of Congress. Big beneficiaries from the foundation each year included political organizations such as Congressional Hispanic Caucus Institute and the Congressional Black Caucus Foundation. In 1998, the Black Caucus Foundation received $82,000 from Fannie Mae.

During congressional testimony, in 2000, former lawmaker Walter Fauntroy, who testified on behalf of the National Black Leadership Council (the national network vehicle of the Congressional Black Caucus), was asked if he had any economic incentive for testifying on behalf of the GSEs. He claimed that his group did not receive any money from Fannie. Financial Services Committee chairman Richard Baker pointed out, however, that the Congressional Black Caucus had recently received $500,000 from Fannie.

Even nonpolitical neighborhood groups funded by the Fannie Mae Foundation helped the company play its power game. When a nonprofit applied for funding from the foundation, it had to supply a list of political contacts within their area or organization. These contacts gave Fannie Mae a roster of influence that grew to four thousand names at its peak.

Trying to wring as much favorable publicity as possible from its donations, Fannie Mae trumpeted them. Johnson himself would travel to Capitol Hill to hand out checks designated for community groups. During one trip to the Senate Caucus Room in 1998, Johnson handed out envelopes containing $2.5 million for Washington, D.C.–based neighborhood groups.

"As the lucky recipients queued up for their money," the *Washington Post* reported, "Senators Chuck Robb (D-Va.) and Paul Sarbanes (D-Md.) and Representatives Connie Morella (R-Md.) and Jim Moran (D-Va.) sang Johnson's praises."

In 1998, the foundation began sponsoring a charity golf tournament at a local golf club, called the "Help the Homeless Golf Classic." "Help the Homeless Walk-a-thons" were another money-raising tradition at the company, and the company sponsored charity basketball games to benefit the homeless as well.

"The whole homeless thing was an example of Johnson's ability to get the company involved in something at just the right time," said a former executive. "At the height of the interest in the homeless problem, he enlisted Tipper Gore, the vice president's wife, to be his partner in the Walk-a-Thon. It was brilliant."

Johnson never forgot the favors people had done for him and his company. On March 23, 1994, for example, at a National Bankers Association reception in the Rayburn House Office Building, Johnson was on hand to present the first-ever Fannie Mae Housing Hero Award.

The recipient? None other than Henry Gonzalez, the Texas Democrat who had withdrawn the safety and soundness bill from the House floor so that Fannie Mae could water down the rules on capital cushions at the company.

"The Housing Hero Award is Fannie Mae's version of the Oscar,"

Johnson said at the ceremony. "It is presented to a star player in the housing arena who serves in elected office and who uses that office as an activist seeking to create housing opportunities for all low-, moderate-, and middle-income Americans. Henry Gonzalez fits that profile perfectly."

The next day, on the House floor, Barney Frank described the award ceremony for the Congressional record. The inscription on the award plaque read as follows, Frank said:

Fannie Mae Housing Hero

Chairman Henry B. Gonzalez for his lifetime efforts to extend the American dream of homeownership to families across Texas and throughout America.

Presented with gratitude by James A. Johnson, Chairman and Chief Executive Officer.

Gonzalez did not live long enough to see how his efforts on behalf of Fannie Mae turned the American dream of homeownership into a nightmare. He died in November 2000.

⇌

Fannie Mae did not limit its outreach to politicians in need of photo ops or community organizers in need of money. The company also enlisted the aid of academics whose research papers on housing issues helped shape the policy debate that was so crucial to the preservation of Fannie's status quo.

The company did this mainly through its financial backing of two academic journals, *Housing Policy Debate* and the *Journal of Housing Research*. The publications, both published quarterly, included papers on a broad spectrum of housing issues. More than 325 authors contributed to the academic journals between 1990 and 1997, Fannie Mae documents show.

The publications were immensely powerful in driving housing policy. The Institute for Scientific Information's *Journal Citation Reports*, now owned by Thomson Reuters, ranked *Housing Policy Debate* the most influential publication in the field of urban studies.

But the publications rarely brought real scrutiny to Fannie and Freddie, ignoring such issues as whether they were, in fact, lowering borrower costs as they claimed. Instead the articles focused on affordable housing ("To Whom Should Limited Housing Resources Be Directed?" asked one paper, published in 1994) and trends in housing ("Housing Finance in Developed Countries: An International Comparison of Efficiency," published in 1992).

Fannie Mae also published its own series of studies on housing, known as Fannie Mae Papers. In these reports, Fannie would ask prominent academics to discuss topics near and dear to the company's heart. In March 2002 Joseph Stiglitz, a Nobel Prize winner, and Peter Orszag, who would later become the head of the Congressional Budget Office under Obama, along with Jonathan Orszag, published a paper entitled "Implications of the New Fannie Mae and Freddie Mac Risk-Based Capital Standard." The noted academics pushed back against the companies' critics who argued that both Fannie and Freddie posed significant risks to the taxpayer.

For example, their paper concluded that even though Fannie and Freddie held much smaller capital cushions than other financial institutions, these would never have to be used. "The probability of a shock as severe as embodied in the risk-based capital standard is substantially less than one in 500,000—and may be smaller than one in three million," the authors wrote. "If the probability of the stress test conditions occurring is less than one in 500,000, and if the GSEs hold sufficient capital to withstand the stress test, the implication is that the expected cost to the government of providing an explicit government guarantee on $1 trillion in GSE debt is less than $2 million."*

---

*In November 2008, as Obama's Congressional Budget Office chief, Orszag would again be tasked with estimating GSE risks. This time, even though the analysis would not be paid for by Fannie, Orszag would again be proven wildly optimistic. He predicted that "there was more than a 50 percent chance that Fannie's and Freddie's future losses would not exceed those already recognized, but there was almost a 5 percent chance that the added losses would total more than $100 billion." In fact, the number as of mid-2010 had exceeded $140 billion.

In November 2003, shortly before Fannie Mae's accounting scandal broke, R. Glenn Hubbard, dean of the Graduate School of Business at Columbia University, authored one such paper defending Fannie Mae's risk management.

Fannie Mae's financing of academic research on such a large scale meant that few housing experts were left to argue the other side of any debate involving the company. Any discussion involving Fannie Mae in these papers was designed to defend the status quo.

One bank lobbyist was interested in hiring academics to write papers that might take a different point of view on housing issues. But most of the experts in the area had been co-opted by Fannie Mae. "I tried to find academics that would do research on these issues and Fannie had bought off all the academics in housing," the lobbyist said. "I had people say to me are you going to give me stipends for the next 20 years like Fannie will?"

The answer was no. The discussion was over.

CHAPTER FIVE

Fannie Mae will never impose a cost on the American taxpayer, which is exactly what Congress intended to ensure when it passed the 1992 Act.

—JAMES A. JOHNSON, chief executive of
Fannie Mae, testifying before the House of
Representatives, Washington, D.C., April 17, 1996

The self-promotion machinery at Fannie Mae was clicking on all cylinders in 1996, with the company claiming to have helped more than 2 million families realize their dreams of homeownership the year before.

Helping millions of homeowners meant increasing the number of loans that Fannie bought from lenders. And between 1993 and 1996, Fannie's portfolio of loans that it kept on its own books doubled from $156 billion to almost $300 billion. From March 1996 through December of that year, the company's loan portfolio grew by almost 10 percent.

Between the loans that it held and the mortgages that Fannie Mae packaged into securities and sold to investors, the company touched fully half of all home loans originated across America. But the risks associated with Fannie Mae's mortgage purchases were also growing. According to OFHEO's 1996 annual report, the percentage of loans the company purchased with a loan-to-value ratio of greater than 90 percent rose from 6 percent in 1992 to 19 percent three years later.

The interest Fannie earned on the loans it purchased and the revenues it generated from the securities it sold to investors translated into record earnings at the company in 1996.

As the company's earnings soared, so too did Jim Johnson's pay. In 1995, he received $5.1 million, a compensation package lush enough to vault him into the very top tier of corporate America. Not only was Johnson's pay more than double that of Leland Brendsel, his counterpart at Freddie Mac, it put him on a par with the most famous CEO in the United States—Jack Welch of General Electric. Johnson's compensation was also roughly equal to that of Walter Shipley, one of the nation's top bankers and head of the prestigious Chase Manhattan Bank.

But unlike GE, Chase, and other fully private companies whose results depended upon providing a product or service that customers wanted to buy, Fannie Mae's earnings benefited enormously from its government associations and perquisites. Just as those benefits contributed mightily to the company's income, so too did they boost Fannie Mae's executive pay.

Since no one had ever tried to assign a monetary value to the benefits Fannie received, the role they played in the company's performance and its pay practices remained a mystery to most outsiders.

To insiders, however, these benefits were well known. So as 1996 dawned, Johnson's top concern remained the privatization threat, the possibility that the government might decide to cut Fannie Mae loose from its long-standing federal moorings.

Such a threat was more real than ever in 1996 because the U.S. Treasury was close to releasing its long-awaited analysis of whether Fannie Mae and Freddie Mac should be privatized. The Treasury's report was one of four required by Congress when it enacted the 1992 Safety and Soundness regulation. All four reports were supposed to have been produced by 1994, but by early 1996, none had yet been published.

That spring, rumors began flying around Washington that the

Treasury's report would indeed discuss the merits of ending Fannie's special government perks. Such a recommendation would have at its heart the goal of eliminating any possibility that the taxpayers would have to rescue the company if it got into trouble. The old privatization monster that Johnson had successfully beaten back over the years seemed about to resurface.

As usual, spending money was Johnson's solution to this problem. And in the first six months of 1996, Fannie Mae spent $1.9 million on lobbying efforts. (This may seem paltry by today's standards and it is. But in the mid-1990s this was real money and, as *Roll Call* pointed out, it put Fannie Mae in the lobbying big leagues, a group topped by Philip Morris at $11 million.)

Treasury's report was already two years overdue when Johnson testified before a subcommittee of the House Banking Committee in April 1996. As if to preempt a possibly damaging report from Treasury, Johnson rhapsodized about Fannie Mae as the All-American good-deeds-doer.

In his testimony, Johnson cited numerous studies showing that Fannie Mae reduced consumers' mortgage costs by between one quarter and one half of one percent. Johnson made no mention of the fact that Fannie Mae had funded much of the research that drew these conclusions.

"Fannie Mae's presence in the market will help save Americans who buy homes this year between $7 and $14 billion," he proclaimed. Best of all, these benefits came at no cost to the taxpayer, he said.

The proverbial free lunch. Except this one, according to Johnson, was real.

And yet, he continued darkly, some in our midst argue that it is time to change Fannie's special status, to withdraw its federal charter. Before abandoning the current system, Johnson said, we must analyze whether a new approach will reduce homebuyer costs and help low-income families as much as Fannie's does.

The testimony was reasoned and coolly argued. Behind the scenes, though, Johnson and his cohorts took the usual brass-knuckles approach to heading off a disastrous Treasury finding.

They had to, because they knew Treasury's report indeed argued that privatizing the mortgage giant and its colleague Freddie Mac was an option worth considering. Both Fannie Mae and Freddie Mac had received advance copies of the Treasury analysis.

Richard Carnell, assistant secretary for financial institutions at the Treasury, tasked staffers to draft the report. One was Edward DeMarco, a career public servant.

The report, finally scheduled to be released on May 15, outlined a roadmap for the privatization of Fannie Mae and Freddie Mac. It also detailed the risks to the taxpayers that the companies represented.

In May, Fannie and Freddie executives demanded meetings with Treasury officials to discuss the report's findings; two such confabs took place at Treasury. Given the increasingly charged political environment, Treasury Secretary Robert Rubin, a long-time friend of Jim Johnson, delegated management of the report to Lawrence Summers, deputy secretary of the Treasury. He convened the meetings and hosted Tim Howard, Fannie's chief financial officer, and Robert Zoellick, its executive vice president. Between 1985 and 1993, Zoellick had been a former senior aide to James Baker when he headed both the State Department and Treasury.

Over two days, the meetings with Fannie Mae took place in the mornings and those with Freddie Mac and its chief executive, Leland Brendsel, in the afternoons. For Treasury staffers it was a marathon.

According to a person who attended, Howard and Zoellick argued strenuously against the report's conclusion. It was "unacceptable," they said.

As the meetings dragged on, it became clear that the privatization roadmap was never going to see the light of day. After the meeting concluded, Summers demanded that the staffers rewrite the report.

The participant recalled Summers's comments after the meeting. "Nobody has bullied me in my adult life the way that Larry did on this one," the staffer said.

Summers and Zoellick met again privately to discuss the position Treasury would take on privatization. After that meeting Zoellick was seen in the halls of Treasury "floating with euphoria."

Fannie Mae had triumphed once again.

When the report was issued two months later, Treasury was bland and noncommittal on the merits of privatizing the two mortgage behemoths. "Firm conclusions regarding the desirability of ending or modifying government sponsorship of Fannie Mae and Freddie Mac are premature," the report said, resorting to Washington's default position of recommending further study of any situation that could kick up a political firestorm.

After manipulating the Treasury to achieve the outcome it desired, Fannie Mae made the following statement: "The Treasury recognized the many uncertainties associated with the analysis [of privatization issues] and the great risks of tinkering with a system that works well."

⇌

While Johnson had successfully beaten back Treasury's straight talk on privatization, across town, in Washington, D.C.'s less genteel southwest quadrant, another storm cloud for Fannie Mae was forming. At the Congressional Budget Office, the arm of the government set up to provide objective and nonpartisan analyses to help lawmakers make budgetary decisions, a lonely official was scrutinizing Fannie's and Freddie's operations. CBO, like Treasury, had been asked by Congress to analyze the companies and consider "the desirability and feasibility" of privatizing them.

Because the work done by CBO almost always relied on facts and figures, its analysis would be quantitative, not based on the soft and fuzzy claims of helping homeowners reach their dreams that Johnson and others at Fannie Mae repeated ad nauseam.

Among the fuzziest of those claims also happened to be the one that the company made most stridently—that Fannie Mae served the American public by passing along to borrowers all of the cost savings the company received from its government association. This was Fannie's crucial rationale for maintaining the status quo and the lucrative perquisites that went with it.

"The golden goose was the fact that you had the government guarantee," a former executive said, "and as long as you didn't screw it up you could make good livings."

But no one had ever tested Fannie Mae's claims that it passed on all those cost savings to the home-buying public. So in 1995, Marvin Phaup, deputy assistant director of CBO's special studies division, set out to determine two things: the amount of the subsidy received by Fannie Mae and Freddie Mac as a result of their implied government backing and how much of it they passed on to borrowers.

Phaup and his CBO colleagues going up against Fannie Mae? It was the quintessential David versus Goliath story, Washington-style.

Phaup, who had been at the CBO since 1976, was keenly interested in how the government budgeted for various federal activities. In 1985, he had done an analysis of the government-sponsored student loan company, known as Sallie Mae. In that piece, he concluded that between 1982 and 1985, Sallie Mae had received a government subsidy worth around $40 million.

As Phaup well knew, Fannie Mae and Freddie Mac were mighty companies with friends in high places. But that did nothing to dampen his enthusiasm for the project.

So Phaup sharpened his pencil and started scrutinizing Fannie and Freddie. He began his analysis with just one assistant; using longitudinal data on bond prices compiled by academics, he compared the differences in borrowing costs investors charged to Fannie and Freddie with those levied on other financial institutions.

Because investors perceived that Fannie and Freddie would be rescued by Uncle Sam if they ever got into trouble—an accurate assessment, as it turned out—the companies paid less to borrow money in the market than comparable private institutions did.

But what was a benefit to Fannie Mae was a cost to those providing the implied guarantees—the taxpayers. And it was this cost that Phaup hoped his research would quantify.

Over the next year, Phaup worked his analysis looking for

missteps or errors. To test his conclusions, he turned to a handful of academics; they confirmed his conclusions.

Phaup had begun to get a glimpse of the benefits Fannie received from the government's implied guarantee—and they were huge. By Phaup's reckoning, the benefits accruing to Fannie Mae and Freddie Mac from their government ties amounted to $7 billion in 1995, which was by no means an unusual year.

Seven billion dollars was a lot of money in 1995. But Phaup's report contained another bombshell: Contrary to the claims made by Fannie and Freddie, the companies passed on to borrowers only about two thirds of the billions in benefits they received. Fannie and Freddie kept $2.1 billion for themselves and their shareholders.

Put another way, for every $3 in savings that Fannie and Freddie received, they delivered $2 to homebuyers, while $1 stayed in the companies' tills.

Suddenly it became clear to Phaup and others at CBO how Fannie Mae could pay its executives as much as it did. Equally evident: Holding on to so much of its subsidy let Fannie Mae fund its elaborate self-preservation scheme, make its massive charitable contributions, pay for its extensive "political outreach," and hire academics to write favorable studies about its role in the mortgage market.

The report concluded that Fannie and Freddie were an extremely costly way to help homeowners across America. "Scant evidence exists of public benefits from the government-sponsored enterprises that would justify a retained taxpayer subsidy that is more than $2 billion annually," the report stated drily. Moreover, CBO questioned Fannie's and Freddie's claims that if their federal charters were revoked, mortgage markets would become less stable and more volatile.

Based on an authoritative analysis of irrefutable figures, the report's message was clear: The money these companies were reaping from their implied guarantees allowed them to distort the political process. Taxpayers were essentially, if unknowingly, handing the companies billions of dollars each year with which they funded their protection game. Phaup had stripped away the façade erected by Fannie and Freddie to make the companies appear to exist solely for the benefit of homeowners.

The CBO report also concluded that because the perks associated with their government backing were largely unknown to those outside Fannie and Freddie, the companies were free to determine how much of those subsidies they kept for themselves. Phaup came up with a term for this—because they retained a lot of the benefits, Fannie and Freddie were "spongy conduits."

But an even more significant cost than the $7 billion highlighted by Phaup and his associates was the expense associated with backing Fannie or Freddie if either should get into financial trouble. CBO did not put a figure on that cost but noted that the federal government had failed to assess fees on either company to contribute to a fund that might cover losses if Fannie or Freddie failed.*

Phaup's report even noted the rich executive pay awarded to high-level officials at both Fannie and Freddie. Reporting that the top five executives at Fannie held $44 million worth of its stock at the end of December 1995, CBO said: "In the context of a government-sponsored enterprise, in which management controls taxpayer subsidies to a significant extent, those compensation agreements can be inconsistent with the interests of taxpayers and the government."

Having laid out this disturbing arithmetic, the CBO report arrived at its explosive conclusion: "Congress may want to revisit the special relationship that exists between the government and Fannie Mae and Freddie Mac."

During the months that Phaup conducted his research, he would regularly send his findings to Fannie Mae and Freddie Mac for feedback, as Treasury had done. The reports would come back with a wide range of criticisms, he recalled years later, but never would they dispute the numbers that Phaup had come up with. Neither would they offer an alternative analysis that might have resulted in a lower implied subsidy.

---

*Had such a fund existed by the mid-1990s, the hundreds of billions of dollars in costs to bail out Fannie and Freddie in 2008 might well have been covered.

Instead, what came back from Fannie were the old clichés about the important role the company played in the mortgage market and how removing its subsidy would be the equivalent of levying a tax on housing.

"In some ways it was surprising to me how ineffective their counter was," Phaup said in 2010. "I thought their arguments were really flimsy."

Even more surprising, given Fannie's reputation for brazen assaults on its critics, was the fact that early on, the company did not seem overly concerned about Phaup's work. Perhaps it was because Johnson viewed CBO staff as accountants, unimaginative bureaucrats obsessed by numbers and unable to see the greater good that Fannie Mae provided to millions.

"Fannie Mae was so powerful, they really didn't take this very seriously at first," Phaup recalled. "It could have been hubris—'Who is this guy?' and 'He's writing about how much we cost?' They didn't take us too seriously at the beginning. Or even halfway through."

Banal people like these could not possibly threaten Fannie's empire, could they?

Moreover, whatever CBO recommended still had to be weighed by Congress. And Fannie's friends there were legion.

Finally, if worse came to worst, the company could always send its henchmen to see June O'Neill, the head of the CBO, to get her to back down on the report. Such a strategy had worked with Larry Summers at Treasury, after all. Of course it would work with the diminutive female economist who headed the Congressional Budget Office.

Nevertheless, as the months passed and Phaup continued his work, the CBO began to sense increasing agitation at Fannie Mae. The company requested meetings with O'Neill but she dodged them. If Fannie Mae had hoped complaining to CBO would chill its researchers' ardor, it was wrong. "The more they pushed back the more we were motivated," Phaup said. "We thought, at last! A worthy opponent!"

By May 1996, CBO's report was finished. The implied government subsidy awarded to Fannie and Freddie was enormous and the amount of it that they kept was huge. It was the first time anyone had quantified what the companies received from taxpayers and how much they hoarded.

Knowing that his "worthy opponent," Fannie Mae, would be likely to attack his report with politically charged language, Phaup had written the report more colorfully than was typical for a CBO paper.

"This paper had much more personal voice in it than CBO usually tolerates, and that was a factor of the pushback we received from the company," he said. "We were inspired to make it rhetorically effective because we knew it was going to mostly be attacked politically with rhetoric."

Fannie Mae knew it had trouble on its hands. That May, O'Neill received a phone call asking if Fannie executives could meet with her to discuss the report's findings before she went to Capitol Hill to deliver it to Congress. She agreed.

"They were outraged by this report or so they said," O'Neill recalled years later. "They said it was unfair, untrue and could they come and see me? So Frank Raines and Bob Zoellick came and met with me and the people from CBO. All of us had the same feeling—that we were being visited by the mafia."

But rather than demolish CBO's argument using irrefutable arithmetic of their own, Fannie's henchmen made the same tired claims that the company was not backed by the government and received no subsidies at all. The best the executives could do was present soft counters to CBO's hard facts.

The CBO staffers in the meeting were stunned that Fannie failed to marshal a compelling defense. "They kept reciting the same thing over and over again probably for an hour, or an hour and a half," O'Neill said. "The general tone was you cannot publish this."

Finally she thanked Raines and Zoellick for coming and told them the report would be published as written.

"I told them 'we stand by this work and we think it is fine,'" O'Neill recalled. "And I said 'we are going to come out with it.'"

Phaup attended the meeting, of course, and was surprised at the reaction from Raines and Zoellick. "Their arguments didn't resonate," he said. "I think they were unaccustomed to dealing with a place like CBO where argumentation matters and threats about what we can do to you in the next election is sort of a badge of honor to be worn among those directors."

O'Neill said she was proud to defend the study. "It was really a terrific report," she said later. "Very well done. It met any standards of academic excellence."

But Fannie Mae did not go quietly. Unable to attack the report on the merits, Johnson and his advisers decided to cast doubt on the CBO analysis by attacking its authors.

"This is a case of policy wonks piling their own prejudices on top of faulty analysis," fumed David Jeffers, Fannie's national spokesman, in the *Washington Post*. "If these digit-heads could figure out a better way of delivering credit to millions of families with the use of private capital markets, while paying the government billions of dollars in federal taxes, then they can get a real job in Washington."

Jeffers told the *New York Times* the CBO report was "the work of economic pencil brains who wouldn't recognize something that works for ordinary home buyers if it bit them in their erasers."

Fannie Mae did not limit its character assaults to discussions with reporters. Johnson himself traveled to Capitol Hill to meet with lawmakers, according to a financial services lobbyist with knowledge of the discussions. "He was going door-to-door to members of the banking committee in the House saying that it was very sad that Marvin Phaup was having personal problems of the mental sort," the lobbyist recalled. "It was totally untrue and very ugly."

Years later, after O'Neill had left public service and become a professor of economics at Baruch College in New York, she remembered the slurs Fannie Mae visited upon CBO. "It was amusing," she said, "but it was also telling that they should be waging this war against an agency that was doing its job."

⇌

Although Fannie had been unable to stop CBO from publishing its report, the company knew that it would have a second chance to undermine its thesis when O'Neill, the CBO director, presented the research to Congress in June.

To that end, Fannie visited with staffs of every member of the House Banking and Financial Services Committee, providing each group with a detailed analysis of the work the company had done in their district, all the mortgages it had financed. In addition, Fannie gave the lawmakers harsh and pointed questions they could ask O'Neill when she testified about the CBO report.

This was clearly not going to be your routine congressional hearing.

Anticipating the fireworks that were sure to erupt, a standing-room-only crowd awaited O'Neill when she arrived in the hearing room for her ten A.M. appearance on June 12, 1996. Audio of her testimony and ensuing questions from lawmakers was transmitted to an overflow room where another crowd had gathered.

"You can always sell tickets to a hanging," Phaup said later.

Seated with Phaup before members of the House Banking Subcommittee on Capital Markets, Securities, and Government-Sponsored Enterprises, chaired by Richard Baker, a Louisiana Republican, O'Neill outlined what the CBO researchers had found.

First was the $7 billion subsidy. But that was only the beginning.

"The chief problem with Fannie Mae and Freddie Mac today is that the value of the subsidy and its allocation among potential beneficiaries are not under the control of the U.S. government," O'Neill testified. "Furthermore, because the economic interests of management are closely aligned with those of shareholders, the housing GSEs have an incentive to retain a portion of the economic benefit for themselves rather than pass all of it on to home buyers."

O'Neill marched on, stating that Fannie's and Freddie's operations were so complex that Congress had little way of knowing what risks the companies were taking. "The inability of the Congress to monitor the fiscal activities of the GSEs, combined with their incentives to retain some of the subsidy, creates an environment in which some portion of the benefit intended for housing is bound to be diverted to unintended uses."

Wrapping up her prepared remarks, O'Neill said that Fannie and Freddie had served a very useful service for years. Among their greatest achievements was their demonstration of how local housing markets could be funded by investors willing to buy mortgage-backed securities.

Now, she argued, the private sector could take over for Fannie and Freddie. "Accordingly, the Congress may want to revisit the special relationship that exists between the government and Fannie Mae and Freddie Mac," O'Neill said. "If the Congress decides to modify that relationship in order to reduce the ability of the housing GSEs to control the benefits of sponsored status, then a variety of policies are available that would do so."

Having concluded her remarks, O'Neill prepared for the questions from subcommittee members. "Before I went to testify, one of Baker's staffers called me and said, 'I should tell you in advance that Fannie Mae has sent over scripts for each one of the members to get up and read when you come,'" O'Neill said later.

All of these members had benefited from Fannie's fund-raising and public outreach efforts. And while several of the members declined to carry water for Fannie—Floyd Flake and Rick Lazio were two that O'Neill remembered—the majority rose up to defend the company.

"Most of the others, each one rose in unison and said more or less the same thing," O'Neill said. "I stuck as best I could to 'just the numbers ma'am.' In terms of Fannie Mae, ours was just an assessment of what was going on."

The toughest cross-examiner of all did not even have a seat on the subcommittee. Bruce Vento, a Minnesota Democrat, attended the hearing as a member of the House Banking

Committee. He lit into O'Neill, asking why the government should consider changing its relationship with Fannie given all the good works the company performed so admirably.

"That was the worst that I saw June take in public," Phaup recalled.

It was perhaps not a coincidence that a Minnesota Democrat would swoop into the hearing to defend Jim Johnson's Fannie Mae. And it was classic Fannie to have others do its dirty work. It was also characteristic of Johnson, according to one person who dealt with him over the years. "If you said: 'No, Jim. We're not going to do that,' he'd hang up the phone and two minutes later some growling son of a bitch would call you," this person said. "Johnson wanted to remain above it all."

But O'Neill hung tough in the face of Vento's bullying. She believed in the report because she knew it was rigorous and based on fact, not the fiction that Fannie Mae trotted out whenever its motives or practices were questioned.

A month later, Zoellick, the Fannie Mae executive who had helped to strong-arm Treasury into rewriting its report, responded to the CBO report in congressional testimony. Pay no attention to the billions in benefits reaped by the company as outlined by the CBO, he said, Wizard of Oz–like. "Fannie Mae, like the rest of the business world, is an example that the whole can be greater than the sum of its parts," he intoned. "In the lexicon of business, the corporation 'adds value' beyond the mere sum of its inputs (or advantages). Once one acknowledges this dynamic analysis— instead of the static, accounting-type straitjacket most typified by CBO's report—it is apparent that the benefits Fannie Mae provides to the public and its shareholders exceed the alleged numbers assigned to its charter advantages."

Needless to say, Congress decided against privatizing Fannie Mae and Freddie Mac, even though it was armed with the CBO estimate of the $7 billion subsidy and the huge amount of that the companies held on to. It was the first of many missed opportunities to protect taxpayers from the disastrous collapse of both companies in the late summer of 2008.

But the CBO report had succeeded in one important way—shifting the Fannie and Freddie dialogue away from total fantasy and bringing it one step closer to reality. Like the child in the story of "The Emperor's New Clothes," O'Neill, Phaup, and their colleagues at the CBO had dared to tell the truth about two immensely powerful companies. The courage of O'Neill and Phaup emboldened others in government to begin scrutinizing the companies' operations more closely.

And the scorched-earth tactics that Fannie had used to combat the CBO's efforts also seemed to backfire. Instead of persuading observers that CBO was wrong, Fannie's strident criticism drew attention to the conclusions made by Phaup and his colleagues. Had the company more or less ignored the study, it might have died with little fanfare.

"Those attempts at ridicule—maybe people did laugh somewhere but I didn't hear it," Phaup said years later. "I think they really helped promote our story by their response. That was a big surprise. How could the Wizard of Oz resort to caricatures of ad hominem attacks? They were bullies."

Equally important, CBO's efforts provided cover for other government studies and analyses of Fannie and Freddie. These included efforts by the Government Accountability Office and the Federal Reserve Bank of Minneapolis.

Phaup is now a research scholar at George Washington University where he also teaches federal budgeting. Looking back on the 1996 battle with Fannie Mae, he said: "The personal attacks from Fannie Mae never really affected me very much. It was a difficult fight but it was made much easier by the fact that June O'Neill was very protective and continued the tradition of fierce independence at the CBO."

Few at Fannie Mae seemed to recognize that the CBO report had, ever so slightly, transformed the climate in which the company operated. Inside the Fannie bubble, the weather was fine.

As the company noted in its annual financial summary for 1996, none of the four studies required by Congress and published that year recommended privatizing the company. Not the

General Accounting Office, Treasury, or CBO made such a recommendation, Fannie said.

The CBO had come closest—it said that given the cost to the taxpayer of the Fannie Mae subsidy, Congress might want to revisit the special relationship the company had with the government. It wasn't really CBO's place to recommend privatization—the budget office's purview was to analyze the costs of budget items to the government, which its report did.

But HUD, the company's erstwhile overseer, took the opposite tack, recommending against full privatization of the company. HUD did, however, suggest that the issue of removing Fannie's federal charter be reexamined "periodically."

Even though it had successfully run the privatization gauntlet, Fannie continued its lobbying efforts with the help of no fewer than thirty-six registered lobbyists in 1996. The company gave almost $200,000 to political parties that year while its employees contributed almost $113,000 to congressional and presidential candidates.

That September, Johnson published a book entitled *Showing America a New Way Home: Expanding Opportunities for Home Ownership*. An encomium to Fannie Mae chock-full of bromides about why every American deserved a home, the cover had a picture of Johnson sitting on the steps of a pristine cottage complete with American flag flying from its porch.

"The book is a blueprint for how to take down the walls, brick by brick, that keep would-be home buyers from realizing the American dream of homeownership," Johnson was quoted as saying. "Major economic and social forces have come together to fuel a powerful momentum for change, offering a unique opportunity for a major increase in homeownership during the next decade."

On the back of the book, housing notables praised its contents. Among them was Mozilo, the Countrywide Financial cofounder whose company supplied Fannie with the most loans. "Jim Johnson has been the most vocal and active leader in closing the shelter gap and repairing the important fabric that binds our great country," he said. Dianne Feinstein, the Democratic senator from

California, weighed in with this: "Homeownership is the corner-stone of the American Dream. Jim Johnson's book is a roadmap toward making that dream come true for more Americans."

⇌

Years later, amid the credit crisis, a former Fannie Mae executive looked back on the company's years of dominance. "There are so many lessons for how missions get warped and the latent conse-quences," he said. "How the housing market and the public pri-vate partnerships morphed into an institution that is corrupt or corrupting at more than the margins."

As the architect of that institution, a company with a no-holds-barred approach to lobbying, silencing critics, defanging regula-tors, and protecting its rich government subsidy, Johnson had a legacy that extended far beyond Fannie Mae. Wall Street firms, mortgage lenders, homebuilders all took a page out of the Johnson playbook. And when their operations got into trouble in the credit crisis of 2008, most were, like Fannie and Freddie, bailed out by taxpayers.

"Imitation follows success and Fannie Mae was hugely suc-cessful in carrying that model forward, independent of the under-lying merits of what they were doing," Phaup said after the credit crisis erupted. Speaking of the large financial institutions that were rescued in 2008, he said: "Now we have created a whole new generation of government sponsored enterprises with implied fed-eral guarantees. The cancer isn't gone—now it has metastasized."

CHAPTER SIX

*Experimentation and the financial service industry's
determination to tap new markets has long proved
that credit can be extended well beyond what skeptics
at any given time in our history deemed feasible. These
past few years have seen the industry accepting new
challenges and addressing lingering issues that had
impeded progress.*

—Eugene Ludwig, Comptroller of the Currency,
May 10, 1996

Precisely a decade before the horror show of 2008, a dress
rehearsal took place when a raft of subprime mortgage lenders
failed, causing billions in losses.

Subprime 1.0, as it might be called, was not the full-blown disaster of a decade later. But it had all the same elements: anything-goes lending, aggressive accounting practices, somnambulant credit-rating agencies, and a merry band of Wall Streeters willing to package loans, no matter how dubious, for sale to unwitting investors.

Unfortunately, Subprime 1.0 was a red flag that regulators, lawmakers, and housing policy wonks determinedly ignored.

⇆

Since the end of World War II a host of regional lenders had made it their business to deal with borrowers that other banks would not touch. Perhaps the borrowers had no credit history or a few blemishes in prior loan repayments. Or maybe their income was irregular because bonuses comprised a big part of their earnings or they worked in seasonal businesses that paid them unevenly.

These small lenders had built their operations on local advertising and a high client "touch." Being family-owned, they were cautious in their analyses of the properties they were lending against and made sure they had enough of the borrower's money tied up in the home to provide a margin of safety that would protect them if the borrower hit the skids.

Some of the bigger names in the business were Advanta, United Companies Financial, Metropolitan Mortgage, the Money Store, and Aames Financial. Some of these companies had issued stock to the public, but they were no high fliers.

That all changed in 1995.

Metropolitan Mortgage of Miami, like many of its peers, was built to serve the needs of nontraditional borrowers. Founded in the 1950s by Walter Falk, an entrepreneur on the Florida mortgage scene who received the first mortgage brokerage license issued by the state, Metropolitan made loans to higher-risk borrowers while trying not to lose money. It was a family business; Falk's son Joe joined in 1978.

Since they knew that their business could succeed only if the borrowers made the loan payments they had agreed to, Metropolitan typically required that applicants provide a cash down payment covering half the amount needed to buy a property; Metropolitan would lend them the other half. To reduce the risk that inflated appraisals might present, Metropolitan employed their own appraisers. This way, the assessor's interest was aligned with that of the lender; he or she was not just focused on getting the deal done.

As a result of its hefty down-payment requirements, Metropolitan's borrowers had enough of their own money in the property— what Wall Street calls "skin in the game"—to ensure that they would be likely to keep up their loan payments. The significant down payments, known as equity in the properties, meant that if the borrowers could not make the payments, they could usually get a friend or family member to help. If all else failed and Metropolitan had to repossess the house, the Falks were pretty confident that they would not lose money in a foreclosure sale.

Metropolitan had one problem: It could only make as many loans as it had the capital for. So, the company took the loans it made, combined them, and sold them to a network of individual investors. When the investors bought the loans, Metropolitan had ready cash to start the lending process all over again.

While Metropolitan's "microsecuritization" lending model was effective, it was no growth machine. Identifying investors who would buy their loans was labor-intensive and firms like Metropolitan had to spend a great deal of time building their networks of potential buyers, allowing the Falks to originate new loans and start the process over again. Beating the bushes for capital kept the Falks from making more and more loans.

Like Elmer Fudd envisioning a duck à l'orange dinner when stalking Daffy Duck, Wall Street saw the promise of a profit feast in these firms. They could first provide the lenders with warehouse lines of credit so that they could make more loans; then Wall Street would move on to the rewards of bundling their mortgages into securities that they could sell to clients. Fees could be generated each step of the way.

In addition, Wall Street knew that its close relationship with these companies would provide it with valuable inside information about the performance of the loans in the portfolios. Finally, if all went well, Wall Street saw rich fees generated by bringing the firms public. Once they had outside capital from stock-market investors, earnings growth among these lenders could increase geometrically.

So, Wall Street firms like Bear Stearns and Lehman Brothers began offering warehouse lines of credit to Metropolitan and its rivals. Just as a lender for a paper mill, or any other manufacturer, provides loans for that manufacturer to fund their inventory until it is sold, banks and Wall Street expanded their credit-line commitments to these lenders so that they could originate a predetermined dollar amount of loans before packaging and selling them to investors. Once the firm's "warehouse" was full, it could either sell the loans to banks or begin to securitize them and sell them to investors.

Each new firm that was assigned a warehouse line from Wall Street represented a new opportunity to expand this nontraditional mortgage lending business. Between 1994 and 1997, subprime mortgage origination boomed, growing from $35 billion to $125 billion. By late 1995, nearly one in five mortgages qualified as subprime.

It was clear that the strengthening economy and the focus on increasing opportunities for new "homeownership" was working.

As these small companies employed their new lines of credit, they saw their earnings grow. Slowly, the "stories" of lenders like Metropolitan became more attractive to stock-market investors. To Wall Street this meant one delightful thing: It was time to bring these hot new "growth companies" public.

When the industrial giants of yesteryear issued shares to the public, it was usually because they had grown so large and were so capital intensive that they needed a great deal of equity to support their debt issuance. But companies like Metropolitan had a more compelling and personal reason to go public: It was a way for the founders, who often were getting close to retirement age with no real succession plan, to create a nest egg of not inconsequential size.

Wall Street investment bankers knew that dangling this carrot in front of family-run subprime lenders would have them rushing to issue public shares. And because investors buying into new stock offerings typically required that existing management stay in place atop the companies during their first few years as a publicly traded enterprise, Wall Street knew that the executives, with one eye on their retirement prize, would be incentivized to supercharge their companies' growth initially.

While large banks and their large investment banking counterparties continued to see the mortgage-lending business as staid, conservative, and respectable, investment bankers at smaller firms like Lehman Brothers, Bear Stearns, Alex Brown, Oppenheimer &

Co., and Friedman, Billings & Ramsey recognized that the changes in underwriting standards brought opportunities to package, pool, and securitize the loans and enrich themselves too.

But subprime lending was not limited to homebuyers. By the middle of the 1990s the word "subprime" represented to bankers a huge opportunity to finance all manner of consumer purchases. If new credit scoring tools, underwriting systems, and lending standards were reliable enough to generate subprime mortgages, surely such loans could be made to people shopping for used cars. By early 1996 analysts were highlighting that the $60 billion market for subprime used-car loans would grow about 15 percent for the next three years. Driving this growth, said analyst Kevin O'Brien of Alex Brown, was a dearth of affordable new cars and the fact that "almost a quarter of Americans had some blemish on their credit histories."

Unlike a home, which stays put if the borrower skips town, automobiles are harder for lenders to repossess. Even if they can get a car back from a deadbeat borrower, its value would almost certainly have fallen dramatically. To compensate for these risks, used-auto lenders typically charged interest rates ten to fifteen times the rates that prime borrowers might receive.

In spite of this cushion for loss, used-car dealers often required loans to be approved by a financing company before a car left the lot. Because the approval process took a day or two, this resulted in many lost sales.

Under pressure from dealers, used-car finance companies began to employ and rely on the same underwriting technologies and credit scoring models, like Fair Isaac Corporation scores, that had been developed in the mortgage industry.

Mercury Finance was one of the largest and most respected of these subprime lenders. And in a May 1995 profile of the company, a Wall Street analyst from Robert W. Baird & Co. named Mike Milunovich felt so strongly about the quality of management at Mercury, the company's financial controls, and overall prospects that he recommended its stock as a keeper to investors. "It's the kind you want to buy and just put away," Milunovich said. While a typical bank might earn 1.25 percent on its assets and 15 percent on its equity, Mercury was able to earn 9.5 percent on assets and an astounding 44 percent on equity.

Although Mercury stood out in this industry, it was not alone. By the end of 1997, the number of subprime used-car-financing companies had increased from about 25 to about 170. Among these were subprime companies set up by auto giants Ford and General Motors, providing dealers with even more certainty that they would rarely have to turn away a potential customer. Since these finance companies generally pooled the loans they made and sold them to investors, they needed volumes to keep their securitization machinery humming. Knowing this, car dealers grew increasingly willing to risk letting a car roll off the lot before they had a firm commitment from a lender; with so many lenders looking for loans to package, it would only be a matter of days before they were able to get finance approval. In the meantime they had made a sale.

With cheap capital provided by so many lenders, the power shifted from the lender to the dealer. Dealers submitting the borrower's loan documents to their favorite finance companies knew they held considerable leverage over the lender. If the finance company asked to see the due diligence the dealer had performed on the borrower, it could take the loan application elsewhere.

Knowing that the loan would end up packaged and sold to investors unaware of how much due diligence had been done on it, the finance companies more often than not accepted the loans to meet the demand from investors buying their securitizations. As capital flooded the industry, the amount of competition increased; this in turn drove down the quality of underwriting and, of course, the loan's longer-term performance.

As loans began to fail, lenders realized that they had two options. They could buy back the bad loans out of the pools and tighten underwriting standards or they could increase yet again their loan volumes to try to outrun the problems they already had. The first choice would have been prudent but carried a significant cost—it would have taken the lender out of the competition and harmed its reputation.

The second option was the path nearly all of the firms took. But it wasn't until early 1997 that the subprime auto finance market began to reveal to investors that its "too good to be true" opportunity was a charade.

That January, Mercury Finance stunned investors with the revelation that it had booked $90 million in imaginary profits over the previous three years. Moreover, it was in default on $61 million in debt payments. This shocker was immediately followed by news that Jayhawk Acceptance, another industry darling, had charged off $15.5 million in bad loans and was in violation of the terms of its debt covenants. Jayhawk's bankers cut the company off and forced it into bankruptcy.

In April 1997, First Merchants Acceptance Corporation made it a hat trick with its announcement of accounting problems "involving unauthorized entries"; by July, having failed to renegotiate a $200 million warehouse facility, the company filed for bankruptcy. By early 1998, most of the subprime auto companies were out of business, merged into larger businesses, or dying slow deaths.

But even as the subprime auto finance lenders were vanishing beneath the waves, the subprime mortgage frenzy continued unabated. Wall Street's funding of previously obscure subprime lenders had grown the industry from a fractured business of mom-and-pop regional lenders to an increasingly concentrated and legitimized business.

As 1997 drew to a close, the top ten subprime lenders accounted for almost 40 percent of originations across the entire mortgage sector. Some companies, like Household International, Associates First Capital, and Beneficial Corporation, originated mortgages and held them on their balance sheets, as traditional lenders did. Others, like NovaStar Financial, ContiMortgage Corporation, FirstPlus Financial Group, Greentree Financial, and Cityscape Financial, securitized their originations. These companies were the go-go engine that produced the greatest growth in the industry.

But many investors failed to realize that, thanks to accounting rules, there was less to these companies' results than met the eye.

In those days, accounting rules allowed companies that pooled loans into securities to recognize as income today what they expected the security to generate over the life of the pool. This was known as "gain-on-sale" accounting.

Firms like Greentree, which specialized in loans on trailer homes, made money on the difference between the interest payments they collected from borrowers and the interest payments they were obligated to make to the investors in the loan pools they had issued. Since gain-on-sale accounting allowed them to book revenues on income that they had not yet earned, the companies were free to make their own assumptions about what they were likely to generate on their loans. Many were exceedingly generous with these estimates, recording the kind of supercharged earnings growth that investors loved.

But these rosy scenarios became problematic when a borrower defaulted on his loan. If the company that made the loan had assumed it would pay off and it didn't, the lender had to reverse the gains it had already recorded. This problem was not limited to bad loans; if interest rates fell and the borrower refinanced his mortgage, the lender would also have to reverse the gain it had taken. Reversing such gains meant restating past earnings downward, an event that usually took a big bite out of the company's stock price.

Although subprime lenders' reliance on gain-on-sale accounting worried some analysts following the companies, in late 1997 the problem came out into the open.

Cityscape Financial was one of the new crop of subprime lenders that was willing to lend a borrower more than 100 percent of a home's purchase price. Operating in the United Kingdom but headquartered in the United States, Cityscape had sought to protect itself from the restatement risks that emerged if its borrowers refinanced their loans. Cityscape's form of protection was to charge a very high prepayment penalty on borrowers to discourage them from refinancing and paying back their loans.

In July 1997, after almost a year of investigation into Cityscape's exorbitant interest rates, the British government ruled them improper. Suddenly under the microscope, Cityscape's investors began questioning its gain-on-sale assumptions. Between September and November, Cityscape's stock lost 90 percent of its value.

By the end of October, Cityscape announced that it had hired bankers to explore a possible sale. But investors seemed to view Cityscape's problems as a one-off and continued to ignore the risks of aggressive gain-on-sale accounting in a falling-interest-rate environment and among lenders who specialized in providing loans to weak borrowers.

One of the few to raise red flags about the risks to the industry was an analyst at the credit-ratings agency Standard & Poor's. In early October 1997, David Graifman warned that rising competition and increasing demands for earnings growth could be prompting lenders to be even more aggressive than usual in their gain-on-sale assumptions. Graifman's warning that the situation "could be severe enough that even the best companies may be impacted" was largely ignored.

About a month later, Greentree Financial, based in Minneapolis, disclosed that it would take a charge of between $125 million and $150 million against gains on loans from as far back as 1994 and 1995. Investors were stunned—the charge was roughly half the company's income for the most recent year and Greentree had been a stock-market darling whose shares had increased tenfold during the prior six years. In one day it lost almost 30 percent of its value.

Even as investors took a shellacking, many continued to believe Greentree's woes were the result of a miscalculation of how many borrowers would refinance their loans because prevailing interest rates had declined. What most analysts and investors had missed was the fact that Greentree's escalating defaults were largely a result of its recently introduced loan programs requiring down payments of only 5 percent. Greentree was simply following Fannie Mae's lead—the government-sponsored mortgage giant had begun buying low down-payment loans in 1994.

The Cityscape and Greentree warning signs did nothing to curb investors' ravenous appetites for the higher-yielding securities issued by subprime mortgage originators. And early in 1998, more established companies began acquiring the subprime originators, appearing to validate the lending strategy. First Union, a major regional bank, paid $2.1 billion to buy the Money Store, which specialized in home equity loans; Conseco, an insurance conglomerate, bought Greentree for $6 billion.

These high-priced acquisitions solidified investors' views that subprime lenders were legitimate, high-growth enterprises whose shares held promise.

In February 1998, a privately held subprime lender called National Finance Corporation launched a successful home-equity-loan securitization program through Bear Stearns. An unusual company, National Finance had been founded in 1989 by a nineteen-year-old named David Silipigno. This dynamo of the subprime world had transformed his company into a private powerhouse with six hundred employees and a mortgage origination machine that underwrote $250 million in loans in 1997. National Finance's future was so bright, it was expected to triple that amount in 1998.

By providing National Finance with the funding it needed to grow, Bear Stearns seemed to have captured an undiscovered subprime gem that could provide many layers of fees to the brokerage firm. Besides advising Silipigno on securitizations, Bear committed to a $200 million warehouse line of credit to the firm and hoped to bring the company public later in the year.

Unfortunately, a world financial crisis got in the way of Bear's and Silipigno's plans. In the summer of 1998 global markets went into a tailspin; the Russian government had devalued its currency in an attempt to address a debt crisis sparked by the government's defaults on its bond obligations. Investors sold

European and Japanese debt and fled to the relative safety of U.S. Treasury securities. As investors panicked and moved to liquidate risky positions, Long-Term Capital Management, a quantitatively driven hedge fund, imploded. As the Federal Reserve stepped in to orchestrate the orderly liquidation of the fund, markets remained jittery. Investor demand for subprime securitized assets dried up.

This market pandemonium took its toll. Not only did the expected benefits of Conseco's acquisition of Greentree fail to materialize, subprime lenders began collapsing en masse. As mortgage origination volumes fell and faulty gain-on-sale practices became evident, United Companies Financial, Southern Pacific Funding, FirstPlus, Amresco, and ContiMortgage all vanished. It appeared the end of Subprime 1.0 was at hand.

Still, the officials at Bear Stearns hoped their backing of National Finance would produce the returns they had dreamed of. In early 1999, Bear asked bankers from Westwood Capital to visit Silipigno's outfit to conduct due diligence before offering National Finance shares to the public. The bankers went to the company's headquarters near Albany, New York, and toured the loan production facilities and systems. Impressed and excited by what they saw, the bankers felt good about taking on the engagement to sell the firm. At the end of the day they stopped in to visit with Silipigno in his office. They told the twentysomething chief executive that they liked what they had seen of National Finance but wanted to know if there was anything about the company that reasonable buyers would want to know.

With that, Silipigno closed the door to the office, drew the blinds, lowered the lights, and sat the two men at a small coffee table. He produced a photo of a stunning, young blond woman and told the bankers that for the past two years he had been "living in sin."

The bankers eyed each other with smirks; if this was the only problem with National Finance, IPOing the company would be a cinch. Then Silipigno produced another photo, this time of a baby. "This is our son," he said solemnly.

Now the men were becoming concerned—the comely blonde

could have a legal case against Silipigno and might be entitled to a piece of the company he had built over the years. But Silipigno assured the bankers that there was no risk of legal action by the woman. Quietly jubilant, the bankers left, certain that they had found a great company to sell.

But over the coming weeks the due diligence on National Finance continued. Amid train trips to and from Albany, requests for financial statements, tax records, and due-diligence requests, one of the bankers kept stumbling over numbers that would not reconcile. Each time he hit the roadblock, he called National Finance for more information. After receiving it, the numbers still didn't foot.

Finally, he called National Finance again but this time he received a return call from Silipigno. "You can keep trying to reconcile the numbers but you can't make them reconcile because they won't," the founder said.

Silipigno admitted to falsifying loan schedules and bilking Bear Stearns out of $5.6 million. It was his way of dealing with tight market conditions and deteriorating loan performance.

Stunned, Bear Stearns took over the operations of National Finance and decided to shut the company down on December 22, 1998. Years later, Silipigno maintained that his company had misappropriated the money solely to meet its payroll as it waited for the subprime mortgage market to rebound.

At the time, the lead banker on the National Finance deal was stupefied. How could Bear have done such a shoddy job of due diligence on the lender? How could Bear have been so lax about watching over its precious $200 million warehouse line?

Ten years later, Bear's shareholders would wonder the same thing, albeit on a much larger scale.

CHAPTER SEVEN

In the 1930s, at the trough of the Depression when Glass-Steagall became law, it was believed that government was the answer. It was believed that stability and growth came from government overriding the functioning of free markets. We are here today to repeal Glass-Steagall because we have learned that government is not the answer. We have learned that freedom and competition are the answers. We have learned that we promote economic growth and we promote stability by having competition and freedom.

—SENATOR PHIL GRAMM, as legislation
rescinding Glass-Steagall passed Congress,
November 12, 1999

Banks and lawmakers had been chipping away at the Depression-era law known as Glass-Steagall for years, gradually eliminating the bits and pieces that had kept certain financial businesses separate from one another. But in the fall of 1999, the law that had protected consumers and individual investors from rapacious bankers for sixty-six years breathed its final breath. That's when legislation initiated by three Republicans—Phil Gramm of Texas, Jim Leach of Iowa, and Virginia's Thomas J. Bliley—finally struck Glass-Steagall down.

In a photograph in the *New York Times* memorializing the November 12, 1999, passage of the law, President Clinton sits at a table, leaning back in his chair. He beams at a semicircle of lawmakers and regulators who are laughing, cheering, and clapping. Among them is the maestro, Alan Greenspan, chairman of the Federal Reserve Board, and of course Gramm himself.

The party atmosphere continued later when Leach, the chairman of the House Banking Committee, hosted an event for those who had helped push through the legislation. Greenspan and other luminaries, including Treasury Secretary Lawrence H. Summers; John D. Hawke Jr., the Comptroller of the Currency; and Gary Gensler, an undersecretary of the Treasury, shared champagne and cake with reporters, lobbyists, and staffers to celebrate passage of the historic law.

Gramm-Leach-Bliley had been designed not to create a new set of rules to keep up with a changing financial world but rather to kill off an old set. The inscription on the celebratory cake took note of this distinction: GLASS-STEAGALL, R.I.P. 1933–1999.

These festivities certainly stood in stark contrast to the mood captured by a photographer in June 1933 when Franklin Delano Roosevelt signed Glass-Steagall into law. No one was smiling or clapping then—it was the depths of the Depression and the handful of legislators summoned to stand by the president in the Oval Office were somber. Poised to sign the bill, the president looked grim.

Sixty-six years later, the elimination of Glass-Steagall was indeed a cause for celebration on Wall Street. Although lawmakers Gramm, Leach, and Bliley had put their names on what was officially called the Financial Services Modernization Act of 1999, the law was really the work of a corporate empire builder named Sanford I. Weill. The chief executive at Travelers Group, an insurance company, Weill wanted to be able to merge its operations with Citibank, one of the nation's oldest institutions, which was then run by John Reed. The last vestiges of Glass-Steagall made such a merger illegal, however. Insurance companies were barred from operating under the same auspices as a commercial bank or investment firm.

Happily for Weill, he had friends in positions of power to help him overcome these legal obstacles. Robert Rubin, the former

Secretary of the Treasury and a former head of Goldman Sachs, was sympathetic to the needs of big banking institutions. During his term at Treasury, he had often signaled that the financial world was unrecognizably different from that of the Depression years and that the laws under which banks operated should be changed to reflect that fact.

Such a view had been circulating inside the top New York banks for years. Back in 1984, an economist at J. P. Morgan named William C. Dudley had authored an internal treatise entitled "Rethinking Glass-Steagall." In it, Dudley* argued in favor of a pre-Depression world where banks were free to engage in a variety of commercial activities.

In May 1998, before the repeal, Travelers and Citibank announced the merger that would create Citigroup; the deal could never have occurred had Reed and Weill not been certain that Glass-Steagall would soon be history.

As Gramm, Leach, and Bliley pushed through their legislation to repeal Glass-Steagall, only a handful of lawmakers had stood firmly against them. One was Byron Dorgan, a Democrat representing North Dakota in the U.S. Senate. He proclaimed on the Senate floor in the spring of 1999, "I think we will look back in 10 years' time and say we should not have done this, but we did because we forgot the lessons of the past, and that that which is true in the 1930s is true in 2010."

Right around the time of Dorgan's prescient prediction, Rubin left Treasury to return to corporate America. He landed a cushy job as vice chairman of Citigroup, a post that some considered payback for his support in gutting Glass-Steagall. Over the following decade Rubin pocketed more than one hundred million

---

*Dudley's deregulatory views were interesting given that he hailed from the New York Fed, the overseer of some of the nation's largest banks. He left Morgan to work for Rubin at Goldman Sachs, first as a senior economic adviser, then as the firm's powerful chief economist. Coming full circle, Dudley returned to the New York Fed in 2007 as a top adviser to its president, Timothy F. Geithner. When Geithner was appointed Treasury secretary by President Obama in 2008, Dudley took over as president of the New York Fed.

dollars as the bank sank deeper and deeper into a risky morass of
its own design.

⇌

With Glass-Steagall dead and gone, financial institutions were
now free to grow large, extending their tentacles into the farthest
reaches of both the nation's and the world's economies.

Glass-Steagall's demise also opened the door to greater risk
taking among banks. While the law was in place, investment banks
with their proprietary trading desks, which took risks with the institution's money, had been separated from commercial banks. This
was designed to protect depositors, whose money could be at peril
if a commercial bank generated losses trading for its own account.

Now, however, there was nothing to stop a commercial bank
from setting up an expansive proprietary trading operation that
used the firm's money to make bets. Gramm-Leach-Bliley allowed
banks to cobble together all kinds of different, and risky, operations. Its enactment, therefore, was a crucial step on the road to
financial perdition known as Too Big to Fail. It enabled far more
banks to become far too powerful and intertwined.

But the clearest signal that big financial players would no longer be allowed to fail came in the late summer of 1998. That was
when the Federal Reserve Bank of New York, the most powerful
regional bank in the Federal Reserve system, brokered a rescue of
a huge and troubled hedge fund called Long-Term Capital Management. The $4 billion fund had been a victim of market turmoil
that grew out of the decision by Russia to default on its debt in
August 1998.

Because it was so large, Long-Term Capital's woes had roiled
financial markets around the world; its losses imperiled many
institutions that conducted its trades. In a dramatic decision, the
Fed summoned every major Wall Street firm that did business
with the fund to its ornate and fortresslike downtown headquarters. Seated around a huge table in the Fed's wood-paneled boardroom, Fed president William J. McDonough, a former executive
at First National Bank of Chicago, ordered the firms to craft a

rescue package that would stop the run on the fund and calm the markets.

Arranging the bailout of Long-Term Capital was a watershed event, a former New York Fed official said, because when other brokerage firms had gotten into trouble, they had received no help from the central bank. Helping a hedge fund escape difficulties that it had brought upon itself was beyond the pale.

Nevertheless, the rescue was deemed a success and on February 15, 1999, *Time* magazine published a cover story titled "The Committee to Save the World: The Inside Story of How the Three Marketeers Have Prevented a Global Economic Meltdown—So Far." Pictured on the cover were Greenspan, Rubin, and Summers, looking smug and self-satisfied.

"It was a moral hazard moment," the former Fed official said. "Look back to the Drexel Burnham failure in 1990—it wanted a meeting at the Fed something fierce but didn't get it. Eight years later, Long-Term Capital Management sent the message that the Fed was in bailout mode."

As if this welcome message to financial risk takers was not enough, the Fed also began arguing for looser capital constraints on the nation's banks during this tumultuous time. These actions effectively encouraged banks to increase their leverage—and their risk levels—dramatically. This left the banks with a much smaller capital cushion to cover unexpected losses.

After Congress passed the 1992 law known as FDICIA, the United States had the most conservative capital requirements in the world. Its banks had to maintain at least 5 percent of capital to total assets and were restricted in the amount of leverage they could employ in their operations.

But slowly, and imperceptibly to most people, regulators watered down these requirements over the next fifteen years. This dilution came under the guise of giving banks more flexibility or making them better able to compete in international markets.

Tight capital restrictions characterized by FDICIA had grown out of anger over the savings and loan crisis of the late 1980s. It, too, had been brought about by freewheeling bank behavior and had cost the taxpayers $500 million. This was the crisis that had prompted Congress to rethink its regulation of Fannie Mae and Freddie Mac and consider privatizing the mortgage giants.

But as the S and L disaster faded into a distant memory, the mood shifted among regulators, and especially among those at the Fed. Rather than argue that bankers needed to be policed and ridden hard, Fed officials started to believe these executives could be trusted to do the right thing for the system, for their shareholders, and for themselves.

Regulators no longer needed to stand over these institutions with a whip, the Fed argued. After all, what banker in his or her right mind would do something crazy enough to blow up their company?

This view was a key element of the free market philosophy that had taken hold during the Reagan years and became even more accepted during the Clinton administration. Greenspan was the chief proponent of the concept that self-interested individuals operate in ways that benefit an entire group. Therefore, he and like-minded people reasoned, they can be counted on not to act destructively.*

Historically, banks have been closely regulated to ensure that the loans they make and invest in are sound. Regulatory capital requirements assign risk weightings to various types of assets that a bank might hold; the higher the risk in a particular asset, the greater the amount of capital cushion a bank must set aside if it holds the asset on its books.

Regulators divide bank capital into tiers, with Tier 1 being the most conservative measure of a bank's financial footing. Tier 1 capital typically consists of cash held by the bank and proceeds from preferred and common stock it has issued. Lower tiers consist of riskier and less liquid assets.

---

*It was not until 2009, with the financial world in tatters, that a chastened Greenspan finally acknowledged the flaws in his view. By then, it was too late to do anything but ridicule the Maestro for his naïveté.

To be considered well capitalized, a bank must have a Tier 1 capital that is at least 6 percent of its risk-adjusted assets.

The watering down of capital requirements and other restrictions on bank operations began in the mid-1990s with actions taken by representatives of the ten major countries that make up the Basel Committee. This group, named for the city in Switzerland where it meets, consists of central bankers from each country as well as top bank supervisors. In 1988 the committee put out its first recommendations, known as the Basel Accord.

The countries making up the committee were France, Germany, Italy, Japan, Luxembourg, the Netherlands, Sweden, Switzerland, the United Kingdom, and the United States. While the committee proposed common standards for bank oversight, the countries that participated were charged with deciding how to implement and police the recommendations.

In 1996, the Basel Committee implemented a new rule designed to reduce the capital requirements on assets held by a bank in its trading book versus those it held in its portfolio. This gave banks a way to set aside less capital on the risky assets they traded than they put against their buy-and-hold portfolios.

In another signal move, the Fed also imposed a new rule that year allowing banks to include in their calculation of Tier 1 capital any holdings they had in trust preferred securities (TRUPS). These complex instruments had characteristics of both debt and equity. By allowing a debt instrument to be counted toward the least risky calculation of capital, this rule essentially allowed the banks to make their financial statements appear sounder than they were.

Ruling that riskier trust preferred securities could be included in Tier 1 capital calculations, the Fed was relaxing what had been the tightest measure of a bank's financial soundness.

The Fed put forward two reasons that trust preferreds would provide solid capital to support a bank: The securities had long maturities and their issuers had the right to put off the payment of accrued dividends for long periods.

But some regulators disliked trust preferreds because of

their debt characteristics. They resembled liabilities, after all, so if the bank that issued them got into trouble, its trust preferred holders would come ahead of other stockholders in recovering their investments. That would produce a deadly money drain at precisely the moment the bank needed to preserve its capital.

As soon as the Fed allowed trust preferred securities to be counted toward Tier 1 capital, bank holding companies began issuing them in droves. By late 1997, nearly one hundred institutions had issued $31 billion of TRUPS. It didn't hurt that these securities also received favorable tax treatment—the interest paid to a TRUPS investor was tax-deductible to the issuer.

Soon, Wall Street was pooling these securities into trusts that it sold to investors.

The Fed's benevolent capital treatment for trust preferred securities not only increased risks in the banking system, it also had the unintended consequence of encouraging institutions to grow too big and difficult for regulators to unwind in a failure.

For example, these securities helped feed a bank merger boom during the early 2000s, which created ever bigger and more complex institutions. Bank executives who found it too expensive to issue stock to pay for an acquisition could happily issue TRUPS instead.

More important, the money that banks received when they sold these securities to investors helped fuel the mortgage lending boom that was on the horizon. By 2005, with that boom in full swing, TRUPS issuance stood at $85 billion, with more than eight hundred banks issuing them.

Banks were also the most aggressive buyers of TRUPS. Because they were eager to have the preferential capital treatment associated with these securities, small and large institutions alike bought up the trust preferreds. Although regulations limited a bank to tying up only one quarter of its Tier 1 capital in these exotic securities, their immense issuance increased the perilous interconnectedness in the banking system. When banks began to quake in the crisis of 2008, TRUPS investors raced to sell their positions, hobbling the already troubled institutions. This poured fuel on a fire that was well on the way to a conflagration.

The Fed was not alone in relaxing financial standards as the twentieth century drew to a close. Other regulators were also working to loosen the rules the housing finance industry had previously abided by.

The Office of Thrift Supervision, the federal regulator charged with minding the nation's savings and loans, was one of these. In 1996, the OTS changed its interpretation of rules governed by the Alternative Mortgage Transaction Parity Act, a 1982 law that removed restrictions on mortgages with features that differed from the standardized 30-year fixed-rate loan. While OTS had barred finance companies like Greentree Financial and Metropolitan Mortgage from selling loans with prepayment penalties, the regulator eliminated that restriction in 1996.

With companies now able to write loans with prepayment penalties, their issuance skyrocketed. Between 1995 and 2000, adjustable-rate loans were five times more likely to have prepayment penalties and fixed-rate mortgages were twice as likely to have them.

Andrew Cuomo, the governor of New York who was named director of HUD in 1997, was another overseer who believed that it was high time to take a new broom to old rules. As the regulator for Fannie and Freddie, his views held considerable sway.

One of Cuomo's earliest moves was to proclaim that Fannie and Freddie should buy more subprime mortgages. "GSE presence in the subprime market could be of significant benefit to lower-income families, minorities, and families living in underserved areas," he said.

With such marching orders from their regulator, Fannie and Freddie were being told to lower the underwriting standards for the loans they bought or packaged into securities. As such, Fannie and Freddie would no longer restrict themselves to good-quality loans. Pushed to buy subprime loans, the degradation of underwriting standards was now under way.

HUD followed this directive by requesting that the Urban

Institute, a nonpartisan and nonprofit economic policy research organization, conduct research on the current efforts by Fannie and Freddie to finance mortgages for low-income people in "underserved" communities. The report, "A Study of the GSE's Single-Family Underwriting Guidelines," was funded by HUD and published in April 1999.

The report had four authors: Kenneth Temkin, George Galster, Roberto Quercia, and Sheila O'Leary. They canvassed "knowledgeable observers" in the mortgage and housing field in Boston, Detroit, Miami, and Seattle; all had experience dealing with Fannie and Freddie.

While acknowledging that Fannie and Freddie did a fine job financing many home mortgages and noting that the companies' new, more flexible loans helped borrowers who had previously been shut out of the housing market, the authors nevertheless concluded that Fannie and Freddie were not doing enough for low-income borrowers.

"The GSE's guidelines, designed to identify creditworthy applicants, are more likely to disqualify borrowers with low incomes, limited wealth, and poor credit histories; applicants with these characteristics are disproportionately minorities," the study said. "Some local and regional lenders serve a greater number of creditworthy low- to moderate-income and minority borrowers than the GSEs, using loan products with more flexible underwriting guidelines than those allowed by Fannie Mae or Freddie Mac."

The message was clear: Fannie's and Freddie's underwriting standards were too high; low-income loan originations were too low.

Of the four authors on the report, three had extensive ties to Fannie Mae: Temkin, Galster, and Quercia. Galster was a consultant to the company and all three had been on the receiving end of research money from the Fannie Mae Foundation.

The report, like the questioned Boston Fed study before it, made political waves, upping the pressure on Fannie and Freddie to lower their standards on the mortgages they would buy. Indeed, it was just three months after this report emerged that Cuomo announced new and aggressive affordable housing goals for Fannie and Freddie.

Affordable housing goals had been instituted by the 1992 safety and soundness legislation, and in 1999 they required that 30 percent of the housing units financed by the companies' mortgage purchases benefit low- and moderate-income families. Moreover, 30 percent of the housing units financed by their mortgage buys had to be located in urban settings.

When Cuomo announced his initiative in 1999, he raised these goals. Fannie and Freddie were already buying 42 percent of their mortgage loans to benefit low- and moderate-income families, but under Cuomo's new rules, that requirement would rise to 50 percent.

The mortgage purchases would provide housing for 28 million low- and moderate-income families, Cuomo crowed in a press conference announcing the new goals. A veritable friends-of-Fannie lovefest, the event showcased Franklin Raines, the Fannie Mae executive who had tried to intimidate June O'Neill of the Congressional Budget Office, and Charles Ruma, an Ohio homebuilder and president of the National Association of Homebuilders who chaired Fannie Mae's Housing Policy Advisory Council.

Another man at the microphone was Bart Harvey, chairman of the Enterprise Foundation, a Maryland-based nonprofit organization that advocates for moderate-income housing. Enterprise received $11.1 million from the Fannie Mae Foundation over the decade that began in 1993 and had two Fannie Mae executives on its board.

Cuomo predicted great things from his plan. "It will strengthen our economy and create jobs by stimulating more home construction," he said. "It will help ease the terrible shortage of affordable housing plaguing far too many communities, and it will help reduce the huge homeownership gap dividing whites from minorities and suburbs from cities."

And if Fannie and Freddie failed to meet these goals? Cuomo held out a stick: possible penalties of $10,000 for each day that the targets remained unmet.

President Clinton even chimed in on the initiative. "During the last six and a half years, my administration has put tremendous emphasis on promoting homeowners and making housing more affordable for all Americans," the president said in a statement accompanying HUD's press release. Noting that 66 percent of all Americans now owned their homes, he added: "Our housing programs and institutions have been a success. Today, we take another significant step. Raising the GSE's goals will help us generate increased momentum in addressing the nation's housing needs. I congratulate HUD Secretary Andrew Cuomo and the entire HUD team on their efforts in this important area."

Clinton's public-private partnership was ramping up. Regulators were relaxing rules, Fannie and Freddie were inflating their portfolios, homebuilders and subprime lenders were flexing their muscles too. To meet the goals Fannie and Freddie had to buy riskier mortgages, such as those defined as subprime.

Some $160 billion in subprime loans would be underwritten in 1999, up from $40 billion five years earlier. And in another four years, that figure would jump to $332 billion.

Many of these loans wound up in Fannie's and Freddie's portfolios. By 2008, some $1.6 trillion of toxic mortgages, or almost half of those that were written, were purchased or guaranteed by Fannie and Freddie.

In 1999, the growth trajectory that Johnson had dreamed of for Fannie was fast becoming a reality.

⇌

As Glass-Steagall was falling and the Fed and other regulators were easing up on financial institutions, Johnson began preparing for his exit from Fannie Mae. To outsiders, both the company and its chief executive appeared to be doing fabulously. During 1998, Fannie's mortgage financing hit the $1 trillion mark and Johnson basked in the glow of being named Washingtonian of the Year by *Washingtonian* magazine.

But internally, top executives knew the year had been a difficult one for the company. Dislocations in the financial markets stemming from the Russian debt default had taken a toll. Indeed, to make its earnings-per-share targets and trigger the all-important executive pay bonanzas, Fannie had had to resort to accounting fraud.

Because bonuses at Fannie Mae were largely based on per-share earnings growth, it was paramount to keep profits escalating to guarantee bonus payouts. And in 1998, top Fannie officials had begun manipulating the company's results by dipping into various profit cookie jars to produce the level of income necessary to generate bonus payouts to top management.

Federal investigators later found that you could predict what Fannie's earnings-per-share would be at year-end, almost to the penny, if you knew the maximum earnings-per-share bonus payout target set by management at the beginning of each year. Between 1998 and 2002, actual earnings and the bonus payout target differed only by a fraction of a cent, the investigators found.

Investigators uncovered documents from 1998 detailing the tactics used by Leanne Spencer, a finance official at Fannie, to make the company's $2.48 per-share bonus target. That year, Fannie Mae earned $2.4764 per share.

In a mid-November memo to her superiors, Spencer forecast that the company was on track to earn $2.4744 per share, just shy of what was needed to generate maximum bonus payments to executives. She described various ways she could juice the company's profits if need be.

"What do I have up my sleeve to solve an earnings shortfall?" she asked rhetorically. Then she proceeded to answer, detailing three options that would generate $6 million in earnings. One proposal was to return to Fannie's income statement $1.8 million previously set aside to cover an environmental tax that it no longer had to pay. Another $1 million came back to the company in the form of miscellaneous income related to loss recoveries among its lenders when loans went bad.

Spencer boasted: "This is how I would solve a small problem."

Instrumental in helping Fannie achieve these earnings and bonus targets was the company's minimal capital requirement.

At the end of 1998, Fannie Mae held capital of only 3.64 percent
of its assets. By comparison, the ratio for banks insured by the
FDIC stood at 8.22 percent at that time.

But 1998 had been tough enough for Fannie that by the time
November rolled around, it looked as though the bonus figures
would fall short.

That month, Thomas Nides, Fannie's executive vice president
for human resources, warned a swath of top managers that earnings growth was coming in weak as the year-end approached.

"You know that as a management group member, you help
drive the performance of the company," Nides wrote in a memo.
"That's why your total compensation is tied to how well Fannie
Mae does each year. *Current estimates indicate that we are exceeding the aggressive EPS target set by our Board of Directors. However, currently we do not expect to exceed the target to as great an
extent as we did last year. As a result, the AIP bonus pool is somewhat smaller than it was last year, which means your bonus may
be smaller than last year.*" The emphasis was Nides's.

The memo achieved the desired result. Fannie Mae executives
wound up exceeding their target in 1998 by accounting improperly for low-income housing tax credits the company received.
The result: 547 people shared in $27.1 million in bonuses. This
was a record—the bonuses represented 0.79 percent of Fannie
Mae's after-tax profits, more than ever before in the company's
history.*

The eighteen directors charged with overseeing Fannie Mae
for both the government and its shareholders received regular
updates on the company's progress toward making its earnings
forecasts. Thirteen of these directors were elected by owners of
Fannie shares while five were appointed by the president of the
United States. Among the appointees one always hailed from the

---

*Executive pay at Fannie Mae was a well-kept secret and the company successfully
  blocked some in Congress, such as Representative Richard Baker of Louisiana,
  from receiving information about salaries and bonuses paid by the company. It was
  only after Fannie was caught cooking its books that details of its lavish executive
  pay came out.

homebuilding industry, another from a mortgage lending business, and a third from the real estate arena.

In 1998, Fannie's board was burnished by the addition of Stephen Friedman, former chief executive of Goldman Sachs, the prestigious Wall Street firm. Brokerage firms like Goldman Sachs flourished from the fees generated by underwriting securities issued by Fannie and Freddie, with fees totaling $100 million a year. With a former Goldmanite on Fannie's board, Goldman was likely to gain even more of the favors the company had to dish out.

In 1999, Johnson joined Goldman's board, stepping into a highly lucrative position that offered rich investment opportunities overseen by the firm and opened doors for Johnson around the world. In 2000, the Goldman board position paid Johnson $50,000, not counting stock awards.

Johnson was still on the Goldman board in 2010, when the Securities and Exchange Commission sued the investment bank for securities fraud relating to its sale of a dubious mortgage security. By that time, Johnson was earning almost $500,000 for his work on the Goldman board.

With Goldman's former head on Fannie's board and Fannie's former chief on Goldman's, a close and mutually profitable association between the two companies was assured. And it was one that would last well into the financial crisis years.

The firm even helped Fannie manipulate its accounting, according to investigators who uncovered a 2001 deal designed by Goldman Sachs to boost the company's earnings. The complex transaction involved a mortgage-backed security that allowed Fannie to "better manage the recognition of income" for accounting purposes. It let Fannie push $107 million in income to future years—providing another cookie jar to delve into when the company needed it.

Goldman received $625,000 in fees for one of the two dubious transactions unearthed by OFHEO investigators, who concluded that the deals "had no significant purpose other than to achieve desired accounting results."

Although the federal investigation into Fannie's accounting

tricks determined that they had begun under Johnson's watch, he was never charged with civil fraud, as his successor Franklin Raines was. In any case, by the time the investigation had been launched, Johnson was long gone.

⇄

The accounting fraud at Fannie went undiscovered until 2005 when an investigation by OFHEO unearthed it. In a voluminous, intensely detailed 2006 report, OFHEO noted that if Fannie Mae had used appropriate accounting methods in 1998, the company's performance would have generated no executive bonuses at all.

A lawsuit filed by the Securities and Exchange Commission in 2006 said the company's 1998 results were "intentionally manipulated to trigger management bonuses."

Although a highly kept secret at the time, Johnson's bonus for 1998 was $1.9 million, investigators determined. It later emerged that the company had made inaccurate disclosures when it said Johnson earned a total of almost $7 million in 1998. In actuality, his total compensation that year was more like $21 million, OFHEO said, referring to an internal Fannie Mae analysis it had turned up.

None of this was mentioned when Fannie Mae announced record earnings for 1998. The company bragged about the $100 billion growth in its portfolio from the year earlier and its record purchases of $188 billion in mortgages, up from $71 billion the year before.

And yet, after a decade running Fannie Mae, Johnson was ready to move on. To help with the transition to a new chief executive, Johnson agreed to remain at the company for a year, as chairman of its powerful executive committee.

Why would he leave Fannie Mae just as all of his hard work was beginning to pay off? Former colleagues speculate that he may have been making himself available for an appointment to run the Treasury Department when the current secretary, Bob Rubin, left government service to return to the private sector.

Rubin's departure was imminent, an open secret in Washington circles. In 1997, Johnson had pushed hard to name Rubin head of the prestigious Carnegie Corporation of New York, a grant-making foundation created by Andrew Carnegie in 1911.

Johnson was chairman of the search committee charged with identifying candidates to head the foundation. As he lobbied for Rubin, others on the committee felt that Vartan Gregorian, a self-made man and brilliant educator who was president of Brown University, was a better candidate.

"They were flabbergasted at the way Johnson ran them around because he wanted Bob Rubin rather than Vartan," said one person briefed on the discussions. "It ultimately worked out, but it was a good example of how Johnson likes being in the club of the elite. That was going to be a great job for someone coming out of the government."

In a rare loss for Johnson, Gregorian got the nod.

Had Rubin been tapped to head the Carnegie Corporation, the former Treasury secretary with close ties to the Clinton administration would have had Johnson to thank for the job. And that, as Johnson knew better than anyone, would have been an immensely valuable chit to have out to Rubin.

Still, Johnson could afford to be patient as he awaited the prize of a cabinet position. During his years at Fannie Mae, making a cool $100 million, he made sure to arrange for an inflation-adjusted consulting contract with the company that began at $390,000 a year. His pension—around $900,000 a year—was secure and so were company-paid perquisites such as a car and driver for him and his wife, office space at the prestigious Watergate complex, and the services of two employees.

And it wasn't as if Johnson would be spending his days bored on the golf course. He was chairman of the prestigious Brookings Institution, and head of the John F. Kennedy Center for the Performing Arts in Washington. Johnson also sat on the boards of KB Home, Target Corp., and United Healthcare and was about to become a director at Goldman Sachs.

Looking back on his years at Fannie Mae in a November 1998 speech at the National Press Club, Johnson once again extolled the virtues of homeownership and his company's role in promoting it. He spoke of the public-private partnership he had been so instrumental in crafting. "American government policies that support homeownership are among the most efficient and effective ever devised," he said. "The American housing finance system, as it has developed and matured over the past 60 years, is at its core a durable and effective partnership between government and the private sector. Fannie Mae is at the heart of this enormously successful public-private partnership."

Just a month later, however, as Johnson prepared to leave the chairmanship of Fannie Mae to his trusted enforcer, Franklin Raines, another threat to the company arose. Clinton administration officials had begun discussing the merits of requiring the company to pay to register its securities. Fannie's exemption from paying these fees was one of the valuable benefits reaped from its government association.

According to the *Washington Post*, Fannie officials called John Podesta, the White House chief of staff, to argue against the idea. He was unreachable, so Fannie asked one hundred mayors and other local officials to call Podesta's private telephone line that day to complain. The idea of forcing Fannie to pay registration fees on its securities died soon thereafter.

It was as though Johnson, even with one foot out the door, was reminding the government that messing with his company was unwise.

After the accounting scandal erupted and the subprime mortgage crisis rocked the economy, some who knew Johnson wondered if he had left Fannie Mae because he saw that the company's growth days were over and that its risk profile was rising.

"I'm not sure he totally saw the handwriting on the wall," said one former executive who worked closely with him. "I think Johnson always moved on. He had all the perks of a big deal. Maybe he felt there were some other fish to fry including getting involved in a presidential election. Remember, in good times you start to believe in your own infallibility."

CHAPTER EIGHT

The recent rise in the homeownership rate to over 67 percent in the third quarter of this year owes, in part, to the healthy economic expansion with its robust job growth. But part of the gains have also come about because innovative lenders, like you, have created a far broader spectrum of mortgage products and have increased the efficiency of loan originations and underwriting. Ongoing progress in streamlining the loan application and origination process and in tailoring mortgages to individual homebuyers is needed to continue these gains in homeownership.

—ALAN GREENSPAN, chairman of the Federal
Reserve Board, addressing America's Community
Bankers, Washington, D.C., November 2, 1999

To regulators at the Federal Reserve Board, the financial crisis of 1998 and the collapse of the giant hedge fund Long-Term Capital Management had been an undeniably terrifying event. Officials at the prestigious New York Fed knew how extraordinary it had been for them to help the hedge fund; they were sensitive to the fact that they had aided in a speculator's rescue and worked hard to downplay their role. A spokesman for the New York Fed even went so far as to complain, off the record of course, that the headline in a *New York Times* article about the event overstated the Fed's role. Never mind that the headline—"Seeing a Fund as

Too Big to Fail, New York Fed Assists Its Bailout"—couldn't have been more accurate.

For years after the rescue, many Fed officials spoke publicly of the lessons to be learned from the disaster. Chief among them were the dangers of increasingly interconnected world markets and economies and the threats of institutions that had grown so large that their failures could imperil the entire financial system.

"It was a humbling and enlightening experience for us all," said Roger Ferguson, a member of the prestigious Board of Governors of the Federal Reserve in a 1998 speech touching on the Long-Term Capital rescue. "It should cause all of us to reassess our practices and our views about the underlying nature of market risks."

But this advice appears to have been for public consumption only because it went unheeded, especially within Ferguson's own organization. Indeed, the Fed seemed to have conducted precious little soul-searching as the 1998 crisis receded into the mists of investors' memories. Like Subprime 1.0, the Long-Term Capital Management event proved to be an opportunity that was ignored by regulators charged with protecting consumers and investors from risky financial institutions and their practices.

One big reason everyone felt they could move on from the LTCM mess was the stupendous performance of the stock market, especially the technology sector. It is an investing truth that rising markets create complacency and in late 1998, with the Dow Jones Industrial Average marching inexorably to the never-before-scaled 10,000 level, investors were especially unworried.

The index of thirty industrial stocks had started off the 1990s at 2,753, but in March 1999 it closed above 10,000 for the first time. Two months later, it had soared another 1,000 points; by the time the decade ended, the Dow stood at 11,497, a gain of more than 300 percent.

Investor enthusiasm for a new communications and commerce tool called the Internet—and for the companies that might capitalize on its applications—were propelling the stock market. All eyes were on tech companies, whose potential profits were deemed by investors to be all but limitless. Initial public offerings of companies with no profits, few revenues, and the vaguest of business plans were oversubscribed by investors eager to get in on the ground floor of the next hot stock.

It was a bubble that would create tens of billions in losses and considerable angst when it popped in 2000. But while the good times were rolling, top financial regulators like Alan Greenspan exulted over the wonders of technological advancements. Although it was obvious to many that the technology stock mania would end badly, Greenspan and his colleagues at the Fed refused to tamp down the euphoria. They could have raised margin requirements, for example, increasing the amount of their own money investors had to put up to buy stock using borrowed funds.

In addition, even as they ignored the stock market bubble, these very regulators were laying the groundwork for a subsequent, far more virulent mania in the credit markets. They did this by siding with the banks who wanted to loosen the capital strings that bound them, too tightly they thought, in this brave new world.

Unfettered capitalism coupled with the ownership society—where individuals were invited to participate in the wealth creation engine of the financial markets—had become a potent combination. It had produced riches for corporate executives like Jim Johnson and considerable wealth for individuals, and had replaced federal deficits with an unheard-of government surplus, generated largely from taxes paid by investors on their market gains.

The belief that the free market could police itself better than any government regulator had already taken hold. So, even as Ferguson and other Federal Reserve officials paid lip service to the important lessons of the 1998 crisis, their actions ignored them. Instead of heightening the scrutiny of risky practices among the big banks they oversaw, the Fed backed these institutions' desires to reduce capital requirements and increase their leverage and profits. Instead of reining in financial institutions in areas that could result in losses, Fed officials loosened them.

In other words, the Fed was busy becoming a pushover, not a policeman.

"It was explicit in those years, if you worked inside the Fed, that you were partners with the banks," said a former Fed official. "You were not adversaries."

One of the banks' crucial partners at the Fed, albeit behind the scenes, was Ferguson, the vice-chairman. From 1997 when he joined the Federal Reserve as a governor until he resigned to return to the private sector in 2006, Ferguson was a strong advocate for the banks among global financial regulators.

President Clinton appointed Ferguson vice-chairman of the Fed in 1999. He began his career as a lawyer at Davis, Polk & Wardwell, advising some of the nation's largest banks on mergers and acquisitions, initial public offerings, and syndicated loans. Davis, Polk was closely linked to the Fed; years later, during the financial maelstrom of 2008, the firm would also advise the New York Fed on its various bailouts.

Ferguson was also the Fed's point man on the Basel Committee, the group of central bankers and international financial regulators that meets regularly to discuss and hammer out standards and practices followed by banks around the world. And according to those who interacted with him in this capacity, he consistently pushed for rule changes requested by the nation's largest banks and that were beneficial to them.

In 1998, when the Fed governors voted 5–0 to approve the megamerger of Citibank and Travelers, Ferguson abstained. His wife, Annette Nazareth, was a managing director at Smith Barney, a Travelers unit, when the application was being considered.

In a speech in October 1999 to the Bond Market Association in New York City, Ferguson outlined his preference for less, not more, regulation. "Heavier supervision and regulation of banks and other financial firms is not a solution, despite the size of some institutions today and their potential for contributing to systemic risk," he said. "Increased oversight can undermine market discipline and contribute to moral hazard. Less reliance on governments and more on market forces is the key to preparing the financial system for the next millennium."

This desire for decreased regulatory oversight took on sinister overtones in 2003 at a crucial moment in Basel Committee discussions about reducing capital requirements for large banks.

The FDIC pushed for a belt-and-suspenders approach to capital requirements, arguing for the retention in the United States of a measure called the leverage ratio. Against immense pressure from other regulators, the FDIC prevailed, saving the banking system from far larger losses when the crisis hit. Officials at the FDIC were also worried that the proposed capital changes would vastly, and dangerously, reduce the cushion the banks were required to set aside to cover future losses. Researchers at the FDIC calculated what the reduced capital requirements would mean in a paper they planned to publish. Their findings: Major banks would have to set aside fully 40 percent less capital than under previous rules if the proposal went into effect.

This reduction alarmed regulators at the FDIC. They were, justifiably, concerned about potential losses to their deposit insurance fund that would result from large bank failures and that could end up as obligations of the taxpayers. A 40 percent reduction in capital would leave the banks dangerously exposed to problems in an economic downturn, they reckoned.

As the FDIC researchers neared publication of their paper, they sent it to the Fed for comments as a courtesy among colleagues. Ferguson immediately tried to silence the critics and contacted Donald Powell, the chairman of the FDIC. His message: Do not publish the paper.

It was reminiscent of the difficulties encountered by Walker Todd back in 1993 when officials at the Board of Governors had tried to stop the publication of his paper outlining the dangers of expanding the Fed's ability to rescue troubled institutions.*

*Moving to thwart the free flow of information about regulatory changes or actions was de rigueur at the Fed, as taxpayers found during the financial crisis of 2008. It became especially problematic for the Fed in its rescue of the American International Group, once the world's largest insurer, in the fall of 2008. At that time, the

One reason Ferguson may have wanted to prevent publication of the FDIC paper was that it showed clearly how big banks were going to benefit from reduced capital requirements, putting smaller banks at a disadvantage. As it happened, Powell stood firm and the FDIC published its paper over Ferguson's objections.

The FDIC researchers could not have been more prescient. Among their more accurate assessments were predictions of unusual market downturns, especially the difficulties in predicting them and safeguarding taxpayers against their ill effects.

"No one knows how to measure the hundred year flood plain for a large complex bank," the FDIC said. "Placing exclusive reliance on banks' statistical estimates of the likelihood of these tail events is not an acceptable way to protect the deposit insurance funds or, ultimately, the taxpayer. Even assuming a bank's models are accurate, the capital banks should hold from a social welfare perspective would normally be expected to exceed the capital that the banker calculates to meet his own needs."

This passage got to the heart of what the bankers—and by extension the Fed—had been pushing the Basel Committee to adopt: capital standards that were based upon internal risk assessments provided not by regulators but by the financial institutions themselves. It was the equivalent of allowing a serial speeding driver to set limits on how fast cars should be allowed to go on a highway.

A belief had arisen during the late 1990s that bankers had so improved their risk-management and loss-prediction techniques that regulators could rely on them and their financial models to develop capital standards. Not everyone agreed—certainly the FDIC rejected the notion. But the Fed was among those regulators who were more than willing to put the bankers in the driver's seat. Others were the Office of Thrift Supervision, which oversaw

---

Fed tried to keep secret the names of the big banks that taxpayers' money went to as part of the bailout. The Fed's secrecy and its refusal to turn over information about its actions during the credit crisis has engendered a lack of trust in the institution and has encouraged those calling for a full audit of its actions, something that has never occurred before.

savings banks, and the Comptroller of the Currency, which scrutinized large national banks.

Not surprisingly, when the Basel Committee began discussing ways to improve the standards set more than ten years earlier, in 1988, the tone inside the meetings greatly supported the desires of the nation's largest banks.

Executives at the big banks had watched Jim Johnson's success years earlier in ensuring that capital standards at Fannie Mae would be set exceedingly low. They knew that their profits would be bolstered if they could reduce the amount of money regulators required them to set aside for problem loans. Smaller setasides meant more money to be deployed in lending or purchases of income-producing securities. Banks also recognized what Johnson had—higher profits meant loftier executive pay.

But reducing capital requirements would also leave the banks in a more perilous position if their loans and investments went bad. And thanks to the elimination of Glass-Steagall, banks were now allowed to extend and expand their operations almost without limit. Such expansion increased the likelihood of losses in the years ahead.

The Fed bought into the banks' argument that because losses and bank failures had been rare during the mid- to late '90s, this was evidence that these institutions had become better at managing their risk taking. Top Fed officials ignored one of the most basic lessons in economics—that even though the sun may be shining today, you should set aside money for the inevitable rainstorm.

Others, such as Chairman Greenspan, seemed to have consciously decided that because it rained so infrequently, it wasn't worth discussing such an outcome. In a 2000 speech, he said: "We have chosen capital standards that by any stretch of the imagination cannot protect against all potential adverse loss outcomes. There is implicit in this exercise the admission that, in certain episodes, problems at commercial banks and other financial institutions, when their risk-management systems prove inadequate, will be handled by central banks."

When discussions about changing capital rules began percolating in 1999, the first thing the Basel Committee said was that capital requirements were not going to be reduced. Improving risk management was the public spin describing the talks.

In a May 2002 speech in Lexington, Virginia, for example, Ferguson said: "Any regulatory capital standard must, of course, require banks to hold an amount of capital sufficient to get them through, not the worst imaginable, but nevertheless rough times. Competition within the industry and among banking systems of different countries often presses for less. Such pressures must be resisted, as supervisors throughout the world work together to develop a more accurate standard that is sufficiently rigorous and that accomplishes our common goals."

But internally, at meetings in which the new standards were discussed among regulators and market participants, granting the banks' wishes seemed to be the Fed's priority, according to a regular attendee.

The Fed concluded that regulators could use banks' own risk metrics to devise capital requirements because the regulator started from the position that these institutions had learned to estimate losses more reliably than they had in the past.

To some outside the Fed, relying on banks' figures represented, at best, a delegation of an important oversight task and, at worst, a dereliction of duty. "They were going to the industry to get a lot of the data," the fellow regulator said. "They were calibrating their formulas off the banks' data. The Fed would have been hard pressed to even come up with the estimates because only the banks really had the data."

Some regulators argued that instead of relying on banks' estimates of future losses, a better approach would be to determine capital requirements using actual losses that the banks had experienced in the 1980s and 1990s. Applying those real and painful losses to the equation, officials at the FDIC concluded that the new capital requirements proposed under the second round of Basel left little room for error if banks experienced losses outside their own estimates.

"The Fed's worldview was dominated by the big banks," the regulatory colleague said. "If you look back at all the things that were done, all the rulemaking was in the same direction—that the banks knew what they were doing and we needed to rely more on their internal systems."

This view came through loud and clear in meetings at the New York Fed's wood-paneled boardroom where regulators and the big banks discussed the new capital requirements. According to a regulatory official who attended these meetings, the message transmitted to the banks was to fear not, the Fed was on their side.

"At one of the first meetings I went to," this official said, "there were people from the highest levels of all the regulatory agencies, both policy and staff, along with chief risk officers at the top ten banks. The banks were told point-blank the changes were going to be attractive from a capital standpoint."

Although after the crisis Ferguson denied that he and others at the Fed had transmitted a dual message, its existence could not have been clearer to participants in these meetings. In public speeches, at Congressional hearings, Fed officials insisted it had no interest in reducing capital requirements. But behind the scenes, the message to the banks was an emphatic "we understand where you are coming from" and "we're on your side," one participant said.

The Fed also angered its fellow regulators by maintaining a disturbing secrecy about the figures and formulas it was using to come up with the new capital requirements. According to people involved in the discussions, the Fed repeatedly pushed back against the FDIC's desire to publish tables showing the range of effects that capital changes would have on different institutions. These tables showed how the big banks benefited from the proposed rule changes far more than small banks did.

"When you publish a bunch of formulas with a lot of Greek letters it's hard to understand what that means," said one regulator involved in the battle. "They did not want to risk having the small banks get wind of the differences and raising a stink on Capitol Hill."

The FDIC prevailed, however, and the tables were included.

The Fed has always been highly secretive about its operations, routinely arguing that disclosure of its actions and deliberations could threaten the financial system. But some in the regulatory community were disturbed by the Fed's secrecy in the years leading up to the crisis because it seemed to indicate a desire by the Fed to manipulate the debate on crucial decisions. In the pre-crisis days, the information the Fed wanted to withhold was critical to the public understanding of proposed changes to bank capital rules and posed no threat to world markets. As a result, the Fed's actions were dubious at best and manipulative at worst.

⇌

While the vast reductions in bank capital requirements did not ultimately take effect, one change recommended by the Basel Committee on Banking Supervision in 2001, more than any other, opened wide the floodgates for the mortgage securities mania.

This crucial change emerged deep in a January 2001 proposal in a section on asset-backed securities. These instruments were essentially bundles of loans, such as mortgages, corporate loans, car loans, and credit-card receivables, put together by banks and sold to investors. The market for these securities had grown dramatically and banks were not only pooling these loans and selling them, they were also holding them on their own books.

"In view of the vast developments that have occurred in financial markets since the introduction of the 1988 Basel Accord, the Committee recognises the importance in developing a comprehensive capital framework for asset securitisation," the proposal stated. The new framework devised by the committee changed the risk weightings that regulators would apply to these types of securities and the resulting capital requirements that the banks would have to set aside if they held them on their balance sheets.

The framework made two momentous shifts. One significantly reduced the amount of capital a bank was required to set aside on privately issued mortgage-backed securities, such as those issued by Countrywide Financial, New Century, and other lenders. The other vastly increased the importance of the credit-rating agencies, for all but the few global banks that would be allowed to use their "internal ratings based" approach, by tying risk weightings on securitizations to the ratings these agencies assigned to them.

The shifts seemed innocuous at the time. But years later, when the mortgage boom collapsed, these decisions were seen through a different prism, that of the law of unintended consequences.

By reducing the amount of capital banks had to set aside on their holdings of privately issued securities, regulators were essentially encouraging banks to purchase them. And by allowing lower-risk weightings for securities that carried specific grades from Standard & Poor's, Moody's, and Fitch Ratings, regulators were blessing these companies' ratings, forcing investors to rely on them whether or not they were worthy.

The ratings would later prove to be entirely unworthy of investor reliance and would generate hundreds of billions of dollars in losses among institutions that bought securities based on the agencies' lofty grades. In the increasingly complex world of mortgage securities the ratings agencies' models were laughable for what they overlooked. Until well after the rout in subprime mortgages had begun, Moody's mortgage security model did not include information about a borrower's debt-to-income ratio, one of the key predictors of default.

The ratings agencies also made the disastrous decision to accept as gospel the information provided to them by the banks that were putting together the deals. Fitch said that it had "no obligation to verify or audit any information provided to it from any source or to conduct any investigation or review, or to take any other action, to obtain any information that the issuer has not otherwise provided."

Nevertheless, Basel's rule change on risk weightings for mortgage securities codified and legitimized the work of the rating agencies. No one in the central banking and regulatory community bothered to check whether that work should have earned such an endorsement.

Basel's risk weightings for banks fell into four categories, or buckets. The safest securities, such as those issued by the U.S. Treasury, carried a zero risk weight; this meant that banks did not need to set aside any capital to protect against losses in those issues.

At the other end of the spectrum were securities requiring 100 percent capital set-asides; these included unsecured lines of credit extended to borrowers, such as credit-card loans. Other securities, with risk weightings of 20 percent and 50 percent, fell in between these buckets.

For years, private-label mortgage securities issued by individual lenders like Metropolitan Mortgage had carried risk weightings of 50 percent. Only mortgage securities issued by Fannie Mae, Freddie Mac, and other government-sponsored enterprises were considered safe enough by regulators to go into the 20 percent bucket.

But in 2001 the Basel Committee proposed that any asset-backed securities with credit ratings of AAA or AA, regardless of issuer, could also have 20 percent risk weights. No longer did banks have to set aside half of these securities' values in their capital cushion.

In its proposal, the Basel Committee said it had decided to encourage an increased reliance on credit-rating agencies because it would level the playing field among different global participants. "Using external credit assessments for assessing capital against risks arising from securitisation transactions would further promote the Accord's objective of ensuring competitive equality," the committee said. The only proviso was that those doing the assessments must be considered experts "as may be evidenced in particular by a strong market acceptance." Dominating the market, as the three ratings agencies did, provided this evidence.

Never mind that some of the more complex mortgage-related securities, such as collateralized debt obligations, were so new that rating agencies had no meaningful experience assessing their risks.

Once again, regulators were allowing the lead-footed drivers to set speed limits. The ratings agencies, whose AAA imprimaturs were necessary for lower capital set-asides, had only to show strong market acceptance for their assessments to qualify as experts. Regulators made no attempt to determine independently whether the ratings agencies were capable of assigning accurate ratings to these increasingly complex asset-backed securities, chock-full of new types of mortgages made to borrowers for whom there was little or no historic information. It was another abdication of oversight duty that would have dire consequences.

In November 2001, the United States' four top bank regulators followed the Basel Committee's lead. The Federal Reserve, the Office of the Comptroller of the Currency, the Office of Thrift Supervision, and the FDIC published a final rule allowing AAA-rated and AA-rated tranches of private-label securities to carry 20 percent risk weightings. This rule, designed to ease capital requirements of banks, put a regulatory imprimatur on these securities, fueling investor interest in them.

The race to mortgage Armageddon was on. And unlike other rule changes, this one was effective immediately.

Without missing a beat, Wall Street banks began working with the ratings agencies to develop new models that would allow riskier and higher-yielding private-label securities to garner the AAA and AA ratings that were necessary to earn a reduced risk weighting. At the same time, the banks began looking for ways to increase mortgage originations to generate loans that would be securitized and sold to investors.

Because higher-quality borrowers were still at this time the domain of Fannie Mae and Freddie Mac, Wall Street could not hope to compete in this arena. So the big investment firms stepped up their interest in alternative mortgage products offered to subprime or near-prime borrowers.

Subprime lending was already growing fast—between 1997 and 2000, HUD said, the number of home purchase applications backed by subprime mortgages more than doubled, from 327,644 to 783,921. Because such loans would be packaged and sold to investors, the banks did not need to worry about credit risks inherent in the loans.

More important, ramping up these businesses promised a return to serious profits on Wall Street, whose engine had stalled with the collapse of the dot-com stock market, the recession, and economic retrenchment following the 9/11 terrorist attacks. The burgeoning subprime market represented a veritable profit bonanza for Wall Street, generating lending fees, interest payments, loan purchase fees, underwriting revenues, and a path into the lucrative retail lending businesses.

Investors' appetites for these loans swelled. The percentage of mortgage securities made up of loans that exceeded the dollar limits on mortgages financed by Fannie and Freddie—known as nonconforming mortgages—would rise from 35 percent in 2000 to 60 percent in 2005.

The mania had begun. And with the Fed cutting interest rates in the wake of the stock market bust, low borrowing costs and declining yields on bonds drove investors to the comparatively higher returns in mortgage securities. Investors could feel confident buying pieces of these securities. After all, federal regulators had blessed them as relatively low risk from a capital standpoint.

⇌

Why did the Fed so determinedly back the banks on capital requirements and risk weightings? There are two possibilities.

First, like most regulators, the Fed was always eager to expand its regulatory reach and everything about the changes proposed by the Basel Committee was directed at bank holding companies, the only entities the Fed directly oversaw. The recommendations of the committee, if implemented, would elevate the Fed's role in bank supervision.

Then there was the fact that the Fed's people were caught up in a culture where their daily interactions and relationships are with big banks. "They get in sync with the people they talk to and listen to," a regulator said.

It is also possible that some inside the Fed recognized that if they did not do the banks' bidding, their institution would lose its hegemony among central bankers. Charles Kindleberger, the author of the classic 1978 economic text *Manias, Panics and Crashes: A History of Financial Crises,* already saw this as a fait accompli in the spring of 2002. He told a visitor: "Our central bank has historically been master of its own domain. But as the rest of the central banking community matures, ours will be just one central bank in a global central banking community with others more able to exert their will upon us." In other words, the United States' position as global leader in financial services was already waning.

⇌

Between December 2000 and July 2003, the Fed made a crucial decision that, although not fretted about at the time, contributed mightily to the mortgage lending craze. It slashed its Federal Funds rate, the most closely watched interest-rate benchmark, from 6.5 percent to an unheard-of 1 percent.

Then, in the fall of 2001, the Treasury made a move that pushed investors to increase their already sizable holdings in mortgage securities issued by Fannie and Freddie. Stunning most investors, the Treasury announced on Halloween of that year that it would stop issuing its benchmark long-term bonds, those with 30-year maturities.

With no more 30-year issuance, investors looking for longer-term bonds turned to debt issued by Fannie and Freddie as a sort of surrogate for Treasuries. This heightened demand for the companies' securities and allowed them to pump up the debt on their balance sheets and vastly increase their mortgage purchases.

During his last year as chief executive of Fannie Mae, Jim Johnson had pushed Fannie to create a series of debt issues that mimicked Treasury securities that were the most popular among investors. These included those with maturities of three years, five years, and ten years. It was a typically aggressive move by Johnson—no private entity had ever tried to issue large amounts of debt on a regular basis to act as a Treasury substitute.

But with the government surplus requiring less and less debt issuance by Uncle Sam, Johnson had seen an opening. The debt was called Benchmark notes and bonds, and within the first year of their launch, Fannie Mae had issued more than $40 billion worth. The program gave the company "a worldwide premium position in global markets," Johnson told *American Banker* in November 1998.

In 2000, the Fed was quietly considering buying Benchmarks in lieu of Treasuries, to conduct its operations. But internal Fed research raised questions about the possibility that it would be seen as endorsing Fannie Mae debt. The idea died.

By 2001, Fannie Mae's issuance of Benchmark securities had more than doubled to $85 billion.

⇌

It is abundantly clear that the Fed's push to reduce capital standards had nothing to do with improving risk management, as Roger Ferguson and other high-level officials claimed.

Indeed, dangerous risks were already blossoming on financial institutions' balance sheets. And even as the world's central bankers were encouraging a greater reliance on securities ratings assigned by Moody's, Standard & Poor's, and Fitch, some institutions were already finding that their assessments, especially on complex asset pools known as collateralized debt obligations (CDOs), were dead wrong.

Amazingly, regulators charged with overseeing the ratings agencies did not have access to detailed information about the types of loans inside the securities they were rating. Only "qualified investors" are allowed to consult deal documents and performance reports, and bank regulators and the Securities and Exchange Commission were not considered such. Even if they had been, however, the regulators had to ask for permission from an issuer to view the deal performance data and prospectus.

Nevertheless, CDOs were issued—and rated highly—with abandon. The American International Group would almost go bankrupt insuring these types of securities against default. But seven years earlier, a different kind of CDO created immense problems for investors and raised doubts about the reliability of credit ratings.

During the late 1990s, investment banks had begun creating CDOs out of varying types of loans that were supposed to behave differently, or in an uncorrelated manner. The more dissimilar the loans in a pool, therefore, the more risk-averse the pool was, investors believed.

Early CDOs contained loans made to companies leasing aircraft equipment, consumers borrowing to buy mobile homes, commercial loans, and other debts and obligations. The diversification of borrowers coupled with advanced computer modeling in designing the structures gave investors a sense that the securities would perform well even in economic downturns.

This proved false. In a single quarter in 2001, American Express reported $1 billion of losses on CDO investments. On a call with investors, chief executive Kenneth Chenault said: "Many of the structured investments were investment grade, so we thought they had a reasonable level of protection against loss. But, it is now apparent that our analysis of the portfolio did not fully comprehend the risk underlying these structures during a period of persistently high default rates."

After the American Express announcement, the CDO market came crashing to a halt; other investors incurred similarly large losses. But the market did not stay moribund for long. Just a few years later it stirred again, this time with devastating effect.

⇄

As it happened, the credit crisis hit before many of the changes suggested by the Basel Committee and backed by the Fed could be implemented. But as banks wrote down hundreds of billions in bad loans and sought on-the-fly ways to press for accounting changes that would protect from writing down hundreds of billions more, it was evident that relying on the banks' loss estimates to reduce capital requirements would have been a disastrous decision. It would have made the crisis even more devastating than it was.

Clearly, the FDIC's concerns from a decade earlier had been validated.

The Fed's determinedly bank-centric approach in the years leading up to the 2008 credit crisis meant banks were dangerously undercapitalized just when they most needed large cash cushions to protect against losses. But even after it had become clear that the Fed had been wrong to push for relaxed capital standards, the regulator continued to take a pro-bank worldview in its various rescues of big banks hobbled by bad credit decisions. In 2008 and after, every Fed rescue, every Fed solution seemed designed to benefit the major banks at the expense of the taxpayers.

CHAPTER NINE

While predatory lending violates all notions of decency and ethics, it has been largely legal due to previously loose consumer protection laws. This is not only wrong— it is tragic. And it must end.

—ROY E. BARNES, governor of Georgia,
October 25, 2002

Alan Greenspan had extolled the innovative lending practices that helped drive homeownership to new heights across America in 1999. But just a few years later, as the century turned, other regulators saw firsthand how these "innovations" were hurting borrowers. They began expressing their concerns.

State legislators and lawyers in local nonprofit housing aid offices were especially alarmed by the increasing numbers of abusive loans they saw being peddled to low-income, unsophisticated, and in many cases minority borrowers. One of them was William J. Brennan Jr., director of the home defense program of the Atlanta Legal Aid Society.

Brennan, who had helped troubled borrowers protect against foreclosure for more than a decade in his city, had seen a lot of bad actors and dubious practices in mortgage lending. But in the early 2000s, he grew disturbed by the truly rapid increase in foreclosures among the poorest populations in Atlanta. The share of

James A. Johnson, chief executive of Fannie Mae during its crucial expansion in the 1990s. A calculating political operative, Johnson was the anonymous architect of the public-private homeownership drive that almost destroyed the economy in 2008. He was especially adept at manipulating lawmakers, eviscerating regulators, and leaving taxpayers with the bill. (Gretchen Morgenson)

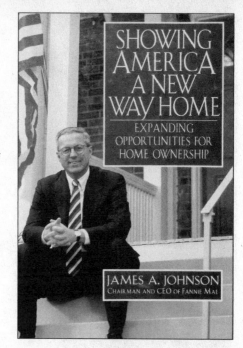

SHOWING AMERICA A NEW WAY HOME
EXPANDING OPPORTUNITIES FOR HOME OWNERSHIP

JAMES A. JOHNSON
CHAIRMAN AND CEO OF FANNIE MAE

Barney Frank, Democratic congressman from Massachusetts and staunch protector of Fannie Mae, almost to the end. Frank requested that Fannie hire his partner in 1991 when Congress was devising regulations for the company. Fannie also made large grants to a Boston charity cofounded by Frank's mother. (*The New York Times*)

Fannie Mae's sumptuous and sprawling headquarters in Washington was designed to resemble the governor's palace in Colonial Williamsburg. (*Getty Images*)

Henry Gonzalez, a Democratic congressman from Texas, was a key supporter of Fannie Mae. When Congress was crafting the 1992 legislation to tighten regulations on the company, he allowed its executives to water down the bill. (*The New York Times*)

Angelo Mozilo, cofounder of Countrywide Financial, the nation's largest mortgage lender until it collapsed under a mountain of bad loans in 2007. He partnered closely with Jim Johnson to become Fannie Mae's biggest supplier and granted Johnson a number of cut-rate mortgages. (*The New York Times*)

Alan Greenspan, former chairman of the Federal Reserve Board, believed that bankers could be trusted to be prudent in their operations. He lauded the increase in homeownership brought about by complex and poisonous mortgages and suggested that most borrowers would be best served by those with adjustable rates. (*The New York Times*)

Walker Todd, research officer at the Federal Reserve Bank of Cleveland, uncovered an obscure amendment in a 1991 banking law that increased the likelihood of taxpayer bailouts. Officials at the Federal Reserve Board in Washington tried to prevent the publication of his findings. (*The New York Times*)

Robert Rubin, a former chief executive of Goldman Sachs and secretary of the Treasury from 1995 to 1999, helped kill off Glass-Steagal, the Depression-era law that had protected taxpayers from rapacious bankers for almost seventy years. He joined Citibank as vice-chairman, earning over $125 million as the company ramped up its risks and then foundered. (*The New York Times*)

Christopher Bond, former Republican senator from Missouri (above), Robert Ney, former Republican congressman from Ohio and convicted felon (right), and Bob Bennett, once a Utah Republican senator (below), benefited from their support of Fannie Mae, receiving generous campaign contributions. (all credits *The New York Times*)

Marvin Phaup, of the Congressional Budget Office, did the first assessment in 1996 of the high-cost government subsidies received by Fannie Mae. Enraged, Fannie executives disparaged Phaup and his work. (*Marvin Phaup*)

June O'Neill, head of the Congressional Budget Office, defended its 1996 study detailing Fannie Mae's rich subsidies and suggested that the government's ties to the company be re-examined. She came under fierce attack in Congress by lawmakers reading from scripts provided by Fannie Mae. (*The New York Times*)

Roger Ferguson (center, with hand raised), a former banking lawyer appointed to the Board of Governors of the Federal Reserve in 1997 by President Clinton. As vice-chairman of the Fed, Ferguson worked to loosen capital restrictions on banks and tried to thwart publication of a regulatory analysis that was critical of relaxed capital requirements. (*Getty Images*)

Celebration time at the White House in 1999 when the Glass-Steagal banking regulation bit the bullet. Banks could now take significantly greater risks. Applauding, from left, are Alan Greenspan, Arthur Levitt, chairman of the Securities and Exchange Commission, and Phil Gramm, Republican senator from Texas. (*Justin Lane*)

Franklin Raines (holding book), former Clinton Budget Director, chief executive of Fannie Mae, and protege of Jim Johnson, was ousted in 2005 amid a massive accounting scandal at the company. (*The New York Times*)

Timothy Geithner presided over the Federal Reserve Bank of New York during the years leading up to the crisis. Its research proclaimed that no housing bubble existed and its regulatory unit was blind to burgeoning risks at Citibank, one of the institutions it monitored. (*The New York Times*)

Marc Cohodes, money manager who bet against the shares of NovaStar Financial. Over five years, he shared damning research about NovaStar with investigators at the Securities and Exchange Commission. They never brought a case; investors lost $1 billion when the company's stock cratered in 2008. (*Marc Cohodes*)

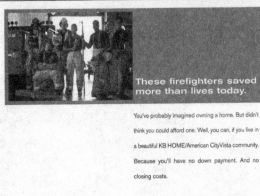

A KB Home ad. Typical of the public-private partnership pushing homeownership, this flyer advertised no-money-down mortgages from Fannie Mae that financed houses built by KB Home in San Antonio. The program generated large losses and high foreclosures.

Armando Falcon, former regulator of Fannie Mae, was subjected to nonstop assault by the company and its protectors in Congress. (*The New York Times*)

William J. Brennan Jr., of Atlanta Legal Aid, helped write one of the nation's toughest state predatory lending laws in 2002. Credit ratings agencies, led by Standard & Poors, were instrumental in killing the law, leaving Georgia borrowers at the mercy of abusive lenders. (*Nancy McLeod*)

foreclosures attributable to subprime lending in the city had more than tripled, from 5 percent in 1996 to 16 percent three years later.

In the spring of 2000, Brennan and his colleague Karen Brown brought some of these devastated borrowers to an open forum in Atlanta sponsored by Housing and Urban Development and Treasury. There, minority borrowers told of unscrupulous mortgage brokers who promoted abusive loans without disclosing their costs.

Victims described a process called equity stripping, where brokers persuaded them to refinance at such high costs that much or all of the equity they had built up in their homes disappeared into lenders' pockets in the form of fees and service charges.

Lenders were also making no pretense of ensuring that the borrowers they targeted could actually pay back their loans, Brennan found. Borrowers with $23,000 annual incomes were receiving loans of as much as $140,000; obviously falsified incomes on loan applications were becoming more and more prevalent.

At first Brennan was baffled by the big jump in these awful loans. But he soon figured out what was behind the boom in predatory lending: Wall Street and its securitization machine.

The process of gathering up mortgages to be packaged into trusts and sold to investors had been around for decades. But the issuance of these securities ballooned after bank regulators deemed them worthy of a smaller capital requirement for the banks that owned them. Securitization was fast becoming the beast that needed constant feeding. It created enormous demand for loans of any sort provided to borrowers of even the smallest means.

In 2001 alone, subprime mortgage originations totaled $7.1 billion in Georgia, an increase of almost 70 percent over the previous year.

"Securitization provided a huge amount of capital that allowed mortgage lending abuses to happen," Brennan said. "There was all this money to lend and yet, there was not in our view, a sufficient number of financially eligible borrowers. The banks were capitalizing predatory lending, and it was a conscious corporate decision to go ahead and make loans to people who can't pay."

Brennan and others who helped troubled borrowers across the

state had a special challenge: Georgia's bankruptcy system was the fastest in the country and anyone working to save a borrower's home from foreclosure had to move quickly. Lenders could call a borrower "in default," foreclose, and take back the home all in as little as four weeks.

The reason for this expedited process is that Georgia, like some twenty other states across the country, is a nonjudicial foreclosure state, meaning that lenders can foreclose and repossess a troubled borrower's home there without having to present the facts to a judge.

Judicial foreclosure states, by contrast, require that a foreclosure be overseen by a judge, slowing the process down and affording some protection against lenders who may not even have the right to remove a borrower from his or her home. But in Georgia, North Carolina, Tennessee, and other nonjudicial foreclosure states, as predatory lending soared, courthouse steps swarmed with foreclosure sales on a monthly basis.

The first Tuesday in every month, Brennan explained, is foreclosure day in Georgia. "From 9 in the morning 'til 4:30 in the afternoon, it's an amazing scene to watch on the courthouse steps across Georgia," he said. And because Georgia has more counties than any other state in the nation but Texas, the same dismal scene would unfold every month at 159 courthouses across the state. "All a company has to do is run an ad once a week for four straight weeks in the local newspaper, send a certified letter to the borrower, and they can auction off his or her home on the courthouse steps," Brennan said.

In addition to realizing that securitization was driving the dramatic increase in predatory lending, Brennan and his small band of legal aid attorneys recognized another pernicious aspect of the loan-bundling process. Compiling thousands of loans into trusts to be sold to investors allowed each participant along the assembly line to deny accountability for predatory loans. Each transfer of the loan—from lender to financier to packager to investors—gave plausible deniability for problems in the mortgages to each of the parties involved.

Most significant, when Wall Street firms provided money to mortgage originators and then turned around and packaged those loans for sale to investors, they could argue that they had no idea the loans were improper. Securitization meant predatory loans could be made and sold to investors with little burden or risk to those on the assembly line.

To Wall Street, it was a beautiful thing. To the borrowers and the investors who bought the loans, it was a disaster that would lead directly to millions of delinquencies and hundreds of billions in losses.

⇆

Listening to borrowers' anguished stories at the Atlanta HUD forum in the spring of 2000 so enraged a state senator named Vincent D. Fort that he stood up and declared that he would put forward a bill in the upcoming legislative session to drive predatory lenders out of his state.

A professor of history and political science at Morris Brown College in Atlanta at the time, Fort had worked against predatory lending before, protesting when banks closed branches in black neighborhoods. Those activities had taken place when he was a graduate student at Emory University. After Fort promised to introduce a bill to stop predatory lending, he asked Brennan for help. Their ideas would become the Georgia Fair Lending Act, a law designed to create consumer protections against high-cost home loans by restricting excessive fees and charges, and providing for penalties if the law was not followed. Those who knowingly broke the law could even face criminal charges.

"We met with the Georgia Mortgage Bankers Association twenty times to hammer out the bill—they said they would support it," Brennan recalled.

But the creation of the law had stirred up a hornet's nest among subprime lenders and their enablers. Among those leading the charge against the law was Wright H. Andrews Jr., a powerful Washington lobbyist who represented the subprime industry. Lobbying for subprime lenders was a family affair for Andrews—his wife, Lisa, was a top executive in government affairs at Ameri-quest, one of the industry's most aggressive and egregious lenders.

Andrews had begun his career in 1973 as chief legislative aide to Sam Nunn, the Democratic senator from Georgia; in 1990, he moved to lobbying, launching his own firm with a partner. Fifteen years later, he was running three different subprime-industry trade groups. All had innocuous, even benevolent-sounding names: the National Home Equity Mortgage Association (of course Ameri-quest was a member), the Coalition for Fair and Affordable Lend-ing, and the Responsible Mortgage Lending Coalition. The three organizations spent $8.3 million lobbying to thwart predatory lending laws during the '90s and early 2000s.

While Brennan and Brown were helping Fort write the Geor-gia law, they met Andrews in Palm Beach at a subprime lending conference. Brennan and a few other consumer advocates had been invited to speak at the confab, which took place in late 2001 at the Breakers, the sumptuous Palm Beach oceanfront resort. The meeting was chaired by Andrews and attended by anyone who was anyone in subprime.

It was clear to Brennan that the conference attendees were watching Georgia's attack on predatory lending with fear and loathing. "So many subprime people were there from every seg-ment and they all were just focused on what [Georgia governor] Roy Barnes was going to do in Georgia," Brennan recalled. "At the very end of the conference Andrews got up and said 'I'm tell-ing you folks we've got to go to Georgia in 2002 and we've got to defeat Roy Barnes's efforts because he's going to pass a law that will be a benchmark for the whole country.'"

Brennan knew then and there that he and his colleagues had a fight on their hands.

Notwithstanding Andrews's call to arms at the Breakers, the fair lending law passed in May 2002 when Barnes, a former law-yer who had brought class actions against abusive lenders, signed the legislation. It went into effect the following October; Georgia now had the toughest predatory lending law in the country.

The subprime industry had only just begun to fight; in late 2002, Andrews and the companies he represented began lobbying Georgia's state assembly to water down the law.

In a time-tested lobbying tactic right out of the Fannie Mae playbook, the industry first claimed that the new law meant Georgia's borrowers would no longer be able to secure a mortgage. Consumers, in other words, would be hurt by it.

One of the first companies to stop making high-cost loans in Georgia was Countrywide, Angelo Mozilo's mortgage machine. In October 2002 Countrywide warned that the Georgia law would undermine the mortgage securities market, with investors requiring premiums to offset the increased risks associated with these loans. A much smaller but even more aggressive lender out of Kansas City, NovaStar Financial, also announced plans to stop lending in the state.

"Mortgage loans made in Georgia are looked upon with suspicion and a number of large secondary market investors are no longer interested in doing business in our state," Wright Andrews wrote in an analysis of the Fair Lending Act published in January 2003. "The time for the General Assembly to act is now to minimize the negative impact of the Act on Georgia borrowers, traditional lenders and the economy."

But the death blow to the law did not come from subprime lenders, as Brennan had anticipated. Rather it was dealt by the credit-ratings agencies, Standard & Poor's, Moody's, and Fitch, which were supposed to be independent assayers of risk in corporate and other types of debt. The very companies that the Basel Committee, in its infinite wisdom, had blessed with new powers just a few years earlier were the ones that killed the Georgia Fair Lending Act, the most aggressive, pro-consumer law in the country.

The day before Christmas, Fitch issued a warning to investors and lenders. It published a comment saying that Georgia was just the beginning of a predatory lending jihad by regulators and that New York, New Jersey, and California each had similar legislation pending. While only 1.3 percent of loans in securitization pools rated by Fitch originated in Georgia, New York, New Jersey, and California made up 2 percent, 3 percent, and 67 percent respectively of the loans in Fitch-rated pools. Fitch's point was clear.

Standard & Poor's was the most aggressive of the three agencies, however. And on January 16, 2003, four days after the Georgia General Assembly convened, it dropped a bombshell. Because of the state's new Fair Lending Act, S&P said that it would no longer allow mortgage loans originated in Georgia to be placed in mortgage securities that it rated. Moody's and Fitch soon followed with similar warnings.

It was a critical blow. S&P's move meant Georgia lenders would have no access to the securitization money machine; they would either have to keep the loans they made on their own books, or sell them one by one to other institutions. In turn, they made it clear to the public that there would be fewer mortgages funded, dashing "the dream" of homeownership.

It was an untenable situation for the lenders who had grown addicted to the securitization money spigot. With S&P shutting it off to abusive lenders, it was only a matter of time before the Fair Lending Act was dead.

To Brennan and other consumer advocates, it was a shocking and devastating moment in the battle against predatory lending.

"We were stunned when we saw the press release," Brennan said. "We thought, where does this come from?"

Standard & Poor's said it was taking action because the new law created liability for any institution that participated in a securitization containing a loan that might be considered predatory. If a Wall Street firm purchased loans that ran afoul of the law and placed them in a mortgage pool, the firm could be liable under the law. Ditto for investors who bought into the pools.

"Transaction parties in securitizations, including depositors, issuers and servicers, might all be subject to penalties for violations under the Georgia Fair Lending Act," S&P's press release explained.

It ended with a warning: "Standard & Poor's will continue to monitor this and other pending predatory lending legislation."

In other words, any states that might have been considering strengthening their predatory lending laws as Georgia did should beware.

Standard & Poor's was correct about the Georgia law—those penalties it had mentioned were a legal design put in place by the law's framers to thwart dubious lending. After all, if you eliminated the "plausible deniability" that securitization provided for participants in the loan pooling process, you would force players at each stop on the assembly line to increase their scrutiny of lending practices. By allowing liability for predatory loans to pass through to each participant in the chain, you could begin to slow down the securitization machinery that allowed fraudulent loans to wreak such havoc among poor and minority borrowers. In addition, such pass-through liability would allow wronged consumers to recover money damages even if the original predatory lenders went bankrupt or disappeared. It would also protect investors by giving them a legal right to put back predatory loans to originators.

It was getting to the very root of the problem Brennan was seeing over and over in his legal practice. The law required everyone involved in securitization to conduct themselves with care and prudence. It was a stroke of genius, from a consumer's point of view, and surely could have become a legal template for other states, as Wright Andrews had predicted.

To Wall Street, the subprime lenders it financed, and the ratings agencies that were paid to grade the securities, the law was a tremendous threat to their profits. Brennan, Fort, and Barnes had recognized that the lenders and Wall Street banks would work to defang the law and they were prepared to engage them in battle. But the consumer advocates had failed to see how the Georgia Fair Lending Act imperiled the increasingly lucrative business of rating mortgage securities, a business that was enriching executives and shareholders of Standard & Poor's, Moody's, and Fitch. After all, if there were fewer loans, there would be fewer pools and fewer pools meant a dearth of deals to be rated by these agencies. They were businesses and had shareholders to consider.

Brennan and his associates had not comprehended that when the Fair Lending Act gored the subprime ox, it also gored that of the ratings agencies. "It was then that we understood perfectly," Brennan said. "S&P makes huge money off subprime lending."

The subprime lending industry did not have to move another muscle. Their lobbyists started circulating S&P's announcement at the statehouse. With S&P refusing to rate securities containing Georgia loans, the law's opponents began arguing that it would close off access to mortgage loans for borrowers throughout the state.

Lawmakers soon began amending the Fair Lending Act and on March 7, 2003, Sonny Perdue, Georgia's new governor who had triumphed over Barnes in the 2002 election, signed a modified version of the law. In addition to gutting many of the consumer protection aspects of the law, the new act pretty much eliminated pass-through liability.

"Standard & Poor's found a way to make what was a wonderful law seem like a bad thing," Brennan said, years later. "It sure seemed like a carefully, well-organized effort by S&P."

Not five months after it was enacted, the toughest consumer protection mortgage lending law in the United States was dead. For subprime mortgage originators a crisis had been averted; their massive profits were once again assured. The lending binge that would drive the economy into the ditch five years later was back on track.

And S&P's fortunes were assured as well. In the first half of 2003, Standard & Poor's led the ratings agencies in subprime loans, according to *Inside B&C Lending*, an industry publication. Standard & Poor's rated $84 billion in securities backed by subprime loans—that was 96.8 percent of the total issuance across the country. Standard & Poor's market share rose 4 percent from the end of 2002 when it rated 93.2 percent of the subprime deals. At 75.5 percent and 65.5 percent respectively, Moody's and Fitch were a distant second and third in this race to the bottom.

That the ratings agencies could scuttle the country's toughest consumer protection law certainly shocked Bill Brennan and other pro bono lawyers working on behalf of troubled borrowers. But while the story made some headlines, there was little outcry against Standard & Poor's. People were not yet focused on the fact that the ratings agencies were members in good standing of the subprime mortgage club—that they were major beneficiaries, like Wall Street, of the lending boom.

While ratings firms had historically assessed the obligations of corporations well after they were established and operating, in the world of structured securities such as mortgage pools the rating agencies were there at the creation, even defining what the deals should look like to get a top rating. In other words, ratings agencies were the equivalent of narcotics cops paid to look the other way when big drug deals were consummated.

The agencies certainly played this role by helping Fannie Mae and Freddie Mac sell their securities to investors. Indeed, they rated the debt of Fannie and Freddie far higher than would have been the case had the analysis been done with a colder eye. Even as Fannie and Freddie were amassing enormous risks in their portfolios and among the loans they guaranteed, the ratings agencies' lofty grades reassured investors that the companies' obligations—tens of billions in debt—would be met. This made it easier for Fannie and Freddie to balloon their balance sheets, buying and guaranteeing even more mortgages.

Subordinated debt issued by Fannie and Freddie was a prime example of the ratings agencies' misplaced optimism. This type of debt is junior to other obligations on the companies' books because it can only be repaid after the senior borrowings. For most financial institutions, subordinated debt was considered below investment grade or "junk" in Wall Street parlance, and received a rating of BBB– or lower. But the ratings agencies rated Fannie and Freddie's subordinated debt AA, just below the highest level.

How did the ratings agencies justify these lofty grades? Because both companies enjoyed access to the capital markets even during times of financial stress, the agencies reasoned, they could raise money for their business, come hell or high water. While the agencies did not spell out the reason for this 24/7 access to capital, investors understood it to reflect the implied guarantee of the U.S. government, a guarantee that the Fed, Treasury, Barney Frank, and even Fannie and Freddie had explicitly said did not exist—implicitly or otherwise—for more than a decade.

So, even as Fannie Mae and Freddie Mac executives publicly disclaimed their federal guarantee, the credit-ratings agencies that assessed the companies' securities let investors know they were in no danger of losing money in a failure of either company.*

Standard & Poor's was an especially close partner with Fannie and Freddie, regularly defending them against assaults. Once again, this was a partnership based on mutual admiration and mutually received benefits. Fannie and Freddie were the largest private issuers of debt, exceeding even the combined balance of all fifty states, and the ratings agencies made enormous fees analyzing the companies' debt and mortgage-backed instruments. Every time they issued a security, it had to be rated by two agencies. That meant the ratings agencies were extremely eager to please Fannie and Freddie.

In 2001, S&P seemed particularly intent on downplaying risks in Fannie and Freddie debt. Under pressure from a Republican Congress worried about the companies' possible costs to the government, Fannie and Freddie had announced plans to make more financial disclosures to investors. As part of this agreement, the companies said they would request and release to the public each year a rating that measured any risks they might pose to the government. The rating, which was to measure the companies' financial standing without considering their implied federal

---

*Wrong again. When the U.S. government put Fannie and Freddie into conservatorship in September 2008, preferred securities issued by the companies and purchased by many smaller banks because of lower capital requirements plummeted in value when the government said dividends would no longer be paid on the shares. Between $10 billion and $15 billion were lost by the 27 percent of banks that held these securities. S&P had rated the preferred stock AA– less than a month before the takeover and had taken Fannie Mae off negative watch, affirming a stable outlook for the company three months before it was nationalized.

guarantee, was to come from one of the big credit-rating agencies, known technically as nationally recognized statistical rating organizations (NRSROs).

Fannie and Freddie chose S&P to conduct this analysis for them. The rating would be maintained continuously and S&P would report publicly if the financial strength of either Fannie or Freddie changed.

But the "risk-to-the-government" ratings issued by S&P did little more than reflect the implied federal guarantee and provided no analysis of the companies' capital positions. Both companies received initial ratings of AA–.

All the way through the subprime mortgage boom, as Fannie Mae bought or guaranteed more and more questionable loans, S&P's risk-to-the-government rating on the company barely budged. As had happened so many times before, the ratings agencies failed to warn investors of the impending storm that would swamp these companies. It was not until August 11, 2008, three weeks before Fannie was taken over by taxpayers, that S&P lowered Fannie's risk-to-the-government rating. The ratings agency moved the grade from A+ to A.

⇌

The ratings agencies' failure to recognize risks in Fannie Mae's operations was just one of their many misses in recent history. Indeed, just as Fannie and Freddie chose Standard & Poor's as the agency that would advise investors of their risk to the taxpayers, a corrupt energy company known as Enron was careening toward bankruptcy. Enron's collapse would be yet another black eye for all three ratings agencies. None of them had identified the risks that Enron had taken on—all had rated the company highly until four days before it imploded.

The ratings agencies had missed a crucial element in Enron's operations: For years the company had manipulated its results by moving huge risks off its balance sheet into entities that appeared to be owned by others. But because of the way these entities were structured, when Enron got into trouble, the risks they had held moved back onto the parent company's balance sheet, sinking the entire operation.*

(Fannie Mae had been among the first companies to perfect the art of moving liabilities from its balance sheet to places where investors might not notice them. The hundreds of billions in mortgage-backed securities that the company guaranteed sat in trusts known as Qualified Special Purpose Entities, and were therefore not consolidated on Fannie's books. This was something of a charade, since the company had guaranteed the mortgages in the trusts and would have to pay on them if they did not perform.)

The full effect of Enron's off-balance sheet arrangements was missed by the ratings agencies, leaving the company's investors unprepared for its failure.

Just a few months later, Standard & Poor's, Moody's, and Fitch took another beating when WorldCom, a telecom giant, crashed and burned. All three agencies had assigned conservative ratings on the billions in debt issued by the telecom until a few weeks before it filed for bankruptcy in July 2002.

Moody's took a special slam in WorldCom's collapse because its chairman, Clifford Alexander, sat on the telecom's board. Moody's rated WorldCom debt as a good credit risk until the month before the company filed what was then the largest corporate bankruptcy in history.

In both scandals, billions of dollars were lost by money managers, insurance companies, and other institutions that had relied on the ratings agencies to assess risk in Enron's and WorldCom's securities. And yet, despite these losses, regulators did nothing to reduce investors' reliance on ratings agency opinions or their importance.

---

*In the fall of 2007, as the credit crisis was ramping up, Citigroup and other banks were found to have hidden obligations in a manner similar to the way Enron did. They had created special-purpose vehicles to sell short-term paper to investors; the banks used the proceeds from this issuance to invest in mortgages and other longer-term paper. When investors stopped buying this commercial paper, the banks had to bring the entities' massive losses back onto their own balance sheets. This accelerated the crisis.

After the shocking Enron and WorldCom scandals, Congress started making noise about changing the ratings agency game, eliminating the requirements that insurance companies and banks rely on their ratings, for example. To counter this threat, Moody's, Standard & Poor's, and Fitch trotted out two defenses.

First, they said, it is impossible to identify a con artist who is determined to fool investors. This was surely true for analysts outside a company looking in at its operations. But because the companies worked so closely with the ratings agencies when they were analyzing them, providing reams of proprietary information that other analysts did not get, the ratings agencies' claims of ignorance rang hollow with many investors.

A more important defense for the companies was their insistence that investment ratings were simply opinions. This meant that the agencies should be shielded from lawsuits just as a journalist's views are protected by the First Amendment. Deploying this safeguard against lawsuits allowed Moody's, S&P, and Fitch to escape liability even when they failed abysmally in their assessments.

There was a deep flaw in this argument and once again it related to the extensive access to confidential corporate information that the ratings agencies received during the grading process. Few if any journalists received such details from companies they covered; the ratings agencies were much more knowledgeable about the companies they were rating than a journalist could ever hope to be.

Each time the ratings agencies encountered threats to their favored status—typically after they were shown to have performed miserably in their tasks—they fought back vigorously. But in the wake of WorldCom's collapse and Enron's spectacular failure—it was one of the country's most admired companies not long before it filed for bankruptcy—investor confidence in regulation and corporate practices was severely shaken. Congress took up the issue of ratings agencies yet again.

Weeks after WorldCom failed, Congress implemented a new law, known as Sarbanes-Oxley, designed to forestall future accounting scandals like those that had embroiled the telecom and Enron. This legislation required the Securities and Exchange Commission to investigate the role played by Moody's, Standard & Poor's, and Fitch in the financial markets.

Just as Congress's landmark 1992 legislation had required Treasury, the Congressional Budget Office, HUD, and GAO to assess the practicality of privatizing Fannie Mae and Freddie Mac, lawmakers in 2002 wanted the SEC to determine whether the special treatment provided to the ratings agencies should be rescinded. Unfortunately, there would be no Marvin Phaup or June O'Neill to stand up and declare that the ratings agencies' special treatment should be reconsidered.

The favors enjoyed by the agencies were the result of a 1975 regulation that for the first time codified ratings into the investment process used by banks, insurance companies, and other regulated entities. In the rule, the SEC required that brokerage firms base their capital requirements on investment ratings issued by nationally recognized statistical rating organizations. Three of these were dominant: Moody's, Standard & Poor's, and Fitch Ratings. Because of the rule, the companies enjoyed a duopoly—only two ratings were needed for a security to be sold to investors—and were protected from competitors by the substantial barrier to entry established by the NRSRO rule.

Over the years, the special treatment afforded to the ratings agencies only grew. Money market funds, for example, were soon restricted from buying securities that did not receive one of the top two ratings from an NRSRO. The Department of Education used ratings to set financial standards for institutions interested in dispensing financial aid to students. Under federal law, state insurance commissioners required that the companies they oversaw invest only in securities that received high marks from the ratings agencies.

Last but not least, it was the SEC's 1975 rule that the Basel Committee built upon in 2001, when it let banks set aside a smaller capital cushion to protect against losses in highly rated mortgage securities.

But even as regulators were embedding the work of the ratings agencies into the investment and banking process, the quality of that work was declining. With little in the way of competition, the agencies had no incentive to increase their staffs or improve their rating procedures. Moreover, their business models contained a deeply troubling conflict of interest.

In the 1970s, Moody's, Standard & Poor's, and Fitch had changed their systems to require the issuer of the securities to pay for the ratings they received. In previous times, investors had paid the freight for the agencies' risk assessments. Many market participants believed the companies had become less vigilant than they were when investors paid for the ratings. And among the questions Congress wanted answered was this one: Were conflicts blinding the ratings agencies to corporate disasters until just moments before they struck?

After several months of inquiry, a Senate staff report concluded that the companies "displayed a disappointing lack of diligence in their coverage and assessment" of Enron. The report went on to state that "because the credit rating agencies are subject to little formal regulation or oversight, and their liability traditionally has been limited by regulatory exemptions and First Amendment protections, there is little to hold them accountable for future poor performance."

All true. And yet Congress made no changes to the oversight of the ratings agencies or to the heavy reliance on their often erroneous credit assessments. In Enron's aftermath, lawmakers held hearings, Hill staffers produced a blistering report on the failures of Moody's, S&P, and Fitch, and the SEC conducted its own investigation.

But surprisingly little came of these efforts, even though congressional investigators concluded that "the rating analysts appeared to pay insufficient attention to the detail in Enron's financial statements, failed to probe opaque disclosures, did not review Enron's proxy statements, and failed to take into account the overall aggressiveness of Enron's accounting practices."

Moody's, Standard & Poor's, and Fitch "failed to use the

necessary rigor to ensure their analysis of a complex company, such as Enron, was sound," investigators found. "In some cases, the ratings agencies appeared simply to take the word of Enron officials when issues were raised."

Enron's failure was shocking, all right. But it was not a big enough jolt to change the way the world treated Moody's, Standard & Poor's, and Fitch Ratings. The work of these companies seemed just too entrenched in the financial markets to be subject to any serious overhaul.

In December 2004, after an international agreement to regulate the agencies prompted them to launch a lobbying pushback, the International Organization of Securities Commissions published a voluntary code of conduct for credit-ratings agencies that was meant to deal with conflicts of interest. Roughly two years later, the Credit Rating Reform Act of 2006 was signed into law by President Bush. It required ratings agencies to register with the SEC and be subject to oversight by the agency.

The SEC issued rules in the summer of 2007 requiring Moody's, S&P, and Fitch to implement policies to eliminate conflicts of interest and prohibiting what it called "unfair practices." A nonevent, in other words.

But the timing was noteworthy. The SEC's new rules emerged just as investors began to realize how wildly off beam the ratings agencies had been in analyzing risk in mortgage securities.

⇌

Even as the ratings agencies were facing scrutiny for their failings, they continued to exercise clout defending Fannie and Freddie against a growing chorus of critics in Congress. In 2004 and 2005, after both mortgage finance companies became embroiled in massive accounting scandals of their own, some lawmakers once again raised the possibility of reining in the government-sponsored enterprises to reduce the risk of a taxpayer bailout if they failed. Among the ideas under consideration: strengthening the companies' regulator and giving it the ability to take over Fannie and Freddie if they became financially troubled.

Neither company wanted this outcome, of course. And happily for Fannie and Freddie, the ratings agencies came to their rescue.

When Congress raised the possibility of adding receivership language into legislation, giving Fannie and Freddie's regulator the ability to take over the companies in a crisis, Moody's, Standard & Poor's, and Fitch Ratings all responded. They threatened to downgrade the securities issued by Fannie and Freddie; such a move would generate massive losses for investors around the world that were choking on debt and mortgage securities guaranteed by the companies.

When the U.S. Treasury stopped issuing 30-year bonds, remember, debt issued by Fannie and Freddie had become the trusted alternative. By the end of 2005, investors held a total of $4 trillion in debt issued by the companies and mortgage-backed securities guaranteed by them. United States Treasury debt outstanding, by comparison, was $4.7 trillion at the time.

Downgrading the debt issued by Fannie and Freddie would be devastating to investment portfolios the world over. Nevertheless, officials at all three agencies warned that they would do just that if the companies' regulator received more power over them.

Once again, Standard & Poor's took the lead in defending the status quo for the government-sponsored enterprises. "If Congress ends up changing the relationship with the government, we will reconsider the triple-A ratings we have placed on the GSEs' bonds," said Michael DeStefano, managing director in Standard & Poor's Financial Institutions Group. "Because the rating is highly based on the close relationship between Congress and the GSEs, a departure from that would be significant."

On the topic of the new receivership authority for Fannie's and Freddie's regulator, DeStefano could not be clearer. "Giving the regulator that kind of power over the GSEs is not a good thing for debtholders," he said.

Moody's also murmured about reevaluating the companies' credit ratings if new legislation went into effect. Fitch Ratings chimed in with a press release that read: "While Fitch believes the legislative and regulatory proposals, by themselves, do not have direct ratings consequences, their adoption may be perceived by global investors who rely heavily on systemic support, as a change in the governmental role with the GSEs. Since Fannie Mae and Freddie Mac's business conduct relies heavily on unimpeded market access and favorable pricing, such investor sentiments, if reflected in higher funding costs, could present a change in financial performance and ultimately ratings consideration."

Obviously, these threats were potent. The receivership legislation was never enacted. Just as the agencies' refusal to rate securities that held Georgia mortgages in the wake of the state's tough lending law put an end to that act, their threats to downgrade Fannie and Freddie debt helped ensure that the companies' government backing would remain intact.

By threatening to create titanic losses for holders of Fannie and Freddie debt—and these holders included foreign countries as well as large domestic institutions—the ratings agencies helped shift those losses into the future and onto the shoulders of the U.S. taxpayers.

⇌

If the ratings agencies were doing excellent work on behalf of the banks and Fannie Mae and Freddie Mac, they continued to do shoddy work for investors and taxpayers. After the Basel Committee and the United States' top financial regulators gave the all-clear to issuers of private-label mortgage securities, the credit-rating agencies began developing models to help them assess risk in these instruments.

In 2002, for example, Moody's built a mortgage securitization computer model that analyzed risks in underlying loans. In this model, Moody's considered three types of information. The most crucial was what it called "primary" data, inputs such as loan-to-value ratios, property zip codes, borrowers' credit scores, and whether a loan was a first or second lien. This information was required for each loan in a security if Moody's was to rate it.

The next two levels of data were not required by Moody's; but the agency said if they were provided, they would help it "supplement" its understanding of a borrower's risk profile. One of these was what Moody's called "highly desirable" information, including any cash reserves a borrower had on hand, his or her disposable income, whether the borrower was a first-time homeowner or had filed for bankruptcy recently.

Finally, there was the category Moody's labeled as "desirable"; it included the type of appraisal used to evaluate the property and which company had originated the loan.

Given these categories, it is clear that Moody's was not operating with a full deck. All of this information should have been required before a mortgage security could be rated. The fact that the agency did not demand that lenders provide a borrower's debt-to-income ratio—a prudent lending basic—or the type of appraisal that backed up the loan spoke volumes about how lax the agency was in its analysis.

For as long as there were mortgage loans, prudent lenders had used debt-to-income ratios to measure how financially stretched a potential borrower was. For generations, this metric was a key predictor of mortgage defaults. Moody's did not consider it to be crucial.

Then there was the matter of appraisals. With automated underwriting coming to dominate the industry, it was more crucial than ever to understand the quality of an appraisal backing a loan. If it was a drive-by appraisal or if it had been generated on a computer, the risks of an inflated valuation were far greater than if an actual human being had taken time to visit a property to assess it. Automated valuation models were also notorious for relying on outdated information; in a rising real estate market this did not matter so much, but in a falling market stale data could vastly increase a potential loss on a loan.

Finally, failing to require identification of the company making the loan meant Moody's was ignoring another hugely important piece of the puzzle.

Also troubling was the passivity with which Moody's went about getting the information it needed to make thorough assessments. Indeed, the ratings agencies relied almost exclusively on data provided to them by issuers rather than demanding that the loan packagers provide the information the agencies needed. Just as Fannie and Freddie had disavowed their government guarantee even as they capitalized on it, the rating firms were acting as advertisers while claiming to be investigative journalists.

Moody's acknowledged this, albeit in the fine print of its documents. There, a hedge clause noted that the firm has "no obligation to perform, and does not perform, due diligence with respect to the accuracy of information it receives or obtains in connection with the rating process. Moody's does not independently verify any such information. Nor does Moody's audit or otherwise undertake to determine that such information is complete."

Moody's model also seemed to run afoul of the voluntary code of conduct devised in 2004 by the International Organization of Securities Commissions. That code required that ratings agencies "adopt, implement and enforce written procedures and methodologies to ensure that the opinions it disseminates are based on a thorough analysis of all relevant information available" to them.

By limiting the amount of information they collected from mortgage securitizers, the ratings agencies had no way to see problems in the portfolios they rated before they became full-blown. That the agencies preferred to await the information from issuers rather than seek it out seemed to indicate that they were not the cop on the beat that investors thought they were. Furthermore, their passivity in the information-gathering process practically guaranteed that they would not be ahead of the curve when problems erupted. They would be likely to downgrade only when loan woes became clear and apparent.

CHAPTER TEN

What Congress did turned out to be absolutely brilliant—it created a system that harnesses private enterprise and private capital to deliver the public benefit of home ownership. And it maximizes this public benefit while minimizing the public risk, and without spending a nickel of public funds.

—FRANKLIN D. RAINES, chief executive of
Fannie Mae, May 16, 2000

When Gary Gensler strode into the congressional hearing room on March 22, 2000, to address the House Banking Subcommittee on Capital Markets, Securities, and Government-Sponsored Enterprises, few knew that the words of this obscure Treasury undersecretary would mark a turning point in the fortunes of Fannie Mae and Freddie Mac.

In 2000, the gulf between Wall Street and Washington was still wide, and few on the Street cared what policymakers had to say. Unless, of course, it was Fed chairman Alan Greenspan doing the talking, or the Treasury secretary.

But by the end of that March day, Gensler would bridge the distance between investors and policymakers.

The Subcommittee on Capital Markets was run by Richard Baker, a Louisiana Republican who had come to believe that the mortgage finance giants needed to be reined in. The son of a Baptist minister, Baker had entered Congress in 1987, representing a blue-collar district of Baton Rouge. After graduating from Louisiana State University in the late 1960s, Baker had been a Realtor and then a state legislator.

Baker's chief of staff was Ted Beason, an old friend who had spent thirty-three years on Wall Street in municipal finance. Beason had seen the profitability go out of the municipal bond market after the 1986 tax code changes and recognized that the banks were all buying mortgage-backed securities issued by Fannie and Freddie. In crafting Baker's agenda, Beason highlighted the need for taking a closer look at the companies.

Baker had invited Gensler to opine on a bill he had sponsored to tighten oversight of the mortgage finance giants. Gensler was not an academic or ivory tower denizen; he was a financial markets expert, an eighteen-year veteran of Goldman Sachs who had made partner at the firm by age thirty. An acolyte of Robert Rubin, Clinton's Treasury secretary, Gensler later rose to cohead of Goldman's finance unit.

Now the undersecretary for domestic finance at Treasury, Gensler was seated before the subcommittee to offer his views on H.R. 3703, better known as the Housing Finance Regulatory Improvement Act. Unlike past attempts to curb risks at Fannie and Freddie, Baker had put some teeth in his bill. For starters, it removed the $2.5 billion line of credit available to the companies from Treasury, one of the most significant ties binding Fannie and Freddie to Uncle Sam.

Severing this tie was important to Baker, who was acutely aware of the political reach of Fannie and Freddie and the growing risks to the taxpayer the companies posed. The $2.5 billion line of credit, after all, fed investors' beliefs that the companies would be rescued by the government if they stumbled.

But Baker also knew that his bill would be unpopular among many members of the subcommittee he chaired. The membership was dominated by two factions. First were the "housers"—true believers in government subsidies for housing and supporters of Fannie and Freddie as the best vehicles to provide them. Equally zealous, though, were the members who received campaign contributions funded by the companies as well as the ribbon-cutting ceremonies for projects in their districts.

As Gensler began his remarks, he suggested that he was there not to bury the government-sponsored enterprises, but to praise them. Noting all that the companies had done for homeownership in America, Gensler acknowledged that their government associations made Fannie and Freddie different.

He went on to highlight the companies' huge amount of debt issuance—almost as much as the entire municipal bond market. And, Gensler said, these already substantial debt levels were likely to double from the current $1.4 trillion by 2005. Including the mortgages they guaranteed and securitized, credit obligations owed by Fannie and Freddie were already approaching those of the U.S. government.

Gensler's speech was sober and supportive of the companies. Until, that is, he began reviewing the specifics of Baker's bill. When he came to the idea of revoking the Treasury line of credit, he shocked listeners by throwing his support behind it.

Suddenly, investors had to consider what life would be like if the sweetheart deal between the companies and the government was severed, forcing the thinly capitalized companies to stand on their own. Traders in Fannie and Freddie bonds shuddered as investors contemplated this sea change.

True to form, Fannie Mae's supporters, political allies, and lobbying army leapt into action. The company sent a letter to every subcommittee member claiming that even just considering Baker's bill was raising the cost of homeownership in America. David Jeffers, the Fannie spokesman who had ridiculed the work of CBO, told reporters: "The rise in mortgage costs caused by Treasury's remarks means that about 206,000 families will be disqualified for home loans." Tim Howard, the company's chief financial officer, called Gensler's remarks "inept" and "unprofessional."

Within twenty-four hours of the hearing, the Clinton White House was distancing itself from Gensler's remarks. It downplayed them as a weighing of Baker's bill and not an endorsement of it;

moreover the testimony was simply a restatement of long-standing Treasury policy.

But executives at the big banks that competed with Fannie and Freddie were ecstatic. Keen to protect their profits from encroachments by the two companies that enjoyed government-subsidized lower costs, bank officials saw chinks in the companies' federal guarantee armor.

The battle unleashed by Baker's bill was not just one based on the ideology over public subsidies for these semiprivate institutions. It was also a battle between Fannie and Freddie and the nation's banks. For years, the banks had resented the market power of the companies and hated the fact that they had to hold much higher capital cushions than Fannie and Freddie did. Having to compete with companies that had implicit federal guarantees was another complaint. Finally, none of the banks appreciated being forced to pay Fannie and Freddie the rich guarantee fees, or "g-fees" as they were known, to insure against borrower defaults.

Recognizing the possibility that Baker's legislation might become a game-changing bill, Fannie got busy. Within days, thousands of unsigned "air gram" letters began to arrive on the Hill. The "Coalition for Homeownership" was gathering constituents' signatures on letters to send to Congress, warning it not to pass the legislation because it would increase the costs of owning a home.

On May 16, 2000, less than two months after Gensler's stunning testimony, Baker convened a second subcommittee hearing on his bill. Angered by Fannie's over-the-top response to the previous hearings, Baker opened round two proclaiming: "This is a very important hearing. It literally is a battle over huge fortunes. I speak to the potential liability of taxpayers if everything is not run perfectly. The potential for systemic risk is enormous."

As for Fannie's argument that legislative changes would deny homeownership to 206,000 families, he said it was "about as reckless as it gets in my opinion. I wonder how many hundreds of thousands Chairman Greenspan will impact with his expected [interest-rate] announcement this afternoon? And should we expect the same criticism to be leveled at the Federal Reserve? I don't think so."

In Baker, Fannie and Freddie were up against a new and aggressive adversary. Still, they trotted out the same tired arguments. Leland Brendsel, Freddie's chief executive, was the first to testify at the second hearing. He began by highlighting what would become the central themes of the battle between critics of Fannie and Freddie and the companies themselves.

Those who argued that Fannie and Freddie were thinly capitalized and poised to create some future crisis were fear mongering, Brendsel said. "Not only is Freddie Mac highly skilled at managing risk, we are extremely well-capitalized for the risks we take. Freddie Mac holds enough capital to withstand 10 years of severe, adverse economic conditions—much like the Great Depression."

As evidence, Brendsel pointed to a report recently commissioned by Freddie. It had hired William Seidman, the respected former head of the FDIC, to look at the company's capital requirements. Quoting from the report, Brendsel said: "The risk-based capital standard set forth in the 1992 G.S.E. Act creates a very stringent capital standard, one that could be devastatingly stringent if applied to most other financial institutions." He delivered the coup de grace: "The fact is, if the thrifts had held as much capital relative to risk as Freddie Mac does, there would never have been a thrift crisis."

His company's many innovations "are about making mortgages more affordable, making the mortgage process easier for lenders and borrowers, and opening doors to homeownership," Brendsel said. "Freddie Mac uses technology, such as automated underwriting, to make the mortgage finance system more objective and fair."

Then it was Fannie's turn. Franklin Raines, Johnson's enforcer who had taken over as chief executive when his mentor retired a year earlier, spoke in glowing terms of the ingenious U.S. housing system, funded by a robust secondary mortgage market. "There is a simple reason why the low down payment, long-term, fixed-rate mortgage is so common here and uncommon elsewhere," Raines said. "Most countries do not have a secondary market to buy or guarantee loans that lenders originate, so the lender requires the consumer to pay more up front and more each month if mortgage interest rates rise."

Preaching to the choir, Raines went on to give credit where it was due—to Congress—for this amazing construct. "It was Congress that chartered Fannie Mae and later Freddie Mac as private shareholder-owned corporations, so Congress deserves the lion's share of the credit for the successes of the secondary market and the housing finance system today," Raines said. "What Congress did turned out to be absolutely brilliant—it created a system that harnesses private enterprise and private capital to deliver the public benefit of home ownership. And it maximizes this public benefit while minimizing the public risk, and without spending a nickel of public funds."

As for the company's critics? "Let me emphasize that our concern is not with congressional oversight, the hearings of this subcommittee or proposals to improve the housing finance system," he said. "Our concern is with any actual change in the law that would weaken our charter or impose regulatory burdens that would raise our costs of providing capital to the housing finance system."

Bob Riley, an Alabama congressman, immediately challenged Raines. He pointed out that Fannie had not only taken issue with Baker's introduction of legislation that would eliminate the $2.5 billion Treasury tie, the company had also attacked a Treasury undersecretary for having harmed homeownership simply because he supported cutting that financial bond.

How much had the discussion of the bill actually moved interest rates as Fannie executives had claimed? Riley asked Raines.

Talk of removing the Treasury backstop had increased prevailing interest rates by between 0.20 and 0.40 percent, Raines replied, which in turn increased mortgage costs for consumers. Riley pushed harder, asking Raines to explain how much it would actually cost borrowers to pull the Treasury line. Would it be between half a percentage point and 1.5 points? "Maybe around that number," Raines responded.

But Riley had Raines right where he wanted him. The interest rate on the average 30-year fixed-rate mortgage backed by Fannie or Freddie had actually *declined* slightly between the introduction of Baker's bill and the week following Gensler's testimony. It had fallen from 8.3 percent to 8.26 percent. Riley pointed out this undeniable fact.

The congressman went on to warn Raines that if Fannie hoped to work constructively with Congress, the company had better curb the rhetoric claiming certain members of Congress were anti-housing.

Next up: the matter of those constituent letters imploring so many in Congress to reject the Baker bill. John Sweeney, a Republican from New York, and Donald Manzullo, an Illinois Republican, told of calling some of the folks who had sent the letters. What they found was shocking: These constituents had no idea that their names had been signed to such a letter. Others, meanwhile, explained that they had not been contacted by any coalition but by Fannie itself, while still others said they had specifically asked Fannie not to use their names. Some had no recollection of being contacted at all.

The Coalition for Homeownership appeared to be a coalition of one—Fannie Mae, acting once again through its wealthy nonprofit foundation.

Sweeney's staff walked through the hearing room carrying boxes, which they deposited on the witness table next to Raines. In them were more than two thousand letters received by various representatives' offices arguing against any restrictions on Fannie Mae.

"I feel like the judge in 'Miracle on 34th Street' when they brought in the letters to Santa Claus and put them on the judge's desk," Raines said.

Asked by Sweeney and later by Manzullo to explain, Raines

admitted that Fannie had bought the names of constituents from a commercial list vendor and contacted the constituents. He could not say how much money Fannie had spent on the effort.

Manzullo went on the attack, telling Raines that his staff had called thirty of the letter writers from his district; the first nine they contacted said they knew nothing about the letters.

"Most of my constituents were upset that their good name had been used by your company," Manzullo raged. "I am upset also."

He went on. "I want you to send letters to 2,000 of my constituents apologizing for using their good name. This is bogus lobbying."

Raines responded with defiance: "We will ask for support from people in the United States to support the secondary market," he said. "We will ask them to contact their members to express their point of view. If any letter came to you that was not an accurate expression of the views of a constituent, I'm sorry for that, and we will endeavor in the future to ensure that that does not occur."

The fireworks were over. The hearing was drawing to a close. Because of a pending vote, Raines would soon be excused. But before he was, Carolyn Maloney, a New York Democrat, wanted to ask a question about new product areas Fannie and Freddie might pursue.

"There is one that I would hope that you would take a look at and expand to," she said. "I think it would be appropriate to bring the G.S.E. structure to childcare, an area that has been failed by the private markets. You literally revolutionized home ownership in this country, it is now at an astonishing 70 percent, yet childcare, we can't get the financing. It is not supported. I would like to know, would Fannie and Freddie be opposed to having the authority to buy childcare facility mortgages?"

Raines would have loved to respond to such a softball question, but Baker concluded the hearing, asking that Fannie and Freddie answer Maloney's question in writing.

After almost five hours of testimony the hearing was finally over. Battle lines were clearly drawn between those, like Maloney, who wanted to expand the reach of Fannie and Freddie to execute government policy—her idea was called Kiddie Mac—and those

who wanted the companies out of the business of banking altogether.

The Baker bill was a clear indication to Fannie and Freddie that
their enemies were gaining traction and becoming more emboldened. But as legislation it was not meant to be. Fannie and Freddie used all their tools and called in all their chits to do in H.R.
3703. Over the next year and a half, with the dot-com bust and
the 9/11 terrorist attacks, few were willing to support any process
that might increase economic uncertainty. Fannie and Freddie
enlisted Realtors, homebuilders, and their powerful friends on
the Hill to kill the bill.

For Baker to expect any real reform of Fannie and Freddie was
idealistic, narcissistic, or just plain politically dumb. Washington,
after all, is about stasis. Lawmakers had only recently begun considering the elimination of a 1925 law that required the federal
government to maintain a helium reserve so that a dirigible fleet
could be launched to protect the nation under attack. Was it likely
Washington would get rid of the companies that underpinned the
nation's housing markets—especially given how munificent their
campaign contributions were?

Perhaps more important, how could Baker, a subcommittee
chairman, hope to move legislation when Michael Oxley, an Ohio
Republican who was his own committee's chairman, had little
support for the idea? Oxley understood the game and knew that it
wasn't all about policy or politics. It was about how much money
you could raise for your party, and at that, Oxley was a maestro.

In January 2001, Oxley hosted his annual, invitation-only
fund-raising weekend in Vail, Colorado. Among the lobbyists with
whom he already had close ties was Dan Cohen, who represented
both Fannie Mae and World Savings and Loan. Asked by reporters
if he would accept corporate contributions Oxley was unabashed.
"I don't know why not," he said.

⇔

It was yet another measure of Fannie's arrogance that even as
the company was coming under increased scrutiny by some in

Congress, it kept right on doctoring its financial results as it had since 1998, employing crooked accounting to produce its desired earnings and executive payouts.

In 2001, however, Fannie took its accounting chicanery to new heights, or lows, depending upon your perspective. And it did it with the help of its favorite investment bank, Goldman Sachs.

Goldman had long had strong ties to Fannie Mae. Stephen Friedman, chairman of Goldman Sachs from 1992 to 1994, had been a director of Fannie Mae since 1996. In 2001 Friedman sat on Fannie's Compensation Committee and its Nominating and Corporate Governance Committee. Both areas were seriously compromised by the me-first attitude at the top of Fannie Mae.

Indeed, while Friedman was on Fannie's board, federal investigators said directors improperly allowed the company's executives to set earnings targets they were sure to meet. "As a direct result, senior management reaped ongoing and extensive financial rewards through accounting manipulation," the investigators who wrote the OFHEO report concluded.

In 1999, Goldman had returned the favor of a directorship by offering a seat on its prestigious board to Jim Johnson. It was a classic example of the "I'll-scratch-your-back, you-scratch-mine" mentality among corporate boards. The year Johnson became a director at Goldman, Henry M. Paulson Jr., the man who would oversee the taxpayer bailout of Fannie Mae as Treasury secretary in 2008, took the helm at the investment bank.

Because Goldman did not have a nominating committee at the time, Johnson's appointment to its board was a decision made at the highest levels of the firm. Johnson immediately received the plum board assignment of chairing the firm's compensation committee. This meant that Johnson, in addition to his other board duties, would be in charge of dispensing some of the richest payouts on Wall Street.

Given the immense compensation packages he had received at Fannie Mae, Johnson was not likely to rein in the pay awarded to Goldman executives. In the eleven years that Johnson has been on the Goldman Sachs board, he has been the only director to chair the firm's Compensation Committee.

All of the corporate executives who invited him onto their boards seemed to recognize this—Johnson chaired the compensation committees of every board he sat on over the years.*

Two years after Johnson had joined Goldman's board, an executive in the Wall Street firm came up with an idea that would help the mortgage giant ensure that its earnings would keep growing, even in a declining-interest-rate environment.

That executive was David Rosenblum, an expert in structured finance at Goldman. According to the OFHEO report, in 2001, he outlined a transaction to Fannie Mae that would help the mortgage giant artificially set aside earnings the company could use in the future when it needed help meeting its forecasts.

"Project Libra," Rosenblum called it.

The complex deal would require Fannie to misrepresent the true state of its financial position to investors, but it would also give the firm a way to shift $107 million of earnings into future years when the company might need them. The arrangement had no economic purpose other than rearranging income streams; therefore it violated accounting rules.

The transaction Rosenblum devised and presented to Fannie executives involved what is known as a real estate mortgage investment conduit, or REMIC. It was a pool of mortgages that generated cash flows as borrowers paid down their loans.

Designed to free Fannie from having to abide by generally accepted accounting principles, Project Libra did so by packaging $30 billion of mortgages into pools that would artificially generate cash flows at different times in the future. Fannie would keep 90 percent of the mortgages and sell off the rest to investors.

---

*Compensation at two of the boards whose pay committees he chaired attracted lawsuits by regulators—KB Home and United Healthcare. In both cases, compensation approved by Johnson wound up having to be rescinded. In the case of KB Home, Bruce Karatz, the chief executive and a friend of Johnson's, was convicted of a felony for manipulating his stock option grants and was sentenced to five years' probation in November 2010.

Because interest rates were falling precipitously, Fannie was worried about its future earnings power. Under the terms of the transaction, it was estimated to begin benefiting Fannie's earnings in 2005.

Goldman Sachs suggested the idea to Fannie, federal investigators found. In a November 2001 presentation to Fannie executives, Rosenblum noted only one benefit of the Libra transaction: It allowed them to "better manage the recognition of income" under accounting rules.

Rosenblum's contact at Fannie Mae on the deal was Peter Niculescu, a senior vice president for portfolio strategy who had run mortgage research at Goldman during the 1990s. He directed Project Libra inside Fannie and one year after the transaction was done, Niculescu was promoted to executive vice president of the mortgage portfolio business at the company. An indication of how important his new job was: Niculescu reported directly to the company's chief financial officer, Timothy Howard.

After Fannie decided to go ahead with the transaction, Goldman acted as underwriter on the mortgage pools, selling them to investors. Goldman received $625,000 in fees to underwrite the instruments, the OFHEO report said.

The prospectuses for the securities made no mention of why the manipulative deal was done. Neither did Fannie's annual financial summaries for either 2001 or 2002.

⇌

Even though Richard Baker's attempt to curtail Fannie and Freddie's operations had failed, the drumbeat of criticism about the potential risks posed by the companies was growing ever louder in late 2001. That September, Armando Falcon, director of OFHEO, the companies' overseer, introduced regulatory proposals that would require Fannie and Freddie to abide by conflict-of-interest rules as other public companies did. The following March, OFHEO's deputy director, Jimmy Barton, announced that the agency was tightening its procedures and improving its oversight of the companies' credit and interest-rate risk, derivatives, and internal controls.

It must have been a source of some discomfort to Raines and his cohorts to hear that OFHEO was also adding to its accounting expertise. The agency said it wanted "to provide even more scrutiny to the accounting practices being employed by the Enterprises."

While sweeping legislation to overhaul the companies' regulatory scrutiny had gone nowhere, some lawmakers began to promote smaller and more targeted legislation aimed at reining them in. Christopher Shays, a Connecticut Republican, and Edward Markey, the Democrat from Massachusetts, introduced legislation in early spring 2002 that would end the special exemption on financial disclosures that Fannie and Freddie enjoyed. Other public companies routinely provided investors with extensive details about their operations and results. Why should Fannie and Freddie—among the largest debt issuers in the world—be allowed to keep their investors in the dark?

Arguing for more scrutiny was a burgeoning group of economists at the Federal Reserve and other institutions publishing exhaustively on how these non-free-market enterprises distorted financial markets.

On April 22, 2002, the Maestro stepped into the fray. Addressing a New York conference of the International Institute of Finance by satellite, Alan Greenspan spoke of the economy's resilience in the face of sharp equity market declines, retrenchments in corporate spending, and terrorist attacks.

Still, the proliferation of derivative instruments that banks and Wall Street firms used to hedge and manage risks required some caution, Greenspan said.

"Concerns have been raised about potential counterparty risks in the large interest rate hedging efforts of government-sponsored enterprises," he said. The broader risks for financial markets and the economy result from the perception of government support for these corporations, he continued, which "may induce the counterparties of G.S.E.'s to apply less vigorously some of the risk controls that they apply to manage their over-the-counter derivatives exposures."

Without even mentioning Fannie or Freddie by name, Greenspan had made clear that he believed the companies posed a serious and systemic risk to the financial markets.

It is interesting that the Fed, with its deregulatory bias, would support stronger oversight of firms that competed with the banks it always seemed to go easy on in its supervision.

The political heat on the companies was clearly rising. And by the end of May, the Bush administration threw its weight behind the idea of forcing Fannie and Freddie to increase their disclosures. The Office of Management and Budget sent a letter to the OFHEO director asking him to consider issuing regulations that would force the companies to be more forthcoming in their financial reports. Fannie argued that its disclosures generally met or exceeded those of SEC requirements, but OMB director John Graham said that because those disclosures were voluntary, they could vanish at precisely the time the public needed them most.

Recognizing the dangers of increasingly bipartisan assaults like the Shays-Markey bill, Fannie and Freddie began negotiating with the Treasury, OFHEO, and the SEC. On July 12, 2002, the companies agreed to "voluntarily" register their stock with the SEC; their debt securities, however, were not subject to registration. Fannie had capitulated, giving up just about an inch on a hundred-yard field.

But for every small step forward in eliminating the special perquisites enjoyed by Fannie and Freddie, there always seemed to be one step back. Just four days later, Peter Fisher, Treasury's appointed but not yet sworn-in undersecretary for domestic finance, proclaimed at a subcommittee hearing that both Fannie Mae and Freddie Mac "are well-run."

Fisher supported the "latest voluntary initiative" and suggested "further study of the issue." The legislation introduced by Shays-Markey was not necessary, he said, and he could not therefore support legislation in Congress that would repeal the exemptions the companies enjoyed from registering their debt securities.

Some on the Hill wondered if Fisher's confidence in Fannie's management had anything to do with the fact that, during his transition from Wall Street to Treasury, he had been staying at the home of his old school chum Dan Mudd, Fannie Mae's vice-chairman.

⇆

During the congressional recess in August 2002, an explosive story on Fannie Mae, entitled "Balancing Act," appeared in *Washingtonian* magazine. Its author, Ross Guberman, explained the history and the benefits Fannie received, as well as its arrogant culture. "It's not that the companies are famously well managed," Guberman wrote, referring to both Fannie and Freddie. "It's that investors are sure they'll be repaid—if by no one else, by the U.S. government."

The problem with this, Guberman presciently explained, was that taxpayers might have to bail out the companies if they ever got into trouble. "If housing prices crash or either company stumbles, the taxpayers could be on the hook for hundreds of billions," he wrote. "'It's as if the public had cosigned Fannie and Freddie's debt,' says Lawrence White, a New York University business-school professor and former Freddie Mac director. 'To pay for a very small cut in mortgage rates,' White says, 'the taxpayers bear the risk of a massive bailout.'"

The article was groundbreaking and made even the most jaded Washingtonian take note. Here was a reporter not just laying out the fault lines, the arguments, the lobbying strategies of Fannie and their enemies the banks, but also naming names, ranks, and serial numbers. "It's all a matter of know-who, not know-how," complained Ralph Nader about Fannie's higher ranks. "They've perfected all the techniques of lobbying and pay massive salaries for Rolodex hiring to ensure against any change."

The article also outed a well-known secret among financial service watchers: the existence of a coalition of private mortgage insurers, mortgage lenders, appraiser groups, and banks. Called FM Watch, the group was created in 1999 to draw a line in the sand and prevent Fannie and Freddie from a seemingly endless push to become direct lenders.

Chief executives of Wells Fargo, GE Capital, and American International Group told Guberman about threats they had received from Fannie saying that it would not to buy any more loans from them if they continued to support FM Watch. Rick Carnell, the former Treasury official who oversaw the report on the privatization of Fannie and Freddie, said that years before, when he was a banking committee staffer drafting legislation, Fannie tried to get him to include language suggesting that the government backed its debt while it denied the same to the public.

Called to testify before the full Committee on Financial Services on September 25, 2002, Raines was ready for an assault. He was armed with data showing how important the GSEs were to the functioning housing markets, how much they expanded ownership, how much better they were at mitigating interest rate and credit risk than their fully private counterparts. Of course, he cited the Stiglitz/Orszag paper as evidence that the idea of a taxpayer bailout was ludicrous.

With Enron and WorldCom still fresh in investors' minds, Raines defended Fannie's corporate governance: "Openness. Integrity. Responsibility. Accountability. Fannie Mae puts a premium on upholding these simple, core principles in our corporate mission, business, and culture for an important reason," he said. "Trust is uniquely crucial to our company."

Even before the Sarbanes-Oxley legislation had passed, Raines explained, he had conducted a six-month corporate governance project at Fannie, working directly with its board to develop a "best-in-class model."

Fannie had also asked none other than Standard & Poor's to weigh in on the company's governance practices, he said. "Standard & Poor's gave Fannie Mae a corporate governance score of 9.0 out of a possible 10, saying, 'Fannie Mae's corporate governance practices are judged . . . to be at a very strong level on a global basis of comparison.'" It was the first such score assigned to a corporation. The company was very strong in "financial transparency," S&P said, also citing its highly independent board.

Once again, lawmakers backed down.

Then, just ahead of the Christmas holiday and seemingly timed for Congress's use, the Fed released a two-year-old study disclosing their reluctance to purchase mortgage-backed securities issued by Fannie or Freddie as part of their monetary policy operations. Greenspan's Fed was no longer pussyfooting around the systemic risk posed by the government-sponsored enterprises. The Fed's paper said that its purchase of Fannie and Freddie obligations could "inappropriately foster the ability of the G.S.E.'s to expand their operations; this expansion could further affect credit allocation and increase systemic risk."

As 2003 dawned, few knew that it would be the year that the public-private partnership for homeownership would go truly viral. Having watched the great success of Fannie's take-no-prisoners lobbying and operational tactics, the nation's largest banks knew what they had to do to be heard in Washington. With a Republican in the White House, Washington was an even more hospitable place.

On February 4, 2003, Armando Falcon, the head of OFHEO, sent a letter to Richard Shelby, the Alabaman who was chairman of the Senate Banking Committee, and to House Financial Services Committee chairman Michael Oxley. Ranking Democrats Paul Sarbanes and Barney Frank also received a copy of the letter, which accompanied a newly published paper entitled "Systemic Risk: Fannie Mae, Freddie Mac and the Role of OFHEO."

Walking a fine line to avoid creating market turmoil, the paper made clear that without proper regulatory authorities—including the authority to close down and unwind a failing government-sponsored enterprise—there may be no way of preventing a debt default from leading to "contagious illiquidity" that would "cause or worsen illiquidity problems at other financial institutions."

"A financial institution's direct interdependencies exist through explicit contractual arrangements with other parties—loans, financial derivatives, or credit insurance, for example—that expose

the institution to counterparty risk," the paper stated. "If a significant number of interdependent institutions incur losses or
fail simultaneously, uncertainty about the prospects of the remaining firms, even the solvent ones, and about the likely responses of
other investors in those firms, will also increase. This may make
it difficult for the remaining solvent institutions to issue debt."

Falcon's letter made clear that "the views expressed in the
report are my views and do not necessarily represent the views of
the Secretary of Housing and Urban Development or the President." But the head of OFHEO had not simply attacked Fannie
and Freddie, he had also directly threatened the fastest-growing
business on Wall Street: the sale and trading of derivatives, including credit default swaps.

Less than twenty-four hours later, the Bush White House
demanded Falcon's resignation. In his place they would nominate
Mark C. Brickell. The irony was great and the subtext rich. During the early 1990s House Financial Services Committee chairman
Henry Gonzalez, a Texas Democrat and supporter of Fannie and
Freddie, had tried to halt the unfettered growth of derivative
products. He argued that these instruments, which were hugely
profitable to the big banks that traded them, needed greater scrutiny, consideration, and oversight. His work had been supported
by a young aide named Armando Falcon.

In 1994, Brickell, a managing director at J. P. Morgan, had
testified before Gonzalez and launched a successful lobbying
effort to prevent any real regulation of OTC derivatives. During
the ensuing years, Brickell, a friend of Senator Phil Gramm and
his wife, Wendy, the chairman of the Commodity Futures Trading
Commission, had been responsible for the growth of J. P. Morgan's
derivatives trading business into the largest such business in the
world, with over $29 trillion in derivatives outstanding.

With Falcon on the ropes and Brickell in the wings, the White
House was sending a message—we are lining up behind the big
banks and against Fannie and Freddie.

But Brickell never got the job and Falcon was allowed to hold on.

CHAPTER ELEVEN

Expanding the American dream of homeownership must continue to be our mission, not solely for the purpose of benefiting corporate America, but more importantly, to make our country a better place.

—ANGELO R. MOZILO, chief executive,
Countrywide Financial, Washington, D.C.,
February 2003

The public-private partnership to promote homeownership was eight years young when the stars truly aligned, assuring the biggest housing boom of all time. While some of the partnership's key architects had left center stage by 2003—Jim Johnson and Bill Clinton, for example—the push for homeownership was becoming a runaway train. President Bush added to the partnership, strengthening the faith-based initiatives that allowed growth of down-payment assistance programs through charity organizations. Prevailing interest rates were at 1 percent, regulators and Congress were on board for looser lending standards, and a raft of innovative mortgage loans was floating all kinds of new borrowers. Known as "affordability products," these mortgages vastly expanded homeownership, letting borrowers "own" a home but still pay a fraction of what they would have normally. In the early years of the loan, that is.

Homeownership stood at 68 percent and a record $3.84 trillion in mortgages were written in 2003, triple the amount originated just three years earlier. Wall Street's mortgage securitization factory was on fire as well, with 13.6 million loans purchased and pooled into securities that could be sold to investors around the corner or around the world.

But many members of the partnership, especially those whose companies profited from the program, believed more work was needed. No one felt more strongly about this than Angelo R. Mozilo, cofounder of Countrywide Financial.

Standing before an audience of homebuilders, lenders, and policymakers at the National Housing Center in Washington, D.C., in February 2003, Mozilo made his case. The Bronx-born, rags-to-riches chief executive outlined how the already successful partnership could get even more Americans into homes. Among his recommendations: the elimination of down payments for low-income consumers, the paring back of borrower documentation and paperwork so loans could be approved "in minutes," and the eradication of "egregious regulatory fees, outdated building codes and a plethora of restrictions on land use."

Mozilo's Countrywide had been the first lender to embrace the homeownership push back in 1995 and had therefore been a central player in Clinton's public-private partnership. And since 1998, Countrywide had also become crucial to the corporate fortunes of Fannie Mae and the personal wealth of Fannie employees who received special mortgage deals from the lender. That was the year Jim Johnson had agreed to charge Mozilo's company far lower guarantee fees than its rivals on mortgages Fannie Mae bought from the company and sold to investors.

Having struck that deal with Johnson, Countrywide soon became the biggest single seller of loans to Fannie Mae. A believer in technology, Mozilo's company put a premium on speed in the mortgage process; one of its products designed for Fannie was the Fast-N-Easy loan. It required no documentation of a borrower's income or assets and gave loans to borrowers whose debt-to-income levels were far higher—50 percent—than what was required by other lenders, even those who were quite lax themselves.

Countrywide supplied 26 percent of the loans purchased by Fannie in 2004; three years later, this figure had risen to 28 percent. Billions of dollars in toxic mortgages went straight from Countrywide to the government-sponsored enterprise that would just four years later become a ward of the state.

In 2003, however, Mozilo's company was still very much the envy of the mortgage industry. Between 1994 and 2004, Countrywide's annual earnings had rocketed from $180 million to $2.2 billion. Shareholders watched with delight as their stock jumped fivefold over the period. Where most of his non-bank mortgage lending rivals had gone out of business with the collapse of Subprime 1.0, Mozilo hadn't just survived, he'd flourished.

Mozilo, too, was a beneficiary, pocketing $43 million in salary and bonuses over those years. His stock compensation was even more generous, allowing him to cash in more than $400 million in shares during his tenure at the company. In business circles, Mozilo was a rock star, regularly receiving standing ovations at speeches he made to industry groups. When people spoke of Angelo, or "The Tan Man," everyone knew they were referring to Mozilo.

It was almost incomprehensible that back in 1969, Countrywide had begun as a two-man mortgage shop in Los Angeles. Now it had five hundred offices across the nation generating $400 billion in loans. Doing its part to democratize the home-loan business, Countrywide was the number-one lender to both Hispanics and African Americans.

Having come from the wrong side of the tracks in the Bronx, Mozilo had something of a chip on his shoulder. He prided himself, therefore, on disproving any and all Countrywide doubters. He routinely made brash predictions of mortgage volume he expected Countrywide to generate in, say, five years.

But those who laughed at his forecasts soon fell silent as the company proceeded to achieve them. Then Mozilo would lay out a set of even more aggressive metrics for Countrywide to meet.

Mozilo relished taking on his peers, warning them face-to-face that he would drive them out of business. "He was tough, tough,

tough and very boastful," said a former chief executive of an established financial institution that competed with Countrywide. The first time he saw Mozilo in action was at an industry conference, the executive recalled; the Countrywide chief was on a panel with two other chief executives of giant and respected institutions—Home Savings and Great Western Savings.

"There's Mozilo saying, 'I'm going to blow you guys out of the water, I'm going to whip you guys,'" the executive said. "He was going to take over everything. Countrywide was going to be the last one standing."

Naturally, as Mozilo stood before the Washington crowd that February, even as he acknowledged the strides that had been made in homeownership, he wanted more. Announcing an extension of his company's "House America" program, Mozilo promised to devote $600 billion to mortgage loans for underserved communities through 2010.

"Housing is critical to our nation's welfare and to our communities' well-being," he said. "Let's make sure that the American dream of homeownership is never a cliché, and always our cause, and always our steadfast mission. We have the resources. Together, as partners, let's show the will."

It was a Jim Johnson message delivered deep in Jim Johnson territory. And while some might have thought the crude, rough-around-the-edges Mozilo an unusual candidate to take on the mantle of the smooth and calculating Johnson, the two were more alike than dissimilar.

Yes, they were an odd couple outwardly. Johnson was buttoned-down and Mozilo was flashy. But more important than appearances was their common modus operandi—both were bullies. The only difference was Mozilo liked to push people around himself while Johnson preferred others to do his handiwork.

Thanks to Johnson's aggressive courting of Mozilo years earlier, Countrywide and Fannie Mae were inextricably bound. Millions of risky loans made by Countrywide and sold to Fannie Mae would contribute mightily to the downfall of Johnson's former company. And although Countrywide's collapse would come in

2007, a year before Fannie Mae's, both failures had been set in motion long before by Johnson and Mozilo.

⇌

It was no coincidence that Countrywide's operations were so intertwined with Fannie Mae's and so similar. Both companies had the same goals to achieve and the same enemies to defeat. And for years, Mozilo's friendship with Johnson had given him a front-row seat for the Fannie Mae way—the deep political focus, the co-opting of regulators, the manipulation of public opinion, and extensive granting of favors to friends and potential foes.

Mozilo, a quick study, saw what Johnson had won and set out to copy it. More than any other mortgage lender, Countrywide was at heart a Fannie Mae clone.

While Mozilo needed no instruction from Johnson on expanding his mortgage lender—Johnson was no businessman, after all—Mozilo did learn from Johnson how to adapt Fannie Mae–style tactics to his company.

Countrywide's lobbying efforts, for example, began to accelerate dramatically in 2003, just as predatory lending laws were gaining traction in several states. Back in 1998, the company's lobbying expenditures had totaled a relatively minor $60,000, but by 2003 they had risen to $1.1 million. As the mortgage craze was reaching its crescendo in 2005, Countrywide's lobbying expenditures peaked at $1.52 million.

Countrywide pleaded its case—stopping new lending laws was its key issue—before the Treasury, the Federal Reserve Board, and the House and Senate. Between 1998 and 2007, the company spent $6.6 million lobbying.

In 2005, when Congress was considering changes to consumer bankruptcy laws, Countrywide lobbied in lockstep with Fannie Mae, according to a Hill staffer who witnessed the companies' activities. In a classic Washington bait and switch, changes that some lawmakers had hoped would help consumers by giving them access to a fresh start after bankruptcy soon became co-opted by the credit-card industry. Consumers wound up worse off than they had been before.

"Fannie, Freddie and Countrywide were all lobbying on the same issues," the staffer said. "They were looking for protection in the bankruptcy process and Countrywide had hired a lot of folks to lobby the issues. It makes you wonder—did they know that there were a lot of bad loans out there and that borrowers would be filing for bankruptcy down the road?"

The bankruptcy law barred the courts from getting involved in mortgage foreclosures automatically, giving lenders far more freedom to evict borrowers from their homes.

But Mozilo recognized that lobbying might not be enough. And he soon began inviting people with deep political connections to join his company's board. While before its directors had been obscure businessmen who counted Mozilo as a friend, in 2001 the Countrywide board took on a more political tone. That was the year that Henry G. Cisneros, the Clinton-appointed secretary of HUD from 1993 through 1997, became a Countrywide director. Cisneros was also on the board of KB Home, the giant home-builder where Johnson was a director from 1992 through the first few months of 2008.

In 2004, Robert T. Parry, former president of the Federal Reserve Bank of San Francisco, joined Countrywide's board. Parry became a Countrywide director just three months after leaving the Fed; while at the San Francisco Fed, he consistently acted in the interests of the big banks, according to those who dealt with him.

Directors at Countrywide were paid handsomely for their work. In 2004, the company began granting shares worth approximately $220,000 to its directors; this was in addition to the $70,000 cash stipend. Over time, the payouts rose; by 2007, Mr. Parry was receiving $557,000 a year for his Countrywide board service.

Having a former regulator on his board may also have helped guide Mozilo when it came time to select the most forgiving regulator for his company. In 2006, Countrywide changed from reporting to the Office of the Comptroller of the Currency, a unit of the

Treasury, to the Office of Thrift Supervision. OTS was famous for embracing rather than policing its regulated entities.

Because Countrywide had truckloads of money to dispense in the form of mortgages, sweetheart loans bestowed on friends and on those in power became central to Mozilo's modus operandi. These deals, known in-house as the VIP Program, or the "Friends of Angelo" Program, started in 1998; an expansion of the deals took effect in 2003.

Johnson was an early initiate to the VIP Program. Starting in 1998 and continuing through 2007, Johnson received six cut-rate loans from Countrywide worth a total of more than $10 million.*

Jim Johnson's former partner at the political consulting firm they sold to Lehman Brothers, Richard Holbrooke, who was appointed special representative to Afghanistan and Pakistan in the Obama administration, also received a VIP loan from Country-wide. So did an untold number of politicians, including Chris Dodd, the Connecticut Democrat in the Senate, and Kent Conrad, a Demo-crat from South Dakota. Barbara Boxer, the California Democrat, and Donna Shalala, the former head of Health and Human Ser-vices under Clinton, secured low-cost Countrywide loans as well.

Also receiving special treatment was Alfonso Jackson, secretary of HUD from 2004 to 2008 and a deputy secretary there beginning in 2001; Jackson sought a sweetheart Countrywide mortgage for his daughter as well. (HUD was the agency charged with over-seeing Fannie.) Clinton Jones III, senior counsel to the House Financial Services Subcommittee on Housing, also scored a bar-gain loan.

That many of these recipients were friends of Jim Johnson was no coincidence. Indeed, he often acted as a kind of super-

---

*In August 2009, almost a year after Fannie Mae collapsed into the arms of the U.S. government, Johnson held a dinner party for his high-powered friends at his sump-tuous home in Ketchum, Idaho, near the ski resort of Sun Valley. At the party were Mozilo, Richard Fuld, the disgraced former chief executive of Lehman Brothers, and Vernon Jordan, the confidant of Bill Clinton who is a lawyer and investment banker and was in town for the Sun Valley Writers' Conference.

powered mortgage middleman; upon learning of a friend's home-loan needs, he would call Mozilo on his private line and provide the particulars. Mozilo would hand off the details to loan officers in his VIP Program who were instructed to handle such mortgages with care.

That Countrywide mimicked Fannie's influence-peddling ways was also evident in the case of former Utah senator Robert Bennett. In 1999, Fannie Mae hired Bennett's son to help run its partnership office in Salt Lake City, an office that was supervised by Tim Stewart, an aide to the former senator. Records from 2004 show Countrywide granting twelve special loans to members of Bennett's staff.

Friends of Angelo, it seemed, were also friends of Fannie.

Countrywide also hired the children of politicians and others in power. Paul Pelosi Jr., the son of Nancy Pelosi, the former Speaker of the House, worked as a mortgage broker and sales manager at a Countrywide office in San Mateo, California. In 2007, when the company was on the ropes and beginning a mass of layoffs, Pelosi's name was on the list of those to be cut. According to a former executive with knowledge of the situation, Mozilo personally removed Pelosi's name from the list.

With more than thirty-five thousand employees, it was easy for Mozilo to make a few strategic hires for friends and others in positions to help Countrywide.

⇌

Although Mozilo, with his perennial tan, monogrammed French cuffs, and loud, pin-striped suits, was a parody of the superslick salesman, there was no denying that he and cofounder David Loeb had built an enviable business empire from scratch. Loeb was Mr. Inside, a quiet, deliberate man who was about fifteen years older than Mozilo, Countrywide's Mr. Outside.

The men had met in 1960 when Mozilo was twenty-one, having just graduated from Fordham University with a degree in marketing and philosophy that he had earned at night. He was working at United Mortgagee Servicing Corporation, a company that had taken over a firm started by Loeb. In 1968, when United was taken over, Mozilo and Loeb struck out on their own. With just one office in Los Angeles, they brazenly named their company Countrywide.

Loeb was Countrywide's strategic thinker and risk manager, according to those who knew him, while Mozilo was its leader and builder. "David was a Buddha-like father figure, an incredibly wise and grounded mentor to Angelo," said one former analyst who followed the company from its beginnings. "David was ever the curmudgeonly risk manager and Angelo was ever the optimist. I think they really played well together."

Mozilo's obsession was market share—no matter what, Countrywide was going to be the nation's largest lender. Even in economic downturns, Countrywide moved aggressively to snare market share from rivals.

In addition to selling billions of dollars in mortgages to Fannie Mae every year, Mozilo recognized the importance of being able to issue and sell mortgage securities containing Countrywide loans directly to investors. As such, he was among the first to jump-start the so-called private-label mortgage securities market in 2002. One year later, Countrywide was the fourth-largest issuer of private-label mortgage securities.

With both private investors and Fannie Mae willing and eager to buy Countrywide mortgages, Mozilo soon had access to a cash spigot almost as big as Niagara Falls.

While Loeb remained atop the company, Countrywide's growth was notable. But after he retired from Countrywide in 2000, the company's performance went off the charts. While revenues were $1.7 billion in 2000, by 2003 they had hit $8 billion. The company generated almost 3 million mortgages in 2003 and its earnings were more than double the amount recorded in 2002.

When Loeb died in 2003 at the age of seventy-nine, the controls on Mozilo's bravado and aggressive growth plans were really and truly gone. Countrywide was now a one-man show. And the man running it was one of those people who thought too much of a good thing was never enough.

"David was a reclusive genius; if he had stayed around, I think Countrywide's growth would have been a little more balanced and risk-averse," a former friend recalled. "Countrywide was a rocket ship after David, but in my opinion, knowing the two of them, the company suffered from his absence."

Obsessing about market share meant that as Countrywide's rivals corrupted their lending practices, it would have to do so as well in order to compete. The former finance executive recalled: "To the extent that more than 5 percent of the market was originating a particular product, any new alternative mortgage product, then Countrywide would originate it. I would ask 'why are we originating 182 products?' and the answer I got was we want to be the leader in all products. We might lose business otherwise."

Mozilo's second mistake was relying on investors to finance his securities; this made his company exceedingly vulnerable to a turning off of the cash flow, unlike banks, which used their customers' relatively stable deposits to make loans.

Add in Mozilo's arrogance and the mix became ultra-combustible, not only for his company but for the financial system as a whole.

⇌

In 2004, almost twenty-five years after he and Loeb had first partnered in Los Angeles, Mozilo finally got his wish—Countrywide was the nation's largest mortgage lender, dominating the private-label business. It was generating almost 200,000 mortgages a month and booking revenues of $8.6 billion a year. The company was responsible for 26 percent of the loans Fannie Mae bought in 2004.

Countrywide originated mortgages in three different ways. Some it bought from other institutions; others came from independent mortgage brokers who arranged deals for their clients. Finally, it attracted other borrowers either through Realtors or in television, radio, or print advertising.

The pitch used by Countrywide brokers to lure in customers involved some variation of a promise to provide "the best loan possible." But as many borrowers would learn the hard way, these were the best loans only for Countrywide, not for its customers.

Instead, borrowers were led to high-cost loans that resulted in rich commissions for Countrywide's smooth-talking sales force, outsized fees to company affiliates providing services on the loans, and a roaring stock price that made Countrywide executives among the highest paid in America. Such loans carried punitive prepayment penalties or had interest rates that were set alluringly low at first, only to skyrocket in a few years' time.

For all of Mozilo's talk of wanting to help minorities and low-income people secure a mortgage, the company's systems were designed to increase costs for precisely these borrowers, former Countrywide employees said.

One former mortgage broker in Los Angeles said that Countrywide branches in upscale neighborhoods like Beverly Hills and Santa Monica had to slash their mortgage rates to be competitive with rival banks. But in areas that were predominantly minority, Countrywide's rates were far higher because company executives knew borrowers in these neighborhoods had few if any alternatives.

"I'll put it this way, at Countrywide's Santa Monica branch they lost anywhere from 1 to 2 percentage points on a loan," the former employee said. "If they broke even they were lucky. But in black areas, like the Slauson branch, the average points charged per loan was anywhere from 2 to 4 percentage points. And you were reprimanded for not charging more."

Countrywide's entire operation, from its information technology to its incentive pay, was designed to wring maximum profits out of the mortgage lending boom, no matter what it cost borrowers. For example, the company's computer system default setting excluded a borrower's cash reserves from his or her financial statement. This had the effect of making the borrower appear to be less sound financially and he would be steered away from lower-cost loans into those that were more expensive and more profitable to Countrywide.

Subprime loans were especially lucrative to Countrywide. Internal documents showed that Countrywide generated different profit margins depending on the loan size. Small loans of between $100,000 and $200,000 produced 5 percent profits while slightly larger loans, those between $350,000 and $500,000, generated 3 percent profits. But on subprime loans, which imposed heavy burdens on borrowers like high prepayment penalties that persisted for three years, Countrywide's margins could reach 15 percent of the loan, former employees said.

Certainly, Countrywide jumped on the lax lending bandwagon relatively early. A financial filing made by the company in June 2002 described its "No Income/No Asset Documentation Program." Although it said the program was limited to borrowers with "excellent credit histories," Countrywide acknowledged that debt-to-income ratios of borrowers could not be calculated because of a lack of documentation. Under the program Countrywide would lend a borrower 95 percent of a property's value; these loans were generally eligible for sale to Fannie Mae and Freddie Mac.

But for some in Congress, even this type of loan was too restrictive. In an April 2003 hearing sponsored by the Committee on Financial Services, Maxine Waters, a Democrat from California, implored the housing finance industry to eliminate down payments altogether. These requirements were too onerous; besides that, they were unnecessary.

Waters's "American Dream Down Payment Initiative" would free a borrower from having to put any money down when buying a house. Never mind that history showed borrowers who had no investment in their homes defaulted far more frequently than those who had built up equity in them.

"I think we ought to be encouraging our private institutions, our financial institutions to have more products where you have no down payments," Waters urged. "There are people who will never have a down payment, who make their rental payments every month on time, and they would be just fine if they could get a product that could be offered to them by the people who really do the financing, who do the mortgages."

Waters's plea was music to Mozilo's ears. Although her initiative would never get off the ground, within two years Countrywide would be writing no-money-down mortgages with abandon.

⇌

Had anyone wanted to scratch the surface at the incredible growth machine known as Countrywide, warning signs were certainly evident. In September 2004, for example, internal audits of loans made in a half-dozen of Countrywide's largest regions showed disturbing trends. About one in eight loans in regions as far-flung as Florida, New Jersey, Massachusetts, Idaho, Northern California, and New York was "severely unsatisfactory," failing the company's quality-control checks.

Such checks are required of lenders by HUD, and each quarter a lender's senior management must receive reports identifying their company's deficiencies. These managers are supposed to respond by taking "prompt, effective corrective measures," HUD says.

But if Countrywide took prompt corrective measures that fall, they had no effect. By April 2005, audits of the same six regions showed that the loan performance had gotten even worse—almost one in five loans was severely unsatisfactory, internal documents show.

In fact, unbeknownst to Countrywide shareholders, the company's credit risk-management team had begun warning of the consequences of the company's lending spree. In September 2004, officials in that unit advised top management that risky lending practices were imperiling the company.

In early 2005, a risk-management executive advised Countrywide's president, David Sambol, that the company's strategy "to have the widest product line in the industry" put the company "clearly out on the 'frontier' in many areas." That frontier was a Wild West of high default rates and massive losses.

But instead of curtailing its issuance of these loans, Countrywide stepped up their issuance. Of the loans generated by the company in 2004, more than half were adjustable-rate mortgages, products that lured unsuspecting borrowers in with low teaser rates, only to adjust to sky-high levels in a few years. Such loans, just a year earlier, had accounted for less than one quarter of Countrywide's mortgage production.

Some at Countrywide were proud of the company's anything-goes approach to lending. One top executive drove a car with a vanity license plate that read: FUND'EM. When asked what this meant, the executive said it described the company's loan strategy. The sole criterion used to determine whether an applicant got a loan, he explained, was if a person could fog a mirror.

While Countrywide's risk managers were fretting over its lending practices, consumer advocates also began agitating against its most popular loans, arguing that borrowers had no clue about how poisonous they could be. Robert Gnaizda, general counsel at the Greenlining Institute, a nonprofit in Berkeley, California, became a thorn in Countrywide's side when he began complaining to the company and its regulators about its lending practices.

Gnaizda believed that Countrywide was targeting immigrants and unsophisticated borrowers with incomprehensible loan documents. "The typical borrower for a subprime mortgage reads at the sixth-grade level or below," Gnaizda said, "and that is part of why these instruments were devised. As Alan Greenspan informed us in 2004 when we presented the Countrywide instruments in detail, he said even if you had a Ph.D. in math, you wouldn't be able to see what was helpful or harmful."

But Gnaizda said that Mozilo would routinely reject Greenlining's pleas to underwrite responsible loans, maintaining that Countrywide was doing precisely that.*

Former Countrywide brokers tell wild tales about how dubious

---

*When the SEC sued Mozilo for insider trading in 2009, it cited e-mail messages from the executive expressing disgust for the very mortgage products Gnaizda had complained about. A 2006 e-mail from Mozilo called no-money-down mortgages "the most dangerous product in existence and there can be nothing more toxic." Mozilo settled with the SEC in October 2010, neither admitting nor denying the allegations. He agreed to pay $67.5 million, but most was covered by Bank of America or insurance.

loans ran through the company's machinery. If a loan looked questionable—perhaps the borrower's job was not good enough to generate the required mortgage amount—company officials thought nothing of changing the applicant's information to secure the loan.

"Say the guy is a worker at Baja Fresh fast food and also works for 7-11 at night," explained a former Countrywide broker. "We couldn't state his income on the loan because it wasn't high enough, so we would change his title to manager at each job. With that, the computer system will assume his salary is $100,000, and the loan goes through."

Many of these doctored loans were welcomed with open arms by Countrywide's friends at Fannie Mae. Indeed, documents produced to Congress in 2010 show a concerted effort by executives at Fannie Mae in 2004 to cultivate Countrywide's top executives. Their goal: to assure that the lender would help Fannie maintain profitability.

The "Customer Engagement Plan" drawn up by Fannie Mae targeted Mozilo and fourteen top colleagues at Countrywide. The battle plan detailed the roles and goals of each Countrywide executive and recommended that top Fannie executives, from Frank Raines and Dan Mudd on down, make regular trips to "meet and greet" the lender's management. The plan even urged Fannie Mae executives to arrange to run into Mozilo and his key Countrywide home loan lieutenants at Habitat for Humanity golf tournaments and industry conferences, such as those sponsored by the Mortgage Bankers Association.

Fannie Mae's primary objective from the "outreach strategy": to "deepen relationship at all levels through CHL and Fannie Mae to foster alignment and collaboration between our companies at every opportunity."

The program was a success. In 2005, Countrywide sold $12.7 billion in subprime loans to Fannie Mae and was its second-biggest supplier of what would turn out to be highly toxic paper. By the first half of 2006, almost two thirds of the subprime loans underwritten by Countrywide had loan-to-value ratios of 100 percent; that meant borrowers had put no money down to secure the property.

The brokers who brought these problem loans to Countrywide had a time-tested system for making sure they progressed smoothly through the Countrywide machinery. Envelopes stuffed with thousands of dollars in cash would be hand delivered by some brokers each month to the account managers responsible for seeing that the loans actually closed.

Such payments were only a tiny example of the staggering amounts of money made in the mortgage business at the height of the craze. Among the most successful mortgage brokers were people who had recently sold used cars or cell phones. The stereotype of the twenty-six-year-old mortgage broker driving a red Ferrari and living in a $1.5 million house existed for a reason—there were loads of them. Especially in Southern California, home to reckless lenders like New Century Financial, Long Beach Mortgage, Fremont, Countrywide, and others.

Mozilo, of course, generated immense wealth for himself at Countrywide. From 2003 through 2006, he received $123 million in compensation; and in case this was not enough, Countrywide also paid for Mozilo's country club memberships and for his and his wife, Phyllis's, travel on the corporate jet, a Gulfstream IV. In addition to a residence in Thousand Oaks, California, Mozilo and his wife owned two homes in Santa Barbara and a residence in the desert at the resort town of La Quinta.

Mozilo liked to drive a gold Rolls-Royce or a navy blue Bentley convertible to Countrywide's Calabasas headquarters—until the company got into trouble, that is. Then he started driving a more modest car, so as not to draw attention to himself. It was a rare display of self-awareness. As a former high-level finance official at Countrywide described Mozilo, "His attitude was—'I'm from the Bronx. I made my $500 million and it's your problem if you haven't made yours.'"

⇌

Even as Mozilo was privately lamenting his company's lending standards, Countrywide was looking for new ways to write more mortgages. Just as Jim Johnson had recognized that earnings growth was essential to Fannie Mae's continued success, political influence, and his lush pay packages, Mozilo knew that he had to keep feeding the beast to keep his company's stock price high.

In 2005, Johnson brokered a deal that would boost Countrywide's loan production overnight. It involved a joint venture between Mozilo's company and KB Home, a company on whose board Johnson sat.

KB Home was one of the nation's largest homebuilders; it had begun life in 1957 as Kaufman and Broad, a Los Angeles–based company founded by Eli Broad. In 2001, the company changed its name to KB Home; it was headed by Bruce Karatz, and among its numerous subsidiaries was a mortgage-lending unit that provided financing to prospective homebuyers. Salespeople from KB's mortgage unit were on-site at the company's real estate developments to snare customers as they walked through its model homes.

As early as 2001, KB Home was teaming up with Fannie Mae to offer no-money-down mortgages on developments aimed at low-income, immigrant, or inner-city populations. A development in San Antonio called Lago Vista was an example of the effort. Conceived by Henry Cisneros with KB Home after he left HUD, Lago Vista was a 428-home project that rose in an industrial neighborhood in Cisneros's hometown. The "lake" in the development's name had been a runoff pit for an asphalt producer; it was ringed by a chain-link fence.

Lago Vista was Exhibit A for how Clinton's public-private homeownership push was supposed to work. KB Home joined with Fannie Mae, pitching homes that required no down payments to firefighters, teachers, and police officers. HUD insured the mortgages taken out by Lago Vista buyers.

"Henry decided to go back to his roots, go to the churches and the schools to organize," said Janet Ahmad, president of Homeowners for Better Building, an advocacy group in San Antonio. "They offered sandwiches from the deli and handed out flyers that talked about homeownership. Still, he had a terrible time selling those houses."

The Lago Vista homes sold for between $75,000 and $90,000.

But many of the blue-collar buyers targeted by KB Home and Fannie Mae were unable to keep up their payments. By 2008, defaults had swamped Lago Vista. On one of the development's longer streets, one in five homes had gone through at least one foreclosure. Residents reported high-pressure sales tactics to sign mortgage documents that many did not understand.

When Lago Vista borrowers defaulted, HUD (a.k.a. the taxpayer) had to buy back many of the homes and then resell them at a loss.

KB Home had had its share of regulatory run-ins and its mortgage unit was no different. In June 2005, HUD announced the settlement of an action it had brought against KB Home Mortgage. Without admitting or denying the allegations, the company paid $3.2 million to settle the case; it was the largest fine ever collected by HUD's mortgage review board.

According to HUD, KB Home Mortgage was a regular rogue operator. It approved loans based on inflated borrowers' incomes, failed to include all of a borrower's liabilities when making the loans, did not bother to verify the source of funds used to close the loan, and approved borrowers who were ineligible because they were delinquent in paying federal debts or had unpaid court-ordered judgments outstanding. KB Home Mortgage had also failed to determine that borrowers were not charged excessive fees and did not ensure that the information on the loan statement was accurate.

These practices violated the rules governing loans insured by HUD or the Federal Housing Authority. But they seemed to fit right in at Countrywide.

"KB Home's whole objective was to get the loans signed," Ahmad said. "Over and again we found KB Home would take people who had extremely bad credit, take all their car loans, furniture costs and roll it into a loan that's backed by the taxpayer. Now, HUD and the taxpayers have been saddled with all these failed subdivisions."

A director of KB Home from his early days at Fannie Mae (he joined KB Home's board in 1992), Johnson was a trusted adviser to

Karatz, the company's chief. And in 2005, Johnson pushed the notion of selling the company's mortgage business to Countrywide. The fact that Cisneros, Karatz's former partner at Lago Vista, was on the board of Countrywide didn't hurt either. But Johnson was the prime mover.

"Jim Johnson was a very good friend of Angelo's and he was on our board at the time and he was very much in favor of the transaction," Karatz recalled, years later.

"At that time, there were so many different mortgage products it seemed every month somebody was coming out with a new one," Karatz said. "We were unable to keep up with all of them, to explain it to customers and guide them into the right mortgage program. Thank goodness the company did that transaction."

In the joint venture, Countrywide paid KB Home $42.4 million in cash while KB contributed $15 million. Over the next two years, the venture made thirty-three thousand loans for a total of $8 billion.

KB Home pitched the joint venture as good for its customers. "We believe that the ability of Countrywide KB Home Loans to offer customers a variety of financing options on competitive terms as a part of the on-site sales process is an important factor in completing sales," it said. In 2007, almost three quarters of the KB Home customers who financed their home purchases took out mortgages from Countrywide.

⇌

Johnson, who remained on the KB Home board until 2008, had come full circle. The company on whose board he sat was making money selling mortgages to the very company he had become wealthy running. It was nice that his friend Angelo could benefit from the arrangement as well.

But those benefits, like most of what Countrywide had generated for Mozilo, carried a cost. His prized company's race to the bottom of the lending pit finally caught up with it in 2007 as the subprime crisis gained momentum. That August, Countrywide had a brush with bankruptcy as investors stopped buying its debt and mortgage securities. Six months later, the company was bought in a fire sale by Bank of America, which pledged to clean up Countrywide's practices.

To many observers, it was a shocking end to a compelling corporate success story. "After three decades of being the smartest player in the industry, Angelo finally built up enough hubris that he thought he could outrun a cyclical decline," the former analyst and friend said. "Countrywide could have just stepped back from the market but I don't think Angelo had it in him to step back. It was not in his DNA."

CHAPTER TWELVE

NovaStar delivered its best results ever in 2003. Our focus is on sustaining growth for the long haul, and NovaStar has reached a scale and maturity that will serve us well in the future.

—SCOTT HARTMAN, chairman of the board,
NovaStar, December 2003

As Countrywide's Angelo Mozilo argued for relaxed lending rules and a regulatory retreat, sketchy mortgage companies were springing up around the country, taking advantage of rock-bottom interest rates and Wall Street's burgeoning interest in loans to be packaged and sold to investors. Marc Cohodes, a money manager in Marin County, California, who was always on the lookout for companies with aggressive accounting or dubious business practices, had his sights on one of them. It was an obscure mortgage lender founded in Westwood, Kansas, name of NovaStar Financial.

Years earlier, in the late 1990s, Cohodes had gotten wind of NovaStar. His brother-in-law had worked briefly at the company during its start-up days and had crazy stories to tell. Anyone who worked at NovaStar knew that it was more like a freewheeling frat house than a buttoned-up bank. The things that went on there were nuts, his brother-in-law had said.

"He used to tell me what a crap operation this was, that they would loan money to your animals and that the people were worse than bad," Cohodes recalled. "I think at the time the stock was $2 or $3."

Although NovaStar's shares traded on the New York Stock Exchange, this was no venerable, blue-chip company. One of a crop of new lenders financed by Wall Street that had started up in the 1990s, NovaStar specialized in lending to people with shaky credit histories.

The company was founded in 1996 by a pair of hard-charging entrepreneurs named Scott Hartman and W. Lance Anderson. Hartman was a native of rural Iowa who went to the University of Kansas; Anderson grew up on army bases in North Carolina and Virginia and went to Old Dominion University.

In the early 1990s, Hartman and Anderson worked together at Resource Mortgage Capital, a Virginia-based lender that changed its name to Dynex in early 1997. Hartman was in charge of risk management at the company while Anderson was president of Dynex's single-family home-mortgage operation. When the company was sold in 1996, both men decided to leave and start NovaStar.

Hartman and Anderson had complementary skills. Handling the financial operation, working with Wall Street to arrange financing for their lending operations, was Hartman's job. Anderson, a born salesman, played the role of the company's glad-hander, hiring mortgage brokers, opening offices, and otherwise presiding over NovaStar's all-important expansion.

At first, NovaStar raised money privately from institutional investors like General Electric Capital Corp. But in 1997, the company issued shares to the public, raising $62 million.

From the outset, NovaStar's board paid Anderson and Hartman handsomely. In 1997, when the company generated losses of $1.1 million, both men received almost $700,000 in salary and other pay. They also received generous dividends on the founders' shares and stock options they held, which was unusual.

Like others in the subprime industry, Hartman and Anderson

used aggressive accounting practices that allowed losses on loans made yesterday to be hidden by new mortgages originated today.

Given the demands of these souped-up accounting practices, NovaStar had to underwrite loads of new loans to obscure losses that cropped up when mortgages "seasoned," typically about a year after they were made. But almost before the ink was dry on NovaStar's initial public stock offering, world financial markets seized up. In 1998, as the Russian debt crisis hit and Long-Term Capital Management collapsed, fixed-income markets around the globe became catatonic. Mortgage originations ground to a halt; suddenly, the Ponzi scheme had stopped working and investors in subprime mortgage companies could see how many borrowers were having problems paying their loans. They fled the market.

This was a very real foreshadowing of what would happen on a much larger scale less than ten years later.

NovaStar's business fell off the cliff. But unlike most of its peers, the company survived the crisis.

⇄

After a couple of very lean years, NovaStar's fortunes started to turn in 2000. During the first half of that year, the company's mortgage operation underwrote $34 million in loans. For the same period in 2001, the company generated $394 million in mortgages.

Back from the brink, in mid-2001 the company began paying dividends again. Because NovaStar was structured as a real estate investment trust, the Internal Revenue Service required it to pay 85 percent of its profits to shareholders in the form of a dividend. This made the stock attractive to risk-averse investors— widows and orphans in Wall Street parlance—searching for income-producing shares.

Although NovaStar was not the household name in mortgage lending that Countrywide Financial was, in 2003 the company boasted 430 offices in thirty-nine states. Having moved its head-quarters to the third floor of a sleek glass and stone building in Kansas City, NovaStar was fast becoming one of the top twenty home lenders in the country. An early believer in mortgage origination expediency, NovaStar began offering its network of independent mortgage brokers a new automated underwriting system in 2002 that was built for speed. That April, in an article in *The American Banker*, Anderson boasted about the technology. "In 30 seconds brokers can complete an application and get multiple approvals back, saving them hours," Anderson said. "In a call center environment, it's nice to approve them right on the phone."

Investors were also becoming acquainted with NovaStar—its shares traded as high as $30 in 2003.

Typing NovaStar's stock symbol into his Bloomberg machine, Cohodes did a double take. Could it be that investors were paying $30 a share to buy into a company that would lend money to a corpse? Must have used the wrong stock symbol, he thought.

He hadn't. NovaStar was on a trajectory that would take the shares above $70. Thanks to wheeler-dealer management, unscrupulous mortgage brokers, inert regulators, and a crowd of stock promoters touting its shares, NovaStar's stock market value climbed to $1.6 billion at its peak.

A beefy, street-smart man fond of sports and sports metaphors, Cohodes knew every trick company executives used to make their operations look better than they actually were. He prided himself on being able to smell a corporate rat well ahead of the pack; while his investment strategy included buying shares of companies he believed in, Cohodes's engines really revved when he thought he had uncovered a shadowy enterprise masquerading as an upstanding corporate citizen.

Hoping to profit when suspecting fraud or dubious practices at a company, short sellers borrow its shares in the open market and sell them to a buyer. Known as selling short, the strategy is profitable only if the stock price falls. Then the short seller repurchases the shares for less than he received when setting up the trade, capturing the difference. Once he buys back the shares, they are returned to the brokerage firm from which they had been borrowed.

Selling short is the opposite of buying shares, or going long in

Wall Street parlance, but it carries far greater risks. While those who buy shares can lose their entire investment in the worst-case scenario, short sellers' potential losses can be unlimited. If a stock goes up when a trader is short its shares, he or she must pay more to buy them back to close out the transaction. Until the trade is closed, the potential for losses is infinite and unknown.

Most investors are optimists—buying a company's stock is something people do because they hope it will increase in value— so short sellers are often viewed by corporate insiders with suspicion. Because they are not buyers of company spin, these traders are often criticized in public and refused access to company conference calls and other events where investors meet with management to hear about developments in the business.

Investors who own shares in companies targeted by short sellers often call them un-American. But the strategy is a venerable and valued market pursuit. Furthermore, because short sellers must buy back the shares they have borrowed to close out their trades, they provide a floor for a stock that is plummeting when they step in to purchase it.

But rare is the corporate executive with an appreciation for naysayers, and NovaStar's founders were no different. Anderson and Hartman had contempt for the investors who had bet against its shares and derided them regularly in conference calls. A Web site sponsored by NovaStar backers called NFI-info.net published a picture of a cockroach next to a discussion about investors who had bet against the company's stock.

Sticks and stones was the response from Cohodes and the other investors who were dubious of NovaStar's practices. They felt that their investigations had turned up the truth about the company, facts that would lead to its demise. It was only a matter of when.

Once he was on the trail of a bad actor, Cohodes was unrelenting. When he had amassed a file of evidence, he would often share his research with regulators at the Securities and Exchange Commission in Washington. Other short sellers took their findings to state officials who, because they were closer to these companies' operations and were "boots on the ground" overseers, often acted more quickly than the Feds to shut down frauds.

The nation's top financial cop on the beat is the Securities and Exchange Commission, operating out of a sweeping glass structure in the northwestern quadrant of Washington, D.C. The regulatory agency was created by Franklin D. Roosevelt in response to the Great Crash of 1929 when fraudulent practices at major banks and investment firms were found to have harmed individual investors. "The Investor's Advocate" is how the SEC characterizes itself.

Even though it employs thirteen hundred lawyers to investigate and prosecute fraudulent acts by public corporations, money management firms, and individuals, the SEC is far outmanned and outspent by the institutions it is supposed to police. Short sellers know this and often view themselves as the private-sector equivalents of an SEC gumshoe.

Cohodes figured that if he was right about NovaStar, and he was certain he was, public investors everywhere would be better off if he shared his findings with investigators. The sooner the SEC put a stop to a company's improprieties that were propelling its stock price, the fewer losses investors would incur.

The short sellers would benefit too, of course, if an SEC investigation and civil suit confirmed what they had found. Even the simple disclosure that an investigation into a company's practices had been launched could crush a company's stock.

Still, Cohodes and the other NovaStar critics felt they were on the side of investors. If a company was misleading investors or pretending to be something it was not, Cohodes was happy to help surface the truth. It usually came out in the end anyway; and besides, hurrying along the inevitable could help protect investors from greater damage, he reasoned.

So in February 2003, Cohodes started corresponding with the SEC on NovaStar. He began "throwing things over the wall" as he called it, to Amy Miller, a young attorney in the division of enforcement at SEC headquarters. By this time, loan production at Nova-

Star was clocking $600 million a month, up from $48 million per month five years earlier.

Among the questionable corporate practices that are the easiest to find are those that appear in a company's own financial statements, right there in black and white. With a little determination and expertise, accounting practices that burnish financial results or make earnings appear out of thin air can often be spotted in these publicly filed documents.

Taking his pencil to NovaStar's financial statements in 2003, Cohodes found a raft of red flags. "They made their numbers look however they wanted to," Cohodes recalled. "Not even remotely realistic."

One trick gave the company lots of leeway in how it valued the loans held on its books; the higher the assessment, the better NovaStar's financials appeared. NovaStar used the best possible assumptions in valuing its loans.

A second type of arithmetic used by NovaStar allowed it to record immediately all the income that a loan would generate over its decades-long life. This accounting method completely ignored the possibility that some of the company's loans might default and fail to pay off. Although most companies using this method—known as gain-on-sale accounting—estimated that some portion of the loans would not be repaid, NovaStar assumed that losses on all of its loans would be nonexistent.

This was the same trick that killed off almost all of the Subprime 1.0 companies in the wake of the Russian debt crisis.

NovaStar's ridiculously rosy assumption not only had the effect of padding its profitability with income it had not yet received, it also encouraged the company to make more mortgages, regardless of quality. The more loans it made, the more fees and income the company could record.

After doing some digging, Cohodes found that NovaStar's lending practices were appallingly lax and rife with hidden fees. Promotional memos NovaStar sent out to its army of 16,400 independent and unsupervised mortgage brokers across the country told the tale of easy credit terms. "Did You Know NovaStar Offers to Completely Ignore Consumer Credit!" one shrieked. "Ignore the Rules and Qualify More Borrowers with Our Credit Score Override Program!" boasted another.

Other flyers bragged about NovaStar's technique for hiding the crushing commissions that its borrowers were forced to pay, much of which went to the mortgage brokers who sold the loans. Although regulators forbade this practice of burying costs, Nova-Star encouraged its brokers to add commissions that even their more astute customers could not see. These high costs were a burden to homeowners that in many cases would push them over the brink into foreclosure not long after they received their loans.

Cohodes and other critics felt certain they had found a company whose success was built on deceptive practices. But what they did not recognize was that NovaStar was a microcosm of the nationwide home-lending assembly line that would lead directly to the credit crisis of 2008.

⇔

Patricia and Ricardo Jordan of Atlanta learned the hard way how NovaStar's freewheeling lending practices imperiled unsuspecting borrowers.

The Jordans had purchased their three-bedroom home in a middle-class, African American section of southwestern Atlanta in 1983 for $30,000. Patricia had made many improvements on the property, putting up a fence and installing an attic fan and air-conditioning. The sole breadwinner in the family, Patricia supported her husband, a physically and mentally disabled Vietnam veteran. In 2000, she retired and they lived on Social Security and veteran benefits.

In 2004, she had a 9 percent adjustable-rate mortgage that she wanted to change to a fixed-rate loan. She received an offer in the mail from NovaStar and called the toll-free number.

"I told them I wanted to come out of the adjustable and they said they would give me the fixed rate if I would accept it at 10 percent," Patricia said. "I could have stayed where I was but I told them definitely a 30-year fixed rate."

The Jordans were more or less perfect targets for a lender like NovaStar. They were financially unsophisticated and they were trusting.

Even better, the Jordans lived in Georgia, a state where predatory lenders like NovaStar had free rein. Just a year earlier, subprime lenders and the ratings agencies had eviscerated the Georgia Fair Lending Act, the toughest predatory lending law in the nation. NovaStar had been among the first lenders in Georgia to stop making loans there when the Fair Lending Act was passed. If the law had stayed on the books as it was written, Patricia Jordan would never have gotten roped into the loan that almost wrecked her life.

Jordan knew nothing about the battle over the Fair Lending Act and she signed up for her new NovaStar mortgage right over the telephone. "I had to fax information to them," she said, "my income, my bank statements and stuff like that. Later a man did come to see us from the lender. He had little notes telling you to sign this and sign that."

The loan totaled $124,000; the Jordans used the money to pay off their previous mortgage and credit-card debt they had amassed improving their home.

Unbeknownst to the Jordans, their NovaStar loan was one of the most punitive mortgage products out there—an adjustable-rate mortgage with an initial interest rate of 10.45 percent that would soon explode to 17.25 percent. Even the initial monthly housing payment, including taxes and insurance, was barely affordable: $1,215.33. As documented in their loan file, the Jordans' total monthly net income was only $2,697. Their monthly housing and other debt costs totaled $1,642, so after they paid their debts each month, the Jordans had only $1,055 to live on.

And that was just the beginning. Two years after signing up for the loan its interest rate was set to ratchet up. Only then did Patricia Jordan learn that NovaStar had put her into an adjustable loan, not the fixed-rate mortgage she had been promised.

"I got duped," she said later. "NovaStar had fired a woman and she told me they had done me wrong. They knew how much money we were getting and everything. Next thing I know, I couldn't pay my other bills."

The Jordans sued NovaStar in 2007. As part of the lawsuit, their lawyer found that their loan had been placed in a mortgage securitization trust assembled by NovaStar and sold to investors in November 2004. More than half of the loans in the pool were provided with "no documentation" or "limited documentation" of borrowers' financial standing.

But the Jordans had given NovaStar bank statements and other documentation of their income. The lawsuit would show that NovaStar had inflated their monthly income by $500 to make the loan work. The lender had given the Jordans a loan that went against its own underwriting guidelines and that overrode federal lending standards. It was precisely the type of loan that would have been illegal under the Georgia Fair Lending Act and could have subjected NovaStar to criminal penalties.

The Jordans' was just one loan. There were literally thousands more like it.*

⇔

Because it was not a bank, NovaStar's predatory lending practices were largely lost on state and federal regulators. Regulators should have been on the case since the brokerage firms they were supposed to oversee were providing warehouse lines to lenders like NovaStar. These enablers knew the thinly capitalized lenders would not be able to buy back loans, as they were obligated to do, if they went bad.

Because the company sold many of its loans to Wall Street firms that in turn pooled them and sold them to investors, NovaStar did not worry about conducting the kind of due diligence on its mortgages that was typical of lenders who held on to their loans. So what if the loans failed later? Generating more loans meant more fees now.

*NovaStar later settled with the Jordans, although the terms were undisclosed.

Traditional banks, on the other hand, operated under the scrutiny of financial regulators like the Federal Deposit Insurance Corporation, which was set up to protect depositors after the massive bank failures of the Great Depression. But for companies like NovaStar, the closest thing to an overseer was an occasional state regulator who took action when it discovered the company's independent salespeople were unlicensed.

Massachusetts was one state whose regulators recognized the threats posed by NovaStar's independent and unsupervised branch system. In October 2003, the commissioner of banks in Massachusetts filed a cease and desist order against NovaStar in which it concluded that the company engaged in "acts or practices which warrant the belief that the Corporation is not operating honestly, fairly, soundly and efficiently in the public interest."

Nevada followed with its own cease and desist order in early 2004. NovaStar started quietly closing its operations in Massachusetts and Nevada but the company didn't disclose the regulatory reprimands to investors or the public. Only when the *Wall Street Journal* published a front-page article on NovaStar in April 2004 and mentioned its run-ins with state officials did the company own up to the problems.

The revelations did serious damage to NovaStar's reputation and its stock price, which fell more than 30 percent the day the article ran. Still, the housing market was ramping up and NovaStar was able to persuade many of its shareholders that its mistakes were honest ones and were immaterial to its growing business. The company hired Lanny Davis, a well-connected lobbyist and crisis public relations operative, to run interference for it among investors and reporters. Davis was used to operating in a crucible—he had been special counsel to President Clinton during the Monica Lewinsky scandal.

But NovaStar's problems were not limited to a few aggressive state regulators. In the summer of 2004, the inspector general for the Department of Housing and Urban Development produced a damning report on NovaStar's practices. HUD's inspector general determined that the company's branch system did not comply with federal regulations; among the deficiencies HUD cited was the company's practice of hiring independent contractors as loan officers. NovaStar's branch system, HUD said, was designed to shift risk from the company to the federal government. HUD recommended that NovaStar pay penalties in the case.

NovaStar did not disclose the HUD report to investors.

All the while, Cohodes was continuing to talk to Amy Miller and others at the SEC about NovaStar. He sent them information about the company, including the NovaStar flyers indicating its anything-goes lending practices. He even went so far as to annotate the transcript of one of NovaStar's conference calls with analysts and investors, pointing out to the investigators the many inaccurate public statements made by the company's executives.

Although some of the SEC people he spoke with seemed to recognize the problems in NovaStar's operations, their investigation did not appear to be gaining traction.

"Amy was a very nice person," Cohodes said of the SEC investigator assigned to the matter. "But she didn't know shit about subprime mortgages. We used to have conference calls with her on the gain-on-sale accounting, the crappy loan originations, how NovaStar was playing games with the branches. We would talk about business models. Meanwhile, this thing starts out crazy and goes to outrageous."

The phone calls with the regulators went over the same material repeatedly, Cohodes said, leading him to conclude that Miller and her colleagues did not understand what was occurring at the company. "Whenever they seemed to get it, they would either call up or make contact frantically saying, 'Can you please go over this again?'" Cohodes said. "It was almost like someone was presenting a case to the higher-ups and they would say, 'Are you sure? Go back and make sure.'"

One matter whose importance the agency would surely recognize, Cohodes thought, was a lawsuit showing that NovaStar's leading mortgage insurer, PMI Group, had stopped insuring the lender's loans. Surely this was an indication of the kind of garbage NovaStar was originating and selling. After all, investors rely on mortgage insurers to protect them against losses in the loans they buy from originators like NovaStar, so the fact that its top insurer had stopped insuring the company's loans in 2002 would have definitely alarmed shareholders.

Yet again, shareholders were not told that PMI had washed its hands of NovaStar.

In talks with officials at PMI, Cohodes learned that the insurer had cut off NovaStar when they found that borrowers' incomes had been misrepresented in company loan documents. Meanwhile, during conference calls with investors after PMI stopped insuring NovaStar's loans, Anderson and Hartman said the company's relationship with the mortgage insurer was never better.

Not only did the PMI situation seem to be a pretty good sign that NovaStar's loans were toxic, Cohodes said, the company's failure to disclose that its insurer had walked away seemed a material misrepresentation. He passed the information on to the SEC, including names and phone numbers of people at PMI to talk to for confirmation.

Cohodes also gave the agency information about some NovaStar branches that were either nonexistent or extremely questionable. Opening new offices helped the company persuade investors that business was booming—when it announced its financial results the company always highlighted its burgeoning branch system.

But funky stuff had turned up when Cohodes and some colleagues took a road trip to check out NovaStar's offices. "A posse of us went to Vegas, which was their growth market," he recalled. "We found one branch in a massage parlor, another in a guy's house—it was a complete charade. After that, I wrote to the SEC again and basically said, 'Someone should go in here and make sure these numbers are right.'"

NovaStar had other material problems that it did not disclose. ABN AMRO Mortgage Group, a unit of the large Dutch financial services concern, had been a buyer of mortgages originated by NovaStar. But in 2003 it sued the company, contending that NovaStar had engaged in fraud, breach of contract, and negligence involving phony borrowers and inflated appraisals.

All of this information made its way to the SEC. For the most part, there was no response.

"We'd say, 'Here is what we know,'" Cohodes said. "'We know that PMI did a test on these loans and failed. We know that ABM Amro has sued these guys, we know that PMI will no longer do business with them. We know the loans do not test out. Here are the addresses of branches that are completely fake.' We would go on and on."

To most outside observers, however, NovaStar's operations were running on all cylinders. During 2004, the company wrote $8.4 billion in mortgages; that September, the amount of loans held on its books had reached $10 billion. NovaStar ended that year with six hundred offices.

It was time for Hartman and Anderson to take a victory lap. "The $10 billion mark is a tribute to NovaStar associates and our many partners in the mortgage community," Hartman told a reporter at *Origination News*, an industry publication. "As we continue to grow, we want to pause and thank everyone who is contributing to our progress."

But while the NovaStar executives were busy high-fiving themselves, a unit of Lehman Brothers, Wall Street's largest packager of residential mortgage loans sold to investors, was discovering serious problems in a review of NovaStar mortgages. The findings were so troubling to the Lehman executives overseeing the firm's purchases of NovaStar loans that they ended their relationship with the lender in 2004.

According to documents filed in a borrower lawsuit against NovaStar, Aurora Loan Services, a Lehman subsidiary, studied sixteen NovaStar loans for quality-control purposes. What the analysis found: More than half of the loans originated by NovaStar—56.25 percent to be exact—raised red flags. "It is recommended that this broker be terminated," the report stated.

Among the problems turned up by the Aurora audit were misrepresentations of employment by the borrower, inflated property values, transactions among parties that were related but not disclosed, and unsubstantiated payoffs to individuals when loans closed.

The details uncovered by the Aurora analysis were alarming. One NovaStar loan on a property in Ohio totaled $77,500 even though the average sales price for the neighborhood was $31,685 at the time and the same house had been purchased two months earlier for $20,000.

The appraiser on that loan stated that the property was rented out for $900 a month but Aurora found it generating monthly rent of $475. Another warning sign: A company owned by the borrower received $22,421 from the proceeds of the loan at closing.

In another case, involving a $54,000 mortgage on a Dayton, Ohio, property, the borrower was found to have overstated his income by almost double; neither was the value of the property backed up by supporting documents. Aurora also found "unsubstantiated payoffs made back to the borrower and the broker" on the transaction.

The findings by Aurora seemed to be instances of mortgage fraud.

SEC rules require the disclosure by company management of any information considered material to the company's prospects or an investor's analysis. According to an SEC bulletin issued in 1999, the commission defined materiality this way: "A matter is 'material' if there is a substantial likelihood that a reasonable person would consider it important." Two Supreme Court cases use the same standard.

Surely, Aurora's findings that more than half of the sampled NovaStar loans were questionable would have been an important consideration for the SEC's "reasonable person." Still, NovaStar failed to alert investors or the public at large to the Aurora analysis. Neither did NovaStar publicize the fact that Lehman Brothers, a powerhouse in the mortgage business, had stopped buying its loans.

Increasingly frustrated, Cohodes and the other NovaStar short sellers kept throwing information over the wall at the SEC. In

April 2004, after the *Wall Street Journal* article, NovaStar acknowledged the existence of an informal investigation into its operations
by the SEC. But the inquiry soon seemed moribund.

"We kept going to the government from the time the company
had a $300 million market cap, a $600 million market cap until it
had a $1 billion market cap," Cohodes said, referring to Nova-
Star's rising stock price. "We kept talking to Amy Miller; then she
went on maternity leave. We were talking to her when she was
pregnant; then she had the baby. Then we were talking to her
when the baby was one or two. We would joke that we would be
talking to her about NovaStar when she had three or four kids."

To keep its money machine running at top speed, NovaStar
regularly issued new shares to the public. Between 2004 and
2007, for instance, the company raised more than $400 million
from investors. To those critical of NovaStar's practices, this was
money the company should never have been allowed to raise from
investors who were kept in the dark by the company's disclosure
failings.

Cohodes reckons that over roughly four years, he conducted
hundreds of phone calls with the SEC about NovaStar. Each time,
he would walk them through his points. Sometimes, a higher-up
would get on the phone and contend that while NovaStar's practices were indeed aggressive, the company did not appear to be
breaking the law. Certainly, NovaStar's selective disclosures—it
was quick to report good news but failed to own up to problems
on many occasions—seem to be infractions that the SEC should
have enforced. But its investigation went nowhere.

In any case, by 2006 the wheels had started to come off the
NovaStar cart. The company's net income that year was less than
half the amount it earned in 2005. The company faced a number
of lawsuits, including a class action filed in December 2005
alleging that NovaStar failed to disclose to borrowers the fees
earned by its brokers. Plaintiffs in this case, filed in Washington state, contended that NovaStar had violated consumer protection laws.

Its stock was falling too. By the end of 2006, NovaStar was trading around $30; but in the first few months of 2007, as the money for subprime lenders began drying up and these companies started closing their doors, it plummeted to $5. The company halted its mortgage lending and stopped paying its dividend. NovaStar recorded a $370 million operating loss in 2007 and, by March 2008, employed only fifty-three people. In its heyday, the company had more than two thousand employees.

In March 2007, Anderson expressed optimism to a reporter. "Clearly we're going through a tough time right now. But we think the loans we are originating today will perform very well. We were surprised by the speed and severity of the downturn but I think NovaStar will be a survivor."

Anderson was wrong. NovaStar's loans did not perform well. Later in 2007, the company agreed to settle the Washington state class action, paying $5.1 million to borrowers who had been duped into paying NovaStar's onerous and hidden fees.

Most of NovaStar's borrowers and investors fared badly in the collapse of the company's mortgage unit; from the peak of the company's stock price, roughly $1 billion in market value was lost.

But NovaStar's cofounders did just fine. Between 2003 and 2008, both Anderson and Hartman made $8 million in salary, bonuses, and stock grants.

Neither man was ever sued by the SEC or any other regulator.

As is its custom, the SEC declined to comment on the Nova-Star inquiry or the agency's discussions with short sellers. But documents supplied by the SEC under the Freedom of Information Act show the extensive communications between Cohodes and the agency. Miller, still working at the SEC, declined to comment on the case.

"It would be interesting to see who exactly dropped the ball and why," Cohodes said. "It would be interesting why nothing was ever brought. The S.E.C. should have sent a plane for us to come to D.C. and say: 'How do we make sure this doesn't happen again?' 'How do we train our guys to do what you did, so Joe Sixpack

investor and our entire society doesn't melt down to the center of
the earth again?'"

⇌

NovaStar no longer underwrites mortgages. Its shares were de-
listed by the New York Stock Exchange and now trade over the
counter for under a dollar. The company, a shadow of its former
self, runs a property appraiser and a financial services unit that
provides banking services "to meet the needs of low- and moderate-
income-level individuals."

It is also developing risk-management systems for the mortgage industry—a wonderful paradox given how dicey NovaStar's
mortgages had turned out to be.

In a 2010 annual report to shareholders, Anderson reported
that the company has "several interesting initiatives under way."
Hartman, however, had left the building.

At the end of 2009, NovaStar management concluded that
the company's financial reporting was "not effective" because of a
material weakness in internal controls involving accounting and
disclosure. "A material weakness is a deficiency, or combination of
deficiencies, in internal controls over financial reporting, such that
it is reasonably possible that a material misstatement in the company's annual or interim financial statements and related disclosures will not be prevented or detected on a timely basis," the
company said.

NovaStar had finally confirmed what Cohodes had been telling the SEC for all those years. The company's financial reports
just couldn't be trusted.

CHAPTER THIRTEEN

Home prices have been rising strongly since the mid-1990s, prompting concerns that a bubble exists in this asset class and that home prices are vulnerable to a collapse that could harm the U.S. economy. A close analysis of the U.S. housing market in recent years, however, finds little basis for such concerns. The marked upturn in home prices is largely attributable to strong market fundamentals.

—JONATHAN MCCARTHY AND RICHARD PEACH,
Federal Reserve Bank of New York,
December 2004

With NovaStar, Countrywide, and scores of other lenders working hard to make homeownership easy, it was inevitable that property prices would soon start screaming upward. And from 2000 through 2004, the Census Bureau reported, median home prices rocketed 31 percent. Prices in the hottest real estate markets of Florida, California, Arizona, and Nevada, known as the sand states, were absolute moonshots.

Those who already owned homes were ecstatic that their properties were vaulting in value and many rushed to refinance their mortgages, extracting some of the bounty to buy a vacation home, go on a cruise, remodel the kitchen, or send the kids to college.

Talk of rising real estate prices was ubiquitous. Everyone had a story, or had heard one, about fistfights breaking out at open houses and bidding wars ramping up prices of singularly unremarkable homes. Late-night cable television shows featured pitchmen advising how to get rich by putting no money down on properties. The press picked up on the craze, publishing thousands of stories about a potential bubble in the real estate market.

While many talked of bubbles, few were genuinely disturbed by the rising tide of home prices. It made homeowners, many of whom were experiencing no income growth in their jobs, feel rich, and it bestowed outlandish wealth on the promoters of the homeownership strategy. Homebuilders, lenders, developers, insurers, appliance and furniture makers, even gardeners and housekeepers—everyone rode the wave.

There were naysayers, of course, but they were limited to "unlucky" renters who were not participating in the boom and to a few economists and analysts who got hoarse pointing out the obvious—that trees do not grow to the sky.

Many in the housing industrial complex accused the critics of being elitists, churlishly denying the right of everyday people to grab hold of the American dream. It was a reprise of the Jim Johnson number—"Showing America a New Way Home."

In early July 2001, a 30-page paper emerged from an upstart, six-person financial research boutique called Graham Fisher & Co. Written by an analyst, Joshua Rosner, who had spent nearly a decade building a specialty research sales practice in financial institutions and government-sponsored enterprises for the venerable Wall Street firm of Oppenheimer & Co., the piece was entitled: "Housing in the New Millennium: A Home Without Equity Is Just a Rental with Debt."*

Among Rosner's major points was a deep concern that increasingly easy credit terms offered to homebuyers as a part of the National Homeownership Strategy would vastly increase the leverage of American consumers, leaving them vulnerable to economic ruin if housing prices fell. "The virtuous circle of increasing homeownership due to greater leverage has the potential to

*Coauthor of *Reckless Endangerment*.

become a vicious cycle of lower home prices due to an accelerating rate of foreclosures," the report noted.

Citing rapid increases in no-money-down programs, a degradation of the property appraisal process, and lax lending facilitated by automated underwriting systems developed by Fannie and Freddie and adopted by all the major financial institutions, Rosner warned that an economic disruption could hammer overleveraged borrowers. "The relaxation of credit underwriting standards, coupled with the willingness to spend has created a significant debt burden on the U.S. consumer," the paper said.

His research received little attention that summer, with the exception of an angry phone call from the head of investor relations at Fannie Mae, Jayne Shontell. Within a few hours of e-mailing the paper to portfolio managers and other current and prospective clients, the partners of Graham Fisher heard from Shontell who said she had a long list of inaccuracies in that paper and another that had just been published by a second analyst focusing on Fannie and Freddie.

Shontell reprimanded the researchers for not having submitted their work to Fannie before they sent it to clients; other Wall Street firms did this to maintain a profitable relationship with a company that generated fees as a customer. Going through the "inaccuracies," however, Shontell could point only to differences of opinion. It was another attempt at a Fannie Mae power play.

Regulators in Washington met the "Home Without Equity" report with a dismissive silence. But the following year, Charles Kindleberger, the famed economist and author of *Manias, Panics and Crashes*, the definitive 1978 history of investing bubbles, telephoned Rosner. Kindleberger invited him to the retirement home where he lived in Lexington, Massachusetts, and told Rosner that if he were to compile the fifth revision of his book, he would include the paper in a final chapter on what was obviously shaping up to be a housing mania.

Dean Baker, codirector of the Center for Economic and Policy Research in Washington, was another who stood against the tide.

In a 2002 paper entitled "The Run-Up in Home Prices: Is It Real or Is It Another Bubble?" he warned that home prices were on an unsustainable trajectory that clearly indicated a housing bubble. When it burst, he said, the impact would be disastrous.

"At present market values, the collapse of the housing bubble will lead to a loss of between $1.3 trillion and $2.6 trillion of housing wealth," he wrote. "This collapse will slow the economy both by derailing housing construction and by its impact on consumption through the wealth effect. In addition, millions of families are likely to face severe strains in their personal finances."

Baker drew similar conclusions to those in the Graham-Fisher report, noting the dangers posed by the boom in home equity extraction. Interestingly, this disturbing pattern was one that the economists across town at the Federal Reserve Board were celebrating.

With interest rates low and home prices rocketing, the vast majority of mortgages were cash-out refinancings, which allowed borrowers to take the paper gains generated by the housing bubble and turn them into spendable dollars. The vast majority of these refinancings also resulted in a larger loan amount—at least 5 percent or more, research showed. In 2003 alone, the amount of refinancing transactions totaled $2.8 trillion.

Thinking they had been permanently enriched by the housing craze, millions of borrowers were busily undermining what had traditionally been their best forced-savings plan—a home owned outright, with no mortgage at all. Instead, they used the real estate gains generated by the mania to make up for lagging incomes or to spiff up their lifestyles and keep up with the Joneses. So doing, they were digging themselves deeper into debt.

While this was fine as long as real estate kept rising, Baker recognized what would happen when prices fell: People who had spent their paper gains could be left owing more than their homes were worth. Already, the average amount of equity that homeowners had compared to the value of their homes stood at 55.2 percent, near its low for the postwar period, Baker noted in his 2002 article. "This ratio will plunge precipitously if the housing bubble collapses, leaving many families with little or no equity in their homes," he concluded.

And yet, home equity had long been the biggest source of wealth that Americans enjoyed in their later years or passed on to their children when they downsized. Cash-out refinancings were reversing this pattern.

As Baker pointed out, the situation was made even graver by the fact that the American population was comparatively old, with much of the baby-boom generation on the edge of retirement and getting older by the day. This meant the home equity spenders would have little time to rebuild their nest eggs. "It will also lead to a surge in mortgage default rates, as many homeowners opt not to keep paying a mortgage that exceeds the value of their home," he wrote. "This could place serious stress on the financial system."

Home equity extraction *was* a grievous peril in the housing mania, but those at the Federal Reserve thought it was no peril at all. Indeed, Alan Greenspan and others at the Fed considered home equity extraction to be beneficial to society and the economy. In several speeches, the Maestro rhapsodized about the welcome boost that housing gains were providing to an economy that had been hammered by the stock market crash of 2000. Rather than leveling a warning that home equity extraction meant homeowners were draining their savings, Greenspan applauded the economic stimulus created by the real estate bubble.

"The surge in cash-out mortgage refinancings likely improved rather than worsened the financial condition of the average homeowner," Greenspan said in a speech before America's Community Bankers in October 2004. "Some of the equity extracted through mortgage refinancing was used to pay down more-expensive, non-tax-deductible consumer debt or to make purchases that would otherwise have been financed by more-expensive and less tax-favored credit." He made no mention of the long-term consequences of the cash extractions if home prices fell.

Obviously, Baker's 2002 article had done little to change the dialogue. "I was looking for confrontations because I thought this was a serious issue," he said years later. "I was sending these papers around. I was trying to engage the people at the Fed but they ignored me."

Mostly it was deference to authority, Baker thought. With Greenspan assuring everyone that the world was flat, no one wanted to posit that perhaps it was round.

But there was more at stake in this debate than just a difference of opinion among economists. By ignoring that much of the population was squandering its seed corn, the Fed was utterly unprepared for the degree to which the coming real estate crash would devastate millions of consumers' financial standing.

In 2005 alone, homeowners extracted three quarters of a trillion dollars from their homes, spending two thirds of it on personal consumption, home improvements, and credit-card debt.

The Fed's blindness to this specter was not just philosophical. It was also the result of a surprising dearth of data that would reveal the degree to which borrowers were increasing their leverage when they refinanced. Policymakers had no reliable way to measure how many borrowers were taking equity out of their homes when they refinanced and what they were doing with the money.

Contrary to Greenspan's assertion, the millions of borrowers who were rolling car loans and other revolving credit obligations into their mortgages were engaging in a classic investment mismatch, using long-term debt to buy assets with a short-term life. This would cause stress later on but the Fed had no way of knowing how many Viking stoves, Caribbean vacations, and espresso makers were embedded in U.S. mortgage debt.

Moreover, once the bubble burst and consumers could no longer use their homes as cash machines, they would have to look elsewhere to fund purchases of cars, washing machines, and lawn mowers.

Anyone with a little foresight would have had no trouble seeing where the vast extractions of frenzy-fueled real estate gains would lead: to wrack and ruin. But the Fed did not seem to notice.

Fed economists made other significant miscalculations regarding debt levels in real estate. Their calculations ignored crucial changes in the housing market and therefore downplayed the risks that a real estate crash would pose to consumers and banks.

For example, the Fed's measure of leverage among homeowners was significantly understated. It assessed the total mortgage debt across the country and then divided that by the value of the nation's real estate stock. But in its equation, the Fed failed to eliminate properties that were unencumbered and mortgage-free. This had the effect of understating the outsized risks borne by those consumers who had mortgages.

Because people who owned their homes outright posed no leverage risk to the economy, the proper measure would have compared the amount of mortgage debt outstanding to the value of mortgaged residential real estate. That would have massively increased the average debt levels of those with mortgages, sending up a warning flare. Even when analysts confronted senior economists at the Fed with these issues, they closed their eyes to them.

The Fed and its researchers also failed to recognize that the nation's real estate markets were much more uniform, moving in lockstep rather than with variation, and less diverse than they had been previously. This new uniformity meant that previously heterogeneous real estate markets, those that had risen and fallen based on the health of their regions' economies, were now far more likely to perform the same way. As a result, those who missed the shift to homogeneity in the market were astounded when prices fell throughout the country, hammering mortgage securities that many had thought were diversified because of the regional mix in their holdings.

Two elements contributed to this uniformity: the automation of mortgage underwriting in the United States during the late 1990s and the consolidation of firms writing home loans. While the top twenty-five lenders had accounted for between 10 percent and 15 percent of the mortgage market before the turn of the century, after it, these lenders controlled 85 percent of the market.

Combined with standardized underwriting programs, this development increased the synchronicity among markets that previously had been varied.

All of these flaws in the Fed's data collection and analytics left the steward of the nation's economy clueless about the amount of leverage in the system. It was a decidedly dangerous place to be; the Fed was flying into the biggest credit storm in almost a century without instruments.

⇌

Ben Bernanke, who followed Alan Greenspan as chairman of the Federal Reserve in 2006, signaled the institution's disinterest in identifying or reining in asset bubbles in a speech early in his tenure. He said that the central bank "doesn't really have good instruments for addressing asset price bubbles should they exist, particularly if they are in one particular segment or another." Whereas some might consider this a problem, Bernanke did not. "It's generally a bad idea for the Fed to be the arbiter of asset prices. The Fed doesn't really have any better information than other people in the market about what the correct value of asset prices is."

This was perplexing. With dozens of economists poring over reams of data and churning out papers on their findings, the Fed didn't have any better information than other investors? And why on earth shouldn't those economists try to identify perilous asset price run-ups and tamp them down before they could cause even more damage?

In fact, rather than trying to spot where speculative fervor might be inflating the single biggest asset most Americans claimed, many Fed economists were busy dismissing the existence of a housing bubble during the crucial years of its buildup. A review of papers presented and promoted by Fed economists during the years leading up to the crisis shows what appears to be a determination to discount the idea that there was a mania in housing.

Much of this research was as flawed as the Boston Fed study in 1992 that had given rise to relaxed lending guidelines issued to banks. To serious non-Fed economists, the insistence that there was no housing bubble was a disturbing display of intellectual delusion.

Charles Himmelberg, a senior economist in research and statistics at the prestigious New York Fed, published a paper in September 2005 entitled "Assessing High House Prices: Bubbles, Fundamentals, and Misperceptions." Along with two coauthors, Himmelberg concluded that there was no bubble in real estate and that prices varied among different regions. The paper was wrong on both counts.

Himmelberg and his coauthors provided four reasons why there was no mania. Among them was the old favorite—low interest rates were driving prices higher. And anyhow, the paper stated, "high price growth is not evidence per se that housing is overvalued. In some local housing markets, house price growth can exceed the national average rate of appreciation for very long periods of time."

The paper was careful to note a caveat big enough to drive a truck through. "Our data do not cover and hence do not allow us to comment on the condominium market, which due to its lower transaction costs and higher liquidity may be more vulnerable to overvaluation and overbuilding arising from investor speculation." The condo market was indeed ground zero for the real estate frenzy, and excluding data from its transactions understated speculative activity that was a sign of a bubble.

Also in September 2005, five Fed researchers published a report for the Board of Governors International Finance Discussion Papers. Bubbles are hard to determine, the authors said, but nevertheless they concluded that the impact of a decline in home prices would be manageable because residential property prices are historically stable. Moreover, the amounts that banks were lending on properties—measured by the loan-to-value ratio—fell during the life of the loan, meaning that institutions would likely recover a good deal of value even if a property experienced a default.

"Although mortgage lenders in some countries have significant exposure to house prices, the balance of evidence suggests that this exposure does not, in and of itself, pose a significant risk to financial stability," the authors wrote. "Residential property prices are relatively stable, loans are not typically made for the full value of the property, and loan-to-value ratios fall over the life of the loan. All these factors contribute to low default rates on mortgages and high recovery rates on foreclosures."

Several of the points used by the authors to buttress their conclusion either relied upon outdated assumptions—that residential prices are always stable—or completely ignored industry trends such as the no-money-down programs sweeping through the lending world. These options had actually increased loan-to-value ratios significantly and the cash-out refinancing surge meant many borrowers had little or even negative equity in their homes.

But no Fed study exemplified the see-no-bubble mentality more than the one published in December 2004 by two economists at Timothy Geithner's bank-friendly New York Fed. Entitled "Are Home Prices the Next 'Bubble'?" its authors were Jonathan McCarthy, a senior economist at the New York Fed, and Richard Peach, one of its vice presidents. Riddled with analytical flaws and without consideration of significant information, the paper was a spectacular example of dubious research.

McCarthy was a lifer at the Fed but Peach had previously been an economist at the National Association of Realtors and the Mortgage Bankers Association, suggesting a pro-housing mind-set. In their paper, they concluded that even though housing prices had risen rapidly since the mid-1990s, the upturn was "largely attributable to strong market fundamentals." Fears that a housing collapse could harm the U.S. economy were unfounded, McCarthy and Peach said. "As for the likelihood of a severe drop in home prices, our examination of historical national home prices finds no basis for concern."

Many housing economists ridiculed the paper's methodology immediately. But that didn't stop its authors from presenting it repeatedly at conferences, such as one sponsored in November 2004 by the New York Society of Security Analysts. The paper also gained traction among mass audiences and was cited in the popular press as evidence that real estate prices were not, in fact, bubblicious.

At the time, some in the housing finance world quietly surmised that the paper seemed to have been written with a predetermined conclusion—no bubble—that McCarthy and Peach then labored to support. How else to explain the fact that the authors totally ignored structural changes in mortgage lending brought about by automated underwriting? Or that they failed to incorporate into their analysis onetime societal and industry changes that had inflated home prices: the rise of two-income families and the increasingly relaxed credit signified by no-down-payment programs?

Instead, McCarthy and Peach based their conclusions primarily on the old reliable—low interest rates—and the fact that a bubble *only* exists if investors believe that prices for the asset class—in this case real estate—would be higher tomorrow than they were today. Because it was impossible to get inside investors' minds, and because it could never be the only reason for everyone to be buying homes, that criterion was impossible to meet. Voilà! No bubble.

When it came time to forecast how much the economy could be hurt by a severe decline in home prices, the Fed authors estimated "reductions in consumption of around $150 billion, which is slightly less than 2 percent of total personal consumption expenditures." But this figure did not take into account the hundreds of billions in cash that borrowers had taken out of their homes and that had fueled consumption. During the height of the mania, borrowers were extracting between $600 billion and $800 billion per year from their homes, so an expected decline of $150 billion per year seemed a rosy scenario indeed for a post-boom period.

McCarthy and Peach's conclusion that past declines in home prices had been regional, not national in scope, also ignored the major consolidation in the lending industry. In the past, lending was a fragmented business, with local banks able to compete with large institutions for borrowers. But with the top lenders controlling the lion's share of the mortgage market, this ended up increasing the synchronicity among housing markets that might in earlier years have behaved differently.

As major lenders aggressively reached across the country for borrowers, they did so without any understanding of the ebbs and flows of local economies, a consideration that regional bankers took seriously when they made loans. Standardized underwriting practices of big institutions like Countrywide and Indymac actually served to homogenize lending, making it more likely that regional differences in real estate performance would give way to an industry moving in tandem from coast to coast.

Neither did the paper weigh the impact of the enormous increase in lending to facilitate purchases of second homes. The nation had never before seen such a huge percentage of home sales consist of investment, or vacation properties—the figure reached 40 percent—and to many this was a clear indication of speculative fever. This also suggested that borrowers were extracting the equity they had in their primary residences and deploying it to buy other properties—a dangerous use of leverage if real estate prices turned downward.

The New York Fed officials also maintained in their paper that home price increases were due in part to significant improvements in the quality of homes that were being either built or renovated. But the authors failed to quantify this by examining how much borrowers spent on repairs and renovations.

"They didn't even do the most simple investigation to see if their argument was plausible," Baker said. "If it was true, you would have seen a big increase in repairs and renovation." That increase was not in the data.

In the summer of 2005, Rosner, the author of the "Home Without Equity" report, went to visit McCarthy and Peach to discuss the problems he saw in their paper. After Rosner spent almost an hour running through some of the major weaknesses in the paper, Peach raised his hand to stop the discussion. There's economic research that is done to solve for an unanswered question, he said, and then there is the analysis produced because the director of research comments in a morning meeting that he is sick and tired of seeing the word "bubble" bandied about so liberally in press stories about home prices.

Equally confounding was the way the Fed dismissed an important analysis showing the rising perils of institutions that were growing too large and interconnected to be allowed to go bankrupt. A 2005 book coauthored by Gary Stern, the president of the Federal Reserve Bank of Minneapolis—one of their own—outlined the threats these institutions posed. It was called *Too Big to Fail: The Hazards of Bank Bailouts*, and it made a cogent case that companies that were deemed too politically powerful to fail should be dealt with when times were good, not in moments of crisis. The book also warned that the problem posed by these institutions was already large and becoming more severe.

But the warnings issued by Stern and his coauthor, Ron Feldman, were dismissed as overblown by Frederic S. Mishkin, a professor at Columbia Business School who was soon to become a governor of the Federal Reserve. In a working paper published by the National Bureau of Economic Research in December 2005 entitled "How Big a Problem Is Too Big to Fail?" Mishkin said Stern and Feldman overstated the problem. He argued that heightened bank regulation since the 1991 FDICIA law had forced the nation's banking system to become better capitalized than it previously had been. Sitting on all that capital meant the banks had significantly more to lose by conducting risky activities that would generate losses; they were, therefore, less likely to take chances in their operations. Given the willingness of banks to extend warehouse lines to questionable lenders who did not have the capital to buy back bad loans demonstrated the flaw in this logic.

It was deeply paradoxical, of course, that Mishkin had cited the very law that expanded the federal safety net in 1991 as the reason too-big-to-fail institutions were not a problem. But his was also the same flawed thesis posited by Alan Greenspan that the former Fed chairman was forced to retract after the crisis. Banks were so concerned about their franchise values, and their reputations Greenspan had maintained, that they would never imperil them by lending too aggressively or using excess leverage in their operations.

Mishkin's article was published again in December 2006 in the *Journal of Economic Literature*. By that time he was a member of the Fed's Board of Governors, having been appointed by President Bush for a term set to expire in 2014.

He did not stay long, however; Mishkin resigned in May 2008, shortly after the brokerage firm Bear Stearns collapsed, submitting his resignation in a curt, three-paragraph letter to the president.

In an interview years later, Gary Stern expressed regret that his book and its warnings went unheeded. "Everyone said it was a problem we don't have," he recalled of the reaction his book received at the time. When asked about feedback from his own organization, the Federal Reserve, he said: "There was not as much discussion at the Board of Governors as we had hoped."

$\rightleftarrows$

As if it were not enough that economists at the nation's central bank were blinded to one of the biggest bubbles of all time and writing lazy papers disputing its existence, their colleagues in bank supervision and regulatory policy were also busy lobbying for accounting changes that actually encouraged financial institutions to take greater risks. In addition, the Fed was instrumental in undermining accounting standards that were designed to make banks' balance sheets become more transparent.

When Timothy F. Geithner, a fresh-faced acolyte of Robert Rubin, the master of deregulation, was ushered in to preside over the Federal Reserve Bank of New York in 2003, the banks knew they held all the cards. Geithner's selection committee consisted of executives of most of the institutions that would rely on him later to bail them out.

If corporations are to steer clear of accounting violations when they prepare their financial statements for investor consumption, they must follow rules created by the Financial Accounting Standards Board, an independent entity created in 1973. The board devises accounting standards that a public company must follow so that investors have a clear picture of its true financial standing.

While accounting may seem excruciatingly boring to many, it has also proven to be a battleground where those wishing to obfuscate fight against believers in transparency. Such a battle was waged and lost in 2003 on the matter of off–balance sheet entities, a major contributor to the investor losses in the credit crisis that began three years later.

When FASB goes about writing a new rule or modifying an existing one, it does so in a collaborative fashion, holding public meetings to discuss the issue and asking for comments from anyone with an interest in financial statements. Located in Norwalk, Connecticut, far beyond the Beltway and at a remove from Wall Street, FASB prides itself on its independence. That said, its officials meet with regulators quarterly to keep them apprised of what it is working on.

After Enron imploded in 2001, it opened investors' eyes to the accounting games that could be played when companies set up related entities whose operations did not have to be detailed to stockholders. FASB wanted to tighten up regulations surrounding these entities; it had been accounting gimmickry that allowed Enron to claim that losses in these far-flung entities would accrue to them, not to it.

"Special purpose vehicles" that were supposedly independent because they were only partially owned by the parent company had devastated Enron when the losses in these entities were deemed to belong, in fact, to the energy company and no one else. The migration of those losses back onto Enron's balance sheet was the beginning of the company's death spiral.

In spite of the heightened scrutiny given to SPVs and their off–balance sheet games after Enron, the creation of similar entities had increased tremendously. Called "variable interest entities," they were generally related to the corporation that set them up; their operations, however, were not consolidated in its financial statements. A bank, for example, might create such an entity to make investments that it hoped would create gains for the VIE. The bank would participate at least partially in those gains as the VIE passed through some of its profits.

Questions lingered among investors, however, about who really owned these conduits for profits, who was entitled to receive their gains, and, perhaps more important, who was on the hook to absorb their losses. Finally, stockholders wanted to know whether their operations should be consolidated on the balance sheet of the company that created them.

In December 2003, after much deliberation, FASB came up with a new way to judge when a variable interest entity had to be consolidated and when it did not.

Under significant pressure by financial institutions and their high-level friends at the Fed, FIN 46r, as the new interpretation was called, wound up essentially letting corporations decide whether these entities would appear on their balance sheets. The rule did this by allowing the companies setting up these conduits to estimate the potential for losses that would be generated by them.

Naturally, the companies interested in reaping gains from these kinds of conduits wound up using only the rosiest assumptions of what the losses from their investments might be. These assumptions, in turn, meant the companies creating these entities did not have to incorporate them on their books.

The Fed had lobbied for elements of this rule change that benefited the banks, according to a former FASB official who was there at the time. "The Federal Reserve was closely aligned with the banks; they seemed to be asking for the same things," the official said. "As far as I could see, the Fed was one of the biggest problems, from a standard-setting point of view, of not wanting to provide investors with more transparency."

Almost immediately, major financial institutions that had set up these entities began shifting assets off their balance sheets and away from investors' prying eyes.

One of the main problems with the rule was that it required conduits to be reassessed for potential consolidation only if there was a trigger event that changed the beneficiary of the off–balance sheet entity. This had been pushed by the banks and backed up by the Fed, and it had the effect of allowing corporations that had conduits not to reassess them because they could claim that nothing about their status had changed.

All this is highly esoteric, of course. But the result was that Citigroup and other financial institutions were allowed to set up special investment vehicles, or SIVs, that raised money by borrowing from investors for short periods and investing the proceeds in investments with longer terms. The SIV would pocket the difference between the income generated by the mortgage and the amount paid out to investors who bought its obligations. (Often, as was the case with Citi, the mortgage securities its SIVs purchased were those that it had tried to sell to other investors but they had refused to buy.)

This game worked while the mortgage mania was raging, but in 2007, when losses in subprime mortgages began to spook the markets, investors fled SIVs in general and Citi's in particular. Investors were no longer interested in funding SIVs and asked for their money back. Suddenly, Citi was left with mortgages its conduit had purchased with money borrowed from investors. When it repaid those investors, the mortgages had to be either sold or brought back onto Citi's balance sheet at massive losses.

Citigroup's investors were stunned when the flood of losses and bad assets from entities they were unaware of began backing up onto its books. So were officials at the Federal Deposit Insurance Corporation who had had no idea how many risky assets the bank had shifted, artfully, from its balance sheet. Had the FDIC known about these conduits, it would have required Citigroup to set aside more of a capital cushion for potential losses before they hit, its officials later said.

"There were hundreds of billions of dollars of assets and liabilities parked in this shadow balance sheet that Citi was exposed to, yet they never disclosed it or consolidated it," the former FASB official said. "This is the game that is played. Accounting standard setters create rules and during the development it gets heavily lobbied. Then when the standard gets put up, banks structure things to work around the rules."

Citigroup was not alone in stuffing its SIV with assets it could not sell. From 1992 through 2007, on–balance sheet assets at institutions grew by 200 percent while those stored off balance sheet rose by more than 1,500 percent, according to Joseph Mason, a professor at Louisiana State University.

For a while, anyway, the off–balance sheet entities made the banks' operations and financial statements look far more stable than they actually were. FIN 46r achieved the opposite of transparency, just what the financial institutions and their friends at the Fed had wanted.

⇌

Even as Citigroup was building up its hidden off–balance sheet risks in 2006, its overseers at the New York Fed did nothing to rein the bank in. This, even though the bank had been the subject of a regulatory reprimand just one year earlier.

The largest financial institution overseen by the Federal Reserve Bank of New York, Citigroup was headed at the time by Sanford I. Weill. He was the deal maker who had gotten Robert Rubin and others in Washington to approve a merger of Citi and Travelers eight years earlier, even before they had successfully repealed Glass-Steagall. Rubin was a senior Citi executive, having joined the bank in 1999; he was a mentor to Geithner when the younger man worked under him at Treasury in the 1990s, during the Clinton administration. Now Geithner was president of the powerful and secretive New York Fed.

Weill had cultivated Geithner, inviting him to join the board of the Financial Academy Foundation, a charity Weill ran. After the crisis hit, Weill even approached Geithner about running Citigroup.

In 2006, the New York Fed released Citigroup from a ban on making acquisitions that it had imposed one year earlier. Japanese regulators had uncovered trading irregularities at one of the bank's units and the Fed ordered Citi to clean up its compliance and oversight before it could buy any more companies. Citigroup was always on the prowl for acquisitions because its massive size meant that internal operations could not produce the earnings growth demanded by investors. Only mergers with other large companies could move the profit needle for Citi.

The very year that the Fed freed Citi from the acquisition ban, the company was diving headfirst into risky mortgage-related securities, so imperiling its balance sheet that it would have to be rescued twice by the taxpayers in 2008. The Fed did not seem to notice these risks; in 2006 its head of supervision, William Rutledge, said that Citi had made "significant progress" in improving its compliance and risk management.

Mr. Rutledge was dead wrong.

CHAPTER FOURTEEN

*There is a general recognition that the supervisory sys-
tem for housing-related government-sponsored enterprises neither has the tools, nor the stature, to deal
effectively with the current size, complexity and importance of these enterprises.*

—TREASURY SECRETARY JOHN W. SNOW, testifying
before the House Financial Services Committee
about increasing oversight of Fannie Mae and
Freddie Mac, September 10, 2003

While Geithner and his colleagues at the Federal Reserve Bank of New York were loosening the reins on the banks they monitored, the somnambulant regulator charged with overseeing Fannie Mae and Freddie Mac was starting to stir. It all began with a stunning announcement from Freddie—the kind that usually scares investors witless.

In January 2003, Freddie executives warned that they were delaying the regulatory filing of the company's results for the previous year. Freddie's auditors had questioned the company's accounting practices and, after going back over its figures, Freddie had concluded that the earnings it had recorded in 2000 and 2001 were wrong—they were too low. Results for the current year had to be reexamined as well. An earnings restatement would be in order.

Although it was not clear how much Freddie's earnings had been understated at the time of the disclosure, it was later determined that its profits were off by $4.5 billion over three years. The inaccuracy was problematic because a company's books are supposed to reflect its financial reality.

The flags raised by Freddie's auditors had to do with how the company accounted for the derivatives it used to hedge the interest-rate risks in its vast home-loan portfolio. Prices of mortgage securities moved around a lot in response to changes in interest rates—if they fell, for example, borrowers would be likely to refinance and pay off their existing loans. This meant the income streams on existing mortgages would disappear. Hedging protected against the volatile price swings in mortgage values produced by interest-rate moves.

Usually, investors greeted news of corporate accounting mistakes with dismay, if not horror. But with housing markets booming, and the prospect that Freddie Mac's earnings would actually be higher as a result of the errors, few but the wonkiest followers of financial arcana paid much attention.

Besides, Fannie and Freddie were bigger than ever. Together they were involved in financing mortgages worth $3.4 trillion in 2003, almost half the total home-loan market.

Still, the competitive landscape for Fannie and Freddie was changing. And in early 2003, as mortgage rates hit their lowest levels since the early 1960s, banks and mortgage lenders were feeling economically and politically emboldened. In the weak economy, financial companies were a rare bright spot: Manufacturing was in the doldrums and Silicon Valley had been decimated by the dot-com bust. Washington was relying on financial institutions to support an otherwise hollowed-out economy.

Moreover, as consumers struggled with flat incomes and fewer job prospects, more were withdrawing money from their homes, cashing out the paper profits their properties had generated from rising real estate prices. Large banks raked in considerable profits on these and other consumer loans.

Monthly loan production at Countrywide Financial, for example, now routinely exceeded $30 billion. And it was just one of a throng of financial institutions propelling growth in the burgeoning market for private-label mortgage securities. With Wall Street's help, all sorts of lenders were now able to shovel their mortgages into piles that were bundled and sold directly to investors. These institutions no longer needed to bow down quite so obsequiously to Fannie Mae to sell the loans they made. Other outlets were available.

In 2003, the amount of private-label mortgage securities sold to investors totaled $586 billion, less than a quarter of the total, most of which were issued by Fannie and Freddie. Still, the companies eyed the growth in private-label securities with fear and loathing. They had a right to be worried—just two years later, private-label issuance would hit $1.24 trillion, or 55 percent of the total market.

In addition, Fannie and Freddie were still under siege by the "housers" intent on forcing them to expand their affordable housing goals. Private-label lenders, meanwhile, with their no-money-down mortgages and "affordability products," could argue that they were better at serving the needs of the poor, minorities, and those who had historically been shut out of homeownership.

For the first time in over a decade, Fannie and Freddie seemed somewhat more vulnerable than usual.

One reason for this slight rise in vulnerability was the work of a woman named Anne Canfield, a lobbyist at Canfield & Associates who represented smaller community banks and lenders. As Fannie and Freddie sought to expand their reach in ancillary businesses, Canfield began publishing a twice-monthly newsletter, called *The GSE Report*, noting new developments and activities at Fannie and Freddie.

"We started the *GSE Report* because Fannie and Freddie had a different story for every audience to whom they spoke," Canfield said. "They told investors one story, they told members of Congress and policy makers another. They told the lenders a completely different story and the consumer activists yet another story."

So Canfield and her associates began tracking the various announcements made by the companies and collected them along with news articles and policy journals. Over time, *The GSE Report* became a crucial resource for anyone who was concerned about the growth in Fannie's and Freddie's operations and the threat they posed to the taxpayers.

"People actually thought that I was nuts, that the views I held were completely wrong," Canfield recalled. "This town was so bought into the view that these were wonderful companies doing wonderful things."

While *The GSE Report* had no chance of dethroning Fannie and Freddie, it did put information about the companies into the public domain. It was a classic case of sunlight acting as a disinfectant; instead of simply criticizing the companies, *The GSE Report* used their own pronouncements and actions to show why Fannie and Freddie needed to be monitored.

To push back against the encroachments of private lenders and the work of critics like Canfield, Fannie increasingly relied on its powerful and wealthy foundation to fund both offensive and defensive moves. Jim Johnson had started the practice and his replacement as chief executive, Franklin D. Raines, knew better than to stop it.

In May 2003, for example, housing activists at ACORN issued a press release accusing Wells Fargo, one of the nation's largest banks, of predatory lending. Staging demonstrations at several high-profile locations across the country, ACORN's actions seemed coordinated with the help of Fannie and Freddie. Just before these demonstrations, ACORN had organized picketers in front of the homes of executives at Household International, another private lender that competed with the government-sponsored enterprises.

These were mere skirmishes in an on-again/off-again war between the banks that underwrote mortgages and Fannie and Freddie, which financed them. The relationship between these two powerful factions was characterized by a complex mix of intense rivalry, envy, and interdependence. The banks needed Fannie and Freddie but resented their power and government perquisites; Fannie and Freddie needed the banks and recognized the growing threat that these institutions could sell their mortgages elsewhere.

Even though FM Watch, the coalition set up to monitor Fannie and Freddie, had grown to include nine trade groups and all of the nation's major banks, it had been unsuccessful in many of its fights against the companies.

Fannie Mae had mounted attacks on FM Watch as soon as it set up shop, according to a founding member. Among other efforts, Jim Johnson would call up the chief executives of the banks that had joined the organization—one CEO to another—and warn them not to participate.

Thomas Donilon, Fannie Mae's head of government affairs and therefore its lead lobbying coordinator, also expressed his displeasure with the group and its efforts. According to a person briefed on the discussions, Donilon would regularly telephone William Michael House, the executive director of FM Watch and tell him "you are killing the value of my stock options." Donilon was not joking.

Nevertheless, the balance of power was about to shift dramatically—away from Fannie and Freddie. It was hubris and greed, as it so often is, that triggered the beginning of the end for these two titans.

⇌

Sitting at the witness table in the House Financial Services Committee hearing room on the first Tuesday in June 2003 was Armando Falcon Jr., director of the Office of Housing Enterprise Oversight. Falcon, who had narrowly escaped being fired five months earlier, still ran the bumbling regulator in charge of overseeing Fannie and Freddie. He was there to present his office's annual report to Congress.

Nobody expected much from Falcon's testimony; OFHEO was still the subject of ridicule and contempt. But Falcon soon made it clear that he had grown some spine over the past year. First he announced that OFHEO was thinking of changing the capital requirements for Fannie and Freddie, which had been set artificially low a decade earlier at Jim Johnson's urging. The regulator was also considering ways to beef up analyses of how the enterprises would perform in various economic scenarios, including the worst-case variety. Falcon also reported that OFHEO had issued a "supervisory response" to Fannie in September 2002, asking the company to tighten its hedging practices to more properly protect it from interest-rate risks in its portfolio. Hedging was the same issue that had tripped up Freddie, and OFHEO's disciplinary measure signaled a new assertiveness by the companies' regulator.

Fannie's hedging practices had left the company vulnerable to significant losses if interest rates had risen, OFHEO had found. Luckily, rates had fallen and Fannie's risky hedges had made money for the company. But rates could have easily gone the other way; the potential for this, and the losses that would have resulted, was unacceptable for a government-sponsored enterprise, OFHEO concluded.

Investors for the most part ignored Falcon's report. But to those who watched Fannie and Freddie closely, its implications were clear. Barring Fannie from speculating on interest rates through its hedging operations meant OFHEO was eliminating a crucial tool in Fannie's earnings management kit. "It may be last year's issue," Falcon conceded, referring to Freddie's profit restatement. "But it does impact Fannie's financial flexibility going forward."

Falcon was wrong about it being last year's issue, which became clear days later when Freddie Mac's board of directors dropped a bomb. In the wake of the accounting irregularities disclosed six months earlier, they had forced the resignation of Leland Brendsel, the company's longtime chief executive, and David Glenn, its president, as well as its chief financial officer, Vaughn Clarke. Gregory Parseghian, the firm's chief information officer, was tapped as the new chief executive.

The terms of Brendsel's exit were sweet, as is typical for resigning chief executives—even those caught in a scandal. In return for agreeing to "retire," the board offered him a package worth $24 million, on top of $16 million in unexercised options he was owed.

Glenn was not so fortunate; the board fired him and reclaimed

$11.2 million of restricted stock and options the executive had received. The press release put out by the board was terse: "Mr. Glenn was terminated because of serious questions as to the timeliness and completeness of his cooperation and candor with the Board's Audit Committee counsel."

Rightfully afraid that Freddie's troubles would wash up on Fannie's shores, Raines, the former director of the Office of Management and Budget who had stewarded the company since Jim Johnson's departure, went on the offensive. In an interview with *BusinessWeek* magazine on June 17, 2003, Raines brushed aside questions about Fannie's derivatives accounting. "Everyone who has looked at it, from our external auditors to our regulators, found that we are doing this in a state-of-the-art way," he said. "We are compulsive about managing risk."

Understanding the risks that the accounting scandal posed to the government-sponsored enterprises and the rich perquisites of their charters, Freddie's board hired the law firm of Baker & Botts to investigate. OFHEO, meanwhile, embarked on its own probe.

A month and a half later, after a series of heated meetings between OFHEO and Freddie, Parseghian was fired along with the company's general counsel, Maud Mater. The investigation had turned up evidence that Parseghian was intimately involved in the underreporting of income at Freddie; he had approved derivatives trades personally and signed off on improper accounting as a way to augment profit declines.

The politics surrounding these two powerful companies were heating up again. Still, on Wall Street, investors seemed to believe the din around Fannie and Freddie would soon die down. They failed to recognize that OFHEO seemed bent on flexing its regulatory muscles for the first time and that this heightened oversight would crimp the companies' financial performance.

When Fannie reported its earnings on July 15, 2003, the impact of a tougher regulator was becoming apparent. After a decade of reporting 20 percent annual earnings growth year in and out, Fannie now warned that its executives had "voluntarily" reviewed the company's financial discipline and risk-management practices and would be changing the way they addressed the ups and downs of the business.

That Fannie had any ups and downs in its business was news to many investors, who had known only that the company had constant and reliable earnings growth. Raines, trying to calm investors and defend against what he called a conspiracy of anti-Fannie ideologues, held a two-hour conference call and published "Answers from the CEO" on the company's Web site. To the question: "Can you assure us that Fannie Mae does not have the accounting issues raised in the 'Report to the Board of Directors of Freddie Mac'?" Raines answered with an unambiguous "Yes."

But with Freddie on the ropes, lawmakers interested in reining in the enterprises began stirring in both the House and Senate. Three Republican senators, Chuck Hagel of Nebraska, Elizabeth Dole of North Carolina, and John Sununu of New Hampshire, announced legislation that would limit the activities and portfolios of the enterprises to reduce the risks on their balance sheets. Over in the House, Richard Baker, the Louisiana congressman, promised to move a bill that would transfer oversight of the companies to the Office of Thrift Supervision, a regulator housed within Treasury. Ed Royce, a California Republican, introduced legislation calling for stronger controls over the risk profile of the GSE's balance sheets and of the twelve regional federal home loan banks.

Baker argued that a new exam staff might be better at restricting the companies' practices. He had found twenty cosponsors and fourteen supporting members in his subcommittee. He needed twenty-five to move his bill.

But Fannie's lobbyists were way ahead of the Louisiana lawmaker. Duane Duncan, Fannie's vice president of government affairs and recently Baker's own chief of staff, had already begun meeting with his former boss's colleagues. Robert W. Ney of Ohio refused to support Baker's plan. Ney, who would plead guilty to conspiracy charges in a lobbying scandal in 2006, warned that he would prefer not to rush through legislation that could disrupt the housing market. Ney had received $10,250 from Fannie during 2002.

By late July, Fannie had found the support it needed to neutralize Baker's efforts. But the company faced another threat, this time from the Bush administration, which had expressed a new willingness to work with Baker. The goal: to ram GSE legislation through the Congress.

None other than John W. Snow, the Treasury secretary, set the new tone from the administration. In congressional testimony on September 10, 2003, he urged the creation of a new Federal agency to regulate and supervise the financial activities of the government-sponsored enterprises. "We need a strong, world-class regulatory agency to oversee the prudential operations of the GSEs and the safety and soundness of their financial activities consistent with maintaining healthy national markets for housing finance," he said. The administration wanted that world-class regulator to be in the Treasury Department.

This was bad news for Fannie and Freddie who preferred the underfunded, undermanned, and malleable regulator they had. As both companies knew, any remotely "world class" overseer would almost certainly be interested in raising the companies' capital requirements.

In mid-September, Raines met with Snow about the legislation and promised that Fannie would not fight it. But almost immediately, the company began circulating documents on the Hill highlighting everything the company hated about the bill. It doled out talking points on various issues to Democrats the company knew could be relied upon to throw up roadblocks to the legislation.

In congressional hearings in late September, two of Fannie's most constant defenders questioned Snow's view that the company needed a new regulator. They were Democrats—Barney Frank, the representative from Massachusetts, and Maxine Waters, the California congresswoman.

"I have sat through nearly a dozen hearings where, frankly, we were trying to fix something that wasn't broke," Waters said. "Housing is the economic engine of our economy and in no community does this engine need to work more than in mine. We should do no harm to these GSEs. We should be enhancing regulation, not making fundamental change. Mr. Chairman, we do not have a crisis at Freddie Mac, and in particular at Fannie Mae, under the outstanding leadership of Mr. Frank Raines. Everything in the 1992 Act has worked just fine."

Then Barney Frank chimed in, asking Raines and his counterpart from Freddie Mac, George Gould, whether they felt they had been underregulated over the years. When both men said they had not (surprise!), Frank wondered aloud why Congress was even discussing a new regulator for the companies. "I believe there has been more alarm raised about potential unsafety and unsoundness than, in fact, exists," Frank concluded.

At the same time, the National Association of Realtors and the National Association of Homebuilders were lobbying hard against the proposed Treasury regulator. Allowing it to vet or disapprove new or existing programs could limit the enterprises' ability to meet their mission of funding affordable housing, these groups argued. Of course, they noted that minority and moderate-income households would be hurt the most by a new and tougher regulator. It was right out of the Jim Johnson playbook. Reining in Fannie would only harm the poorest Americans; shouldn't they have the right to reap the rewards of homeownership?

The legislation died; Fannie and friends had beaten back yet another onslaught.

It would, however, be their last hurrah.

⇌

The arguments that low-income Americans would be hurt if a tougher regulator arrived on the scene were tried-and-true at Fannie and Freddie. But as company insiders knew, meeting affordable housing goals was their cross to bear, a necessary evil to be dealt with if they were to keep their lush government perks and pay packages.

An incident from late 2003 underscores how the truth differed from the myth.

Keith Johnson, an executive at Washington Mutual, the big

Seattle savings and loan, was at Disney World with his family when the phone rang. It was an executive at Freddie Mac calling, someone Johnson had dealt with often.

"Keith, we need $6 billion in small multi-family immediately to meet our goals," the Freddie executive said. He went on to explain that Freddie would sell the loans back to WaMu at the same price a few days later.

Johnson listened with interest. He was being asked to rent out mortgages to Freddie, which would treat them as purchases, temporarily that is, to meet the affordable housing benchmarks set by the government.

The WaMu unit Johnson ran was one of the nation's largest originators of loans to finance small, multifamily residential properties. Because mortgages on these apartment buildings and other properties counted doubly toward the companies' affordable housing goals, Fannie and Freddie would regularly court Johnson to buy the loans.

But this was the first time Johnson had received a frantic call requiring what was essentially a wink-wink/nod-nod deal to park WaMu mortgages at Freddie. Rather than account for the mortgages as a loan, which it actually was, Freddie would account for them as a purchase to meet its housing goals.*

Johnson asked what Freddie was prepared to pay WaMu for the favor. "What do you want?" came the response.

Johnson first asked to be given an equal amount—$6 billion—of Freddie's debt in exchange, but was turned down. "How about $100 million in fees?" Johnson said, plucking what he thought was an outrageous number out of thin air.

The Freddie executive didn't blink. "I'll have to run it up the flagpole and call you tomorrow."

Call he did and the next day Johnson had a deal. But this

---

*By making the loans, WaMu had already received credits toward its own obligations under the Community Reinvestment Act, a 1977 law encouraging lenders to make loans in low- and moderate-income neighborhoods. So these loans were counted twice toward affordable housing goals, at least temporarily.

transaction was not an anomaly. Regulators would later find that
Fannie and Freddie, desperate to meet their benchmarks, would
engage in many of these dubious trades with WaMu, Citi, and
Bank of America over the years.

So much for the companies' dedication to showing America "a
new way home."

⇄

In early December 2003, OFHEO released its report on the examination of Freddie Mac. It concluded that "excessive attention and
dedication of corporate resources of a government-sponsored enterprise to management of earnings for the purpose of meeting
securities market expectations, without an additional, overriding
business purpose, is an unsafe and unsound practice."

Clearly, the regulatory heat was on. Payback's a bitch, as the
saying goes, and after years of being dismissed, defamed, and
degraded by Fannie and Freddie, OFHEO was finally getting the
chance to settle some very old scores.

Even though Fannie had won the last round on the Baker bill,
its lobbying tactics had offended some of its supporters on Capitol
Hill. Now, with the damning OFHEO findings on Freddie, many
legislators were looking beyond the lobbying spin put out by both
companies. They were seeing that a weak regulator had allowed
for the growth of what some were calling "the Enrons of the housing market."

But increased political costs were not the only consequence
of the OFHEO report. Freddie was also being forced to increase
its financial disclosures and hold a cash cushion of up to 30
percent more capital than required until it remedied its deficiencies.

The OFHEO report detailed numerous examples of intentional
earnings management, improper accounting practices, and reserv-
ing. It pointed to improper round-trip trades Freddie had made to
mislead investors and trigger bonuses. Also noteworthy was the
disclosure that Parseghian admitted to devising a scheme to

disguise $80 billion in derivatives on Freddie's books because he knew investors were concerned about the size of such holdings at the company.

Given OFHEO's findings that Freddie had managed earnings to trigger executive compensation, it was only a matter of time before the regulator questioned whether Fannie was doing the same. OFHEO had requested that Congress provide it with $4.5 million in funding to investigate Fannie; the probe did not begin until February 2004.

⇌

Even though its regulator was on the warpath, Raines and Fannie's other executives kept up the appearance that nothing was amiss. In mid-January 2004, Raines traveled to the University of Virginia's Darden School of Business to launch an influential new organization housed within the university: the Business Round-table Institute for Corporate Ethics. Raines, cochairman of the institute, said its goal was to "help restore the trust of the American people and American investors in business corporations."

Before the year was out, an accounting scandal even bigger than the one at Freddie Mac would destroy investor trust in Raines's company and lay the groundwork for its demise. Raines, the man overseeing the creation of the Institute for Corporate Ethics, would be driven from his job, accused of a litany of ethical lapses and corporate chicanery that could make an Enron executive blush. Raines's business-as-usual approach at Darden that day was either bravado, denial, or a desperation move.

Perhaps Raines thought he could still rely on the powerful friends in high places that his company had. So what if OFHEO was investigating? Congress called the shots and Fannie had that place locked up.

Sure enough, when Congress held hearings on the oversight of the enterprises at the end of February 2004, Fannie enjoyed the usual stroking from its lawmaker pals.

Among the most vocal was Christopher Dodd, the Democratic senator from Connecticut, who urged Congress not to lose sight of the great deeds Fannie and Freddie had done over the years for everyday Americans. "Like most of us here, this is one of the great success stories of all time," Dodd said, inarticulately. "And we don't want to lose sight of that and has been pointed out by all of our witnesses here, obviously, the 70 percent of Americans who own their own homes today, in no small measure, due because of the work that's been done here."

Dodd seemed to be directing his words at Fed chairman Greenspan, who was on hand to testify about Fannie and Freddie. He was not what Fannie would call a friendly witness; like Treasury secretary Snow, Greenspan and some of his colleagues at the Fed were becoming more critical of the companies.

Just before Christmas 2003, Wayne Passmore, the most influential housing economist at the Federal Reserve Board, had released a draft paper estimating that the subsidy received by Fannie and Freddie was a result of their "implied government guarantee." It was Marvin Phaup of the CBO all over again, only this time it was the omnipotent Federal Reserve doing the talking.

Passmore went on to argue that Fannie and Freddie lowered interest rates for borrowers by only .07 percent; and while their benefits each year were worth between $119 billion and $164 billion, the companies' shareholders retained almost $100 billion of them.

It was well known in Washington that Passmore was tight with Greenspan and that no paper of this significance could have been released without having first been vetted by the Maestro. "The GSEs' implicit subsidy does not appear to have substantially increased homeownership or home building, because the estimated impact of it is small," Passmore wrote.

Aware of the conclusions in Passmore's paper even though it had not yet been published, Fannie arranged to send a warning about it to Greenspan. It came in the form of a letter from the Congressional Hispanic Caucus, a congressional member organization that was one of the GSEs' most constant allies. Fannie had recently donated $1 million to the Congressional Hispanic Caucus Institute, its nonprofit arm. The gift was to fund a research program focused on sixty-three congressional districts in which Latinos constituted over one quarter of the population.

The letter to Greenspan, dated November 21, 2003, was signed by fifteen of the twenty members of the caucus. "Against the backdrop of the distressing fact that Hispanics already lag behind other Americans in homeownership, we ask that you carefully weigh the effect of releasing a report . . . that seems to gloss over the very real benefits of GSEs in its criticisms," the caucus members wrote. The last thing they wanted, they added, was for the Federal Reserve to take an anti-housing stance in the midst of an important congressional debate on policy affecting Fannie and Freddie.

But the Passmore paper was published. And with Freddie's scandal still fresh in people's minds, critics of the enterprises such as Christopher Shays, the Republican representative from Connecticut, lauded it as further evidence that the companies posed more risks than rewards.

Now Greenspan was testifying before the Senate Banking Committee about regulatory reform for Fannie and Freddie. Outlining the Passmore paper's findings, he said: "The Federal Reserve is concerned about the growth and the scale of the GSEs' mortgage portfolios, which concentrate interest rate and prepayment risks at these two institutions." And unlike savings and loans and commercial banks, Greenspan noted, Fannie and Freddie had the thinnest of capital cushions but employed heavy leverage.

Then Greenspan brought up the government guarantee that Fannie and Freddie continued to deny. "Without the expectation of government support in a crisis, such leverage would not be possible without a significantly higher cost of debt," Greenspan said. "I should emphasize that Fannie and Freddie, to date, appear to have managed these risks well and that we see nothing on the immediate horizon that is likely to create a systemic problem. But to fend off possible future systemic difficulties, *which we assess as likely* if GSE expansion continues unabated, preventive actions are required sooner rather than later."

It was a shockingly aggressive, not to mention lucid, performance from Greenspan who was known for testifying in meandering, run-on sentences larded with economic jargon. It was also a watershed event—the first time an esteemed senior official acknowledged that Fannie and Freddie posed systemic risks to the financial system.

But his suggestion that the government take "preventive actions" against Fannie and Freddie was simply that—a suggestion. And it was something that Fannie and Freddie knew how to counterattack.

A far greater threat loomed, however, from OFHEO's newly initiated investigation into Fannie's accounting practices.

Failing to uncover the accounting problems at Freddie Mac in 2003 had been an embarrassment for OFHEO and its leader, Armando Falcon. The regulator had only two companies to oversee; how could it have missed a multibillion-dollar accounting scandal at one of them?

By the spring of 2004, OFHEO had hired the audit firm of Deloitte & Touche to lead an examination of Fannie, and the man in charge of the project had led the investigation into Enron's sketchy accounting just a few years earlier. Clearly, this was a serious probe.

OFHEO had also gotten a boost when the Bush administration proposed increasing the regulator's annual budget from $40 million to $59 million. The White House seemed to be sending a signal that it wanted these companies constrained. At the same time the Republican majority in Congress sought to use the Fed's research and the accounting woes as a wedge to force another shot at legislation to cut Fannie and Freddie down to size.

With the 2004 presidential election in full swing, Fannie's ties to the Bush administration's adversaries were striking. The presumptive Democratic nominee, John Kerry, the senator from Massachusetts, had tapped Jim Johnson as a senior adviser. Johnson had his eye on running Treasury even as he was tasked with compiling a list of potential cabinet members in a Kerry administration.

Other potential members of the Kerry team were Peter Orszag, the young Brookings Institution economist who had coauthored the problematic and overly rosy analysis of the risks posed by Fannie and Freddie in 2002. Kerry was also considering Jim Johnson's friend Robert Rubin as a possible Fed chairman; Tim Geithner, the president of the New York Fed, was another candidate for a senior position that Kerry was said to be considering.

Bush's unpopularity gave Fannie's supporters their greatest hope. All they needed to do was get Kerry into the White House and all of Fannie's problems would disappear. Jim Johnson would be there to help that happen, of course.

⇌

On September 17, OFHEO and Deloitte completed an interim report on their investigation of Fannie, Raines, and his senior management. Two days later, before the release of the report, OFHEO briefed Fannie's board on its findings. On September 20, before publication, OFHEO briefed senior legislative staff on the report. Although it was only a preliminary report, it had turned up a raft of disturbing practices at the company, the largest non-bank financial company in the world.

OFHEO found, among other things, that Fannie had orchestrated a "concerted effort" to develop and adopt accounting policies allowing it to spread income or expenses over multiple reporting periods; that it adjusted financial statements for the sole purpose of minimizing volatility and achieving desired financial results; that it forecast and managed unrecognized income and costs to maintain a "cookie jar" of reserves for bad times; and that it applied discretion to the selection of market rate assumptions in order to achieve desired accounting results.

Much of the manipulation was designed to trigger executive bonuses. Indeed, of the more than $90 million in executive compensation received by Raines from 1998 through 2003, over $52 million was directly tied to achieving earnings-per-share targets through phony accounting.

OFHEO also maintained that Fannie's weaknesses were significant, affecting nearly all areas of the company. Many had existed under previous leadership, the regulator noted, alluding to Jim Johnson but not naming him.

The company, which began as steward of the public trust, had been turned into a high-flying growth enterprise with a vast web of political patronage run for the benefit of its top executives.

It was a stunning report. And it was only the beginning.

On September 23 OFHEO sent a letter to Fannie Mae's board, suggesting that they use their regulatory authority to remove certain executives and, perhaps, directors. Although the OFHEO investigation was not yet complete, its findings were significant and warranted "immediate remedial action." Moreover, OFHEO said, "we must consider the accountability of management and whether we have sufficient confidence in management to fully implement these corrective measures and bring about broad cultural and operational changes."

At the same time, Washington was buzzing with talk that HUD was sitting on a powder keg of information involving Fannie Mae. Apparently the company had bought a throng of poorly documented loans containing phony borrower information, but when Fannie realized the loans were troubled had made the lender buy them back.

Although it was required to report them as bad loans, Fannie did not. This allowed the lender to turn around and sell them to HUD, which pooled them for investors. When the loans went bad, HUD discovered that they had first passed through Fannie Mae.

HUD was also stepping up an investigation into Fannie's partnership offices, the network of patronage and largesse providers. The study demonstrated that the offices, which received preferential tax treatment for nonprofit work, were basically corrupt. A disproportionate percentage of their money had gone to support lobbying efforts and the dispensing of favors in violation of their nonprofit status or reporting requirements.

But Fannie was still able to fight back. In April, at the request of Fannie's lobbyists, Republican senator Kit Bond of Missouri requested that the inspector general of HUD investigate the regulator who was investigating Fannie. By calling OFHEO into question, Fannie hoped to undermine the damaging accounting probe.

But it was too little too late. Fannie now found itself in a perfect storm and even its most powerful friends could not steer it to safety.

Representative Baker then offered his own set of shocking revelations. For over a year, Baker said, he had been battling Fannie for information about how much the top twenty executives at this publicly chartered company were paid. When it received the request, Fannie engaged the services of Kenneth Starr, former solicitor general and the independent counsel in the Whitewater investigation of Bill Clinton. Starr promptly informed Baker's staff that a lawsuit would be filed if the information was released to the public. Anyone who released the information would be subject to criminal proceedings, Starr warned, or House disciplinary action. The threat was never acted upon and was ridiculous on its face.

This litany of bad behavior was too much even for Barney Frank, the Massachusetts Democrat who had defended Fannie for more than a decade. He began ratcheting back his defense of the company. "To the extent that people played games to get bonuses, I am outraged," he said. "To the extent that there was manipulation, that is very wrong and should be penalized."

Still, Frank clung to the notion that the companies were well managed and presented no threat to the taxpayer. "I have seen nothing in here that suggests that the safety and soundness are at issue," he said, "and I think it serves us badly to raise safety and soundness as a kind of a general shibboleth, when it does not seem to be the issue."

On November 15, Fannie missed the deadline to file its financial statements with the SEC. The firm that had long claimed to be perfect was now admitting some problems, albeit not serious ones.

Late that afternoon, with little fanfare and no discussion, Fannie canceled a previously scheduled meeting with senior outside lobbyists and consultants. It was odd for the company to leave itself undefended on the Hill given that budget appropriators at the time were considering whether to fund OFHEO at levels that would support a continuation of the Fannie investigation. As calls were made to confirm the cancellation of the meeting, word came back: "Fannie has shut down their PR and lobbying efforts because their lawyers are telling them to do so." Furthermore, this person said that "at this point, the legal team has moved in and will be directing traffic henceforth."

OFHEO's interim report had been released but still Fannie tried to convince both the Beltway and its largest investors that it was in the clear. OFHEO knew nothing about accounting, Fannie argued; the SEC would be the final arbiter as to their compliance with the complex and arcane rules involving derivatives transactions.

On November 16, Armando Falcon addressed a conference of Women in Housing Finance and was frank about his experiences overseeing Fannie and Freddie. "Your motives, your judgment, your competence, they're often questioned," he said. "You're constantly audited and investigated. What's important is that you just stay focused on doing your job, do the right thing and never bow to political pressures. And in this case I think the agency has done this very well."

Falcon understood what he was up against.

The questioning of Falcon, OFHEO, and their motives was about to get louder. Later that same day HUD gave a limited briefing to certain legislators regarding the investigation report of OFHEO.

Although it's common for an inspector general of a federal agency to release a report or a summary of findings to the regulator and Congress at the same time, it is decidedly uncommon for the release to end up in the hands of one of its subjects. But this report reached Fannie before OFHEO had even seen it, and the night before its release, calls began circulating on Wall Street from a large Fannie shareholder who continued to argue that Fannie's management had done nothing wrong and that the regulator was on a witch hunt. The caller suggested that the inspector general had caught OFHEO trying to leak information to the press to damage the credibility of Fannie and its management. Among the allegations were that Deputy Director Stephen A.

Blumenthal was "gleeful" whenever Fannie's stock price fell. When the redacted version of the report was finally released, it did contain that accusation of Blumenthal's "glee," but, highlighting the bias of the inspector general's report, mischaracterized it. According to a source close to the matter, Blumenthal's "glee" was based on the fact that when regulatory actions were taken they had little direct effect on Fannie's stock price; therefore the regulator could not be accused of negatively impacting the stock. Nevertheless, the mischaracterization of Blumenthal's attitude toward the company became fodder for Fannie's friends on the Hill as they continued to shift blame for Fannie's problems to its regulator.

The report was largely a hatchet job filled with "he said, she said" accusations, many of them were believed to have come from OFHEO's former chief examiner, Scott Calhoun, who had missed the company's accounting problems. Blumenthal had sought to sideline Calhoun in the wake of the Freddie scandal and now it seemed Calhoun was getting revenge through the HUD inspector general.

Barney Frank posted the unredacted report for an hour or so on a House Web site, according to a *Washington Post* article. "The senior management of OFHEO appears to have run roughshod over the judgment of professional staff and seriously compromised OFHEO's credibility as a financial regulator," Frank told the reporter. "It is clear that a leadership change at OFHEO is overdue."

Kit Bond, another Fannie friend, put out a press release castigating OFHEO. "This report reveals that top OFHEO officials have misused their agency and abused the public trust," he fumed. "OFHEO leadership put their personal agenda above the public good and have permanently damaged the integrity of the agency."

Battles flared on the Hill about whether the report should be released publicly. The personal damage to Blumenthal had been done, Falcon had been smeared, and Fannie's interpretation of OFHEO had already captured some support.

"OFHEO's behavior is outrageous," fulminated David Dreman,

one of Fannie's largest shareholders, to a reporter at Bloomberg News. Two days later Barney Frank released a version of the report with troubling allegations about Blumenthal blacked out.

Fannie contended that it had done nothing wrong; the regulator was just going after it because it had failed to find accounting problems at Freddie.

In late 2010, Frank was asked why he was so assiduous in his defense of Fannie and Freddie against their regulator. "I wasn't convinced by OFHEO," he said. "I thought there had become a kind of adversarial relationship between Fannie and Freddie and their regulator." Never mind that regulators are not supposed to be friends with the entities they oversee. Frank's interference with the work of a prudential regulator characterized the increasing politicization of what historically had been independent regulatory oversight.

The tempest surrounding the inspector general's report blew over; Fannie was soon back on its heels as critics forecast that the SEC would determine that the company had violated numerous accounting rules.

Senator Bond had one more trick up his sleeve to benefit Fannie. The administration had proposed an increase in OFHEO's budget to support a larger investigation and examination staff at the regulator, but Bond slipped language into the appropriations bill that would defund OFHEO until Falcon was removed from its directorship.

The battles escalated as 2004 drew to a close. By mid-December rumors circulated that the SEC was nearing its determination on the accounting dispute. Fannie continued to boast of a likely victory in the matter; all was quiet at OFHEO. Representing OFHEO was Stanley Sporkin, the well-respected former federal judge who had been head of enforcement at the SEC as well as chief counsel to the CIA under Bill Casey.

On December 15, the SEC convened a meeting of senior executives from Fannie Mae and their lawyers, OFHEO and their outside counsel, and the SEC's senior accounting staff. As the attendees sat around a table, the SEC's chief accountant, Donald

Nicolaisen, began to answer the long-standing question—was Fannie's accounting for derivatives proper as Raines, his top managers, and their friends had long claimed?

As Nicolaisen began, he picked up a piece of paper and expressed his view in simple terms. Look at this piece of paper, he said; we acknowledge that vagaries in accounting might allow one acceptable interpretation to be on one corner of the page while another quite appropriate approach sat on the opposite corner. But Fannie's accounting? Not even *on the page*, he said. Not even in the area code. Maybe on another planet. That was how far out-of-bounds it was.

Raines sat there stupefied. He'd been knocked out cold.

Fannie Mae would ultimately have to restate earnings in the amount of $6.3 billion. Unlike Freddie, however, Fannie's adjustment lowered its profits by that amount.

That evening, as Fannie Mae employees gathered at the company's holiday party, the SEC issued a press release outlining its findings. "Fannie Mae's accounting did not comply in material respects" with two accounting rules, Nicolaisen said in a written statement. Rather than adhere to generally accepted accounting principles, Nicolaisen continued, "Fannie Mae internally developed its own unique methodology."

The SEC statement ended ominously, with Nicolaisen saying, "It is my understanding that investigations into these and related matters by Fannie Mae's special review committee, the Commission, and others are continuing."

The following day, a Thursday, Fannie's stock fell about 2 percent on the accounting news. The Franklin Raines deathwatch had begun. After all, Raines had promised in hearings on Capitol Hill two months earlier that if anything about the company's accounting was found to be in error, he would hold himself accountable.

Fannie's board met over the weekend to decide the fate of the company's top management. On December 21, after the stock market had closed, OFHEO announced that Fannie was "significantly undercapitalized" and that Raines and its other top management were being replaced.

Raines was allowed to retire and when he did, Ann McLaughlin Korologos, the lead nonmanagement director at Fannie Mae, thanked him for his "many contributions" to the company. The board provided another thank-you to Raines and his lieutenants in the form of absurdly large departure bonuses, approved by OFHEO, as well as lifetime health benefits and full coverage of legal defense costs. This acquiescence by OFHEO was disturbing to many; the regulator seemed eager to put the ugly chapter behind it.

Still, the incident was the first of many times that the heads of organizations accused of improper conduct were not held accountable for the damage they did to shareholders and, later, to taxpayers.

OFHEO's findings that the company was undercapitalized were also significant. Under the 1992 act there were four capital classifications governing Fannie and Freddie: "adequately capitalized," "undercapitalized," "significantly undercapitalized," and "critically undercapitalized." Each level of undercapitalization brought with it a different set of regulatory requirements.

While Wall Street was focused on the executive changes, OFHEO was clearly intending to use its new powers as a way to put the company, its new managers, and its board on a leash as they had done with Freddie less than a year before when its accounting practices had been found severely lacking. First, Fannie Mae would have to, according to the statute, file a timely and acceptable capital restoration plan with OFHEO and meet the benchmarks of such a plan. Second, being classified as significantly undercapitalized gave OFHEO certain authorities it could use, such as limiting the increase in or ordering the reduction of Fannie's obligations, limiting or barring the growth of assets, and requiring the acquisition of new capital. Finally, OFHEO could appoint a conservator if necessary, to oversee the company.

Within weeks there were changes of both senior management and board members. Anne Mulcahy, chief executive of Xerox, had been an outside director and head of Fannie's compensation committee. She resigned, citing time constraints, but within a week joined Citigroup as a director. Later it would be shown that she had raised questions about Fannie's uncanny ability to max out its bonus pools year in and year out, but had done little to follow up on those queries.

Shortly after Mulcahy's resignation Fannie announced it was halving its dividend and replacing the auditors who had signed off on the dubious accounting. KPMG, the old accounting firm, was being replaced by the Deloitte team engaged under the OFHEO investigation.

Finally, Fannie Mae had been humbled. More than a decade of arrogance and hubris had done the company in, at last. But stunning though the scandal was, an even greater peril loomed in 2005, when the days of truly crazy mortgage lending were just getting under way. As Fannie and Freddie jumped feetfirst into this free-for-all, they led the company straight into the worst financial crisis in seventy-five years.

Just three and a half years later, overwhelmed with mortgage losses, Fannie Mae and Freddie Mac would be taken over by the U.S. government. The taxpayer bailout of the companies, an event so many of its defenders in Congress had refused to believe possible, had occurred. Even after the accounting disasters at both companies, no criminal charges were ever filed against any of their employees or executives.

And more than six years after Raines and his colleagues were thrown out of the company, the government was still paying their legal bills. In early 2011, it came out that taxpayers had paid $24.2 million in legal costs so that Raines, Howard, and Spencer could defend themselves in shareholder suits. It was an insult added to a decidedly grievous injury.

CHAPTER FIFTEEN

My hope is that all these stretched borrowers who were saved by home price appreciation in the past are getting out of the pools early and that the Fremont core borrower continues to perform but Fremont refused to make any forward-looking statements so we really got nothing from them on the crap pools that are out there now.

—GOLDMAN SACHS client explaining why he
declined to buy one of the firm's many mortgage
pools containing Fremont loans, November 16, 2006

O f all the partners in the homeownership push, no industry con-tributed more to the corruption of the lending process than Wall Street. If mortgage originators like NovaStar or Countrywide were the equivalent of drug pushers hanging around a schoolyard and the ratings agencies were the narcotics cops looking the other way, brokerage firms providing capital to the anything-goes lenders were the overseers of the cartel.

Just as drug lords know that their products pose hazards to their customers, the Wall Street firms packaging and selling mort-gage pools to investors knew well before their customers did that the loans inside the securities had begun to go bad.

But with the mortgage mania raging and profits still flowing, the investment bankers had no interest in coming clean about the toxic loans they were pouring into the pools. So instead of turning them back to the lenders who had made them, demanding that they be replaced with solid loans, the nation's top brokerage firms used the dubious mortgages as a lever to wring more profits for themselves out of the originators.

It was another example of Wall Street turning lemons into lemonade, for itself anyway.

Before assembling a mortgage pool and selling it to investors, brokerage firms hired independent analytical companies to sample loans that were destined for the security and flag those that were problematic. It was a trust-but-verify approach to this lucrative business, a way for Wall Street to look over the shoulders of lenders whose mortgages they were buying. The due-diligence firms watched for loans that did not meet the specifications outlined in a prospectus, such as geographic diversity, loan-to-value ratios, and borrower incomes.

Armed with loan statistics provided by these samples, Wall Street's investment banks saw in late 2005 and throughout 2006 that the mortgages they were financing and selling to investors were becoming increasingly sketchy. They did not share this information with the investors who bought the pools they were selling, however. Instead, the firms started forcing the lenders producing the diciest loans to accept a lower price for them. Wall Street knew they had the lenders in a box—NovaStar and New Century did not have the capital they needed to buy back troublesome loans, so the lenders were only too happy to sell what were called "scratch-and-dent" mortgages more cheaply to the brokerage firms, who then pooled them into securities that were sometimes sold as pristine.

Rather than pass these discounts on to their customers buying the loan pools, some firms charged the same high prices associated with superior loans. Never mind that pushing these perilous mortgages through the securitization machine guaranteed early and substantial losses for their clients.

It was a colossal breakdown in the duty Wall Street owed to its investing customers. The firms should have either turned back the loans to the originators or charged investors less for them to make up for the additional risks they posed.

Years after the meltdown, investors began to understand what the due-diligence process had uncovered and how badly they'd been burned by Bear Stearns, Merrill Lynch, Lehman Brothers, Deutsche Bank, Greenwich Capital, Morgan Stanley, Goldman Sachs, and other smaller firms. Lawsuits against these firms alleging a dereliction of duty started cropping up in 2010 as investors began to realize that Wall Street's secret loan assessments had identified severe problems in mortgages well before they stopped selling them.*

Goldman Sachs's internal response to these due-diligence reports is especially intriguing because, unlike many other firms, it went negative on the mortgage market in the fall of 2006, well before others in its industry. Using its own money, the firm began amassing major bets against the same dubious loans it was peddling to investors at that time. Goldman, therefore, profited immensely from the losses its clients absorbed, losses its own practices helped to create.

It is unclear whether Goldman put on its hugely profitable and negative mortgage trades because of proprietary information turned up in its due-diligence reports. If that was indeed what happened, its failure to tell clients of the problems in the loans it was selling is even more disturbing.

⇔

*As of early 2011, these cases were still pending. During the meltdown, Wall Street firms argued that they too had been victimized by loose lending, stuck with losses on some of these loans when the music finally stopped in 2008. But the degree to which the firms had been victimized was only by their own greed—the loans they were left with were the proverbial hot potatoes, mortgages they had been unable to off-load quickly enough to investors. Pension funds, Fannie Mae, Freddie Mac, endowments, and other investors that bought hundreds of billions of these garbage mortgages from Wall Street lost far more than the brokerage firms that peddled them; moreover, their purchases had provided millions in fees to the firms over many years.

Wall Street had financed questionable mortgages before, of course. But it was during the mania's climactic period of 2005 and 2006 that these firms' activities as the primary enablers to freewheeling lenders really went wild. No longer were the firms simply supplying capital to lenders trying to meet housing demand across America. Now Wall Street was supplying money to companies making increasingly poisonous loans to people with no ability to repay them. And the firms knew precisely what they were doing.

The relationship forged by Wall Street's most prestigious firm, Goldman Sachs, with one of the nation's most wanton mortgage originators—Fremont Investment & Loan—is a case in point. Fremont, a company with a regulatory rap sheet and a history of aggressive lending, received $1 billion in financing from Goldman in 2005, fully one third of the total it received from all of its Wall Street enablers.

Goldman had begun financing Fremont in 2003 with a credit line of $500 million, but as the mortgage spree ramped up, it doubled that commitment. Goldman did so in spite of a serious run-in Fremont's insurance unit had had with regulators just five years earlier.

With one of its units in operation since 1937, Fremont was no upstart lender like New Century or many of the other mortgage companies cropping up all over Southern California. Based in Santa Monica, Fremont boasted $8 billion in assets and declared its hundredth consecutive quarterly cash dividend in November 2001.

The company was something of a family business. It was overseen by founder and patriarch Lee McIntyre, who had launched the company in 1963 with $800,000 in capital. Lee brought his two sons, David and James, into the business in the 1960s. David ran Fremont's insurance operations while James ran the banking unit.

In 1969, James took up the task of decorating the company's headquarters. He commissioned the world-renowned photographer/naturalist Ansel Adams to print 121 of his silver gelatin photographs of American parks and monuments to hang on Fremont's walls. Some were massive, the size of murals, and Adams worked closely with McIntyre on the installation over five years. It was the largest collection, much bigger than that of any museum, of Adams photographs in private hands.

The photograph collection sent a message to Fremont's visitors that this was not just any financial concern—this was a classy enterprise that paid close attention to detail. When Fremont failed almost forty years later, the artwork would become enmeshed in a fierce battle over Fremont's assets.

Fremont had three businesses: an insurance division specializing in workers' compensation, a savings and loan, and a wholesale mortgage originator. The company went public in 1977.

Fremont's bank—Fremont Investment and Loan—began life as a "tiny little company hustling car loans," according to Murray Zoota, who had taken over as chief executive of the bank in 1983. Over the next ten years, Fremont grew from thirty-eight employees with $40 million in assets to a 960-person operation with $5.5 billion in assets.

In 1992, Lee McIntyre died at the age of eighty-six. Two years later, Fremont swaggered into the subprime mortgage business. By 1996, it was originating $183 million in loans.

Not long after this, subprime crashed and burned, following the Russian debt crisis and the collapse of Long-Term Capital Management. Zoota survived those troubled times but recognized that many of his rivals had not. "It was a gold rush mixed with fool's gold," he told an interviewer from the *Orange County Business Journal*. "Some got rewarded, some are in the cemetery."

Even as its competitors struggled, Fremont Investment and Loan thrived in the weak economy of 1999–2001. Its well-capitalized parent company, Fremont General, had the resources to hire employees for the bank and pick up operations of companies undone in the turmoil.

Fremont Investment and Loan was insured by the FDIC and had relationships with many Wall Street bankers. A "no-frills" institution that offered certificates of deposit and money market accounts but shunned the more prosaic businesses of checking or savings accounts, Fremont generally held on to the commercial loans it made. The residential mortgages it made were quickly sold to investors.

Wall Street firms helped Fremont sell its loans and they were happy to further the company's efforts to become one of the heavy-weights of the subprime world. By 2000, Fremont was a giant in that world, originating $2.2 billion in mortgages. But this was only the beginning; in 2006, when the home-loan frenzy was peaking, Fremont would originate $28 billion in mortgages.

Fremont was "always in front of the parade," Zoota told the *Business Journal* in August 2000. He was right—Fremont was ahead of its rivals when the business boomed, but as subprime hit the skids in 2007, it was also among the first to crash.

⇌

Three months after Zoota's boast, the workers' compensation insurance division of the company was leading a very different type of parade. In November 2000, deeply concerned that the company was teetering on a perilously thin wedge of capital, California regulators took over the insurer. At that time, Fremont Indemnity was the nation's sixth-largest purveyor of workers' compensation insurance.

Had Wall Street cared, this high-profile regulatory skirmish might have provided a warning about Fremont's modus operandi. The case against Fremont was public and available to any institution interested in learning more about the company. But Wall Street looked the other way.

The insurance division was no longer run by a McIntyre family member when the troubles began. David McIntyre was fired from the company in 1989 after one too many feuds with his brother, James, who had taken over Fremont. Louis Rampino, a Fremont employee since 1977, was in charge of the company's insurance unit in 1998.

Fremont Indemnity started hemorrhaging money in 1999; after more than a year of losses, including $247 million in the first three quarters of 2000, state regulators moved in. A special deputy examiner came in to oversee Fremont's operations and barred the company from making any financial decisions without permission from California's Department of Insurance. This meant Fremont had to get approval from its regulator before it could borrow money, strike deals with subsidiaries, or hire new management. Fremont was on a very tight leash.

At the same time, regulators began investigating the company. They would later contend that Fremont had secretly shifted losses on insurance it had underwritten to companies it had partnered with. Fremont's scheme was to load losses onto its partners, known as reinsurers, thereby ramping up its own revenues and triggering lush executive pay packages.

The dubious practices at Fremont began in 1998, three years after California had deregulated the workers' compensation insurance market and just as the subprime mortgage market was crashing. The secret scheme was orchestrated at the highest levels of Fremont General, regulators said; it was led by Rampino.

Rampino told his employees that he wanted Fremont Indemnity to generate $1 billion in premiums by 1999, a sizable increase from the $600 million written during 1998, when he took over as chief executive. Fremont didn't quite make it, generating premiums of $831 million that year. Still, that performance was enough to generate executive bonuses in 1999.

Before the scheme was hatched, Fremont's insurance would cover up to $1 million on each workers' compensation claim it received. Anything over that amount would be borne by the reinsurance companies Fremont had contracted with.

But in mid-1998, Fremont secretly changed the terms of those contracts, shifting responsibility to the reinsurers for any losses above $50,000 per claim. Immediately after making the change, Fremont started writing insurance on much riskier types of businesses, insuring workers in 139 hazardous types of operations that it had previously avoided. To make sure its revenues would grow quickly, Fremont executives pushed its salespeople to give discounts to any entity that would likely generate loss claims exceeding Fremont's $50,000 coverage limits. These losses would then become the responsibility of the company's reinsurance partners.

It didn't take long for Fremont's reinsurers to realize they'd been hoodwinked. One by one, beginning in 2000, they stopped doing business with Fremont. Its business collapsed and soon regulators came calling. In July 2002, California's insurance commissioner barred the company from writing new insurance policies, paying dividends, or withdrawing funds without approval by the regulator.

The company divested Fremont Compensation Insurance that year; the insurance commissioner began liquidating Fremont Indemnity in July 2003.

But few paid attention to the failure of Fremont Indemnity. With the subprime mortgage market raging, Goldman Sachs extended $500 million in credit to Fremont in 2003 and bought $2 billion in mortgages from the company. Only two other firms bought more loans from Fremont that year.

By the fourth quarter of 2003, Fremont General's shares had recovered to $19.00 from a low of $3.40 a year earlier. Wall Street, always eager to accentuate the positive, was clearly focused on Fremont's subprime lending prowess. The fact that the company had been caught in a fraudulent insurance scheme that obliterated one of its operations did not seem to concern Goldman, the company's other financiers, or equity investors.

⇆

Even as Fremont's executives were sparring with the California insurance regulator, the company was rushing to get in front of another parade—the highly lucrative one involving subprime mortgage securitization.

In 2001, mortgage lenders like Fremont understood that the low interest-rate environment was driving investors to securities that yielded more than Treasury bonds and other relatively conservative fixed-income instruments. The Federal Reserve Board's decision to slash interest rates to propel the economy was hurting investors who lived on the income generated by their holdings.

Mortgages, with their relatively higher yields, provided a handy answer to this problem. Many investors, notwithstanding Subprime 1.0, still believed that home loans were relatively conservative instruments. Ratings agencies, blessing the majority of these securities with triple-A ratings, only confirmed this rosy view.

Teaming up with lenders, major brokerage firms like Bear Stearns, Lehman Brothers, Morgan Stanley, and Goldman Sachs pressed them for loans to feed the mortgage securities machine. It didn't hurt that the fees generated by these securities made up for stagnant businesses—such as investment banking and stock trading—that were generating only paltry revenues on Wall Street.

With yield-hungry investors on the prowl for profits, and Wall Street eager to please, the subprime mortgage market started to rouse. The billions of dollars being dangled before cash-strapped lenders were mighty alluring; they knew that tapping those funds could juice their volumes and their profits.

In a world of tough sells, this was not one. The race to the bottom had begun.

Fremont quickly grabbed onto Wall Street's brass ring, taking $1.5 billion in credit from Goldman and two other firms in 2003. One year earlier, Fremont had had no such arrangements.

Between January and April of that year, Fremont issued $1.9 billion in mortgages, mostly refinancings of existing loans and adjustable-rate mortgages. Investors were more than willing to snap up the securities containing Fremont's loans because they offered a higher income stream than more conservative mortgages backed by Fannie Mae or Freddie Mac.

In July 2003, its lending operations in high gear, Fremont announced plans to go national. Certain that its California subprime model could work anywhere, the company headed first to Westchester County, outside of New York City. It opened two offices there, doubling its staff, and over the next three years Fremont would set up shop in Illinois and Florida.

But bricks and mortar were not necessary for Fremont to

expand its reach. Working with thousands of independent mortgage brokers in the same way that NovaStar had done, Fremont
wrote loans in forty-five states and the District of Columbia.

Specializing in riskier mortgages than some of its competitors, Fremont focused on cash-out refinancing and adjustable-rate
loans. Refinancings carried higher risks than so-called purchase
loans given when a borrower bought a home because the amounts
borrowed in refi's were usually based on recent home price appreciation. Those gains could easily prove ephemeral, leaving the borrower with a loan greater than the value of the property underlying
it and the lender possibly facing a loss.

But mortgage lenders who had no intention of holding on to
the loans they made favored refi's for the easy and hefty fees they
generated at little cost. These loans represented repeat business
from existing customers and required no new sales or advertising
expenses. Profits, therefore, were far greater on these loans.

Borrowers, too, were swarming to refinance, either to reduce
their payments because interest rates had dropped or to extract
cash from the increased value in their homes that resulted from
the housing bubble. This cash was "found money," and often went
toward consumption of plasma TVs, new cars, luxury goods, and
home remodeling.

With the Fed on a rate-cutting rampage, demand for
adjustable-rate mortgages with relatively low initial interest costs
had become incendiary. One of a raft of "affordability" products
that Countrywide and other lenders were peddling to counter the
effects of the housing bubble, adjustable-rate mortgages with their
low rates allowed borrowers who'd previously been shut out of
homeownership to join the party.

It is not surprising then that 2003 was the year to remember in
mortgage originations. A record 13.6 million mortgages worth $3.7
trillion were written that year; Wall Street's issuance of mortgage-
backed securities also peaked, reaching $463 billion in 2003.

The top twenty-five lenders underwrote most of these loans.
While these companies had accounted for only 28 percent of new

mortgages written in 1990, by 2003, the top twenty-five were responsible for generating 77 percent of the $3.7 trillion in loans.

The good news was 2003 was a banner year for mortgages. The bad news—for Wall Street anyway—was that the blistering pace simply could not continue. Mortgage originations had been propelled by the Fed's rate cuts, but with prevailing rates at 1 percent, there was little room for further declines. This was meaningful because borrowers who had reached for more home than they could afford would no longer be able to lower their costs by refinancing when rates fell again.

As 2004 dawned, therefore, it had become more and more evident that the mortgage lending machine was sputtering. By midyear, Citigroup, Bear Stearns, and Morgan Stanley had all reported serious declines in their mortgage-backed securities deals. Lehman's volumes had fallen 35 percent from the previous year while Goldman Sachs's had plummeted by more than 70 percent. But instead of serving as a warning to the banks, this hiccup in loan origination only made them redouble their efforts in the subprime arena.

For all of 2004, only $276 billion in mortgage-backed securities were issued, fully 40 percent less than the amount sold a year earlier.

The main reason for this decline was that halfway through 2004, the Fed began ratcheting up interest rates. By the end of the year, rates were at 2 percent, double where they had started.

Wall Street bankers were desperate to halt the decline in mortgage volumes, which spelled disaster for bonuses and even presaged the unthinkable: layoffs.

It was a moment of truth for Wall Street, an industry not known for veracity. The firms that had made so much money on the American dream of homeownership were faced with a decision. Recognizing that the easy money days were over, the firms knew that continuing down the path of big mortgage profits was going to require a more concerted effort, greater creativity. Wall Street, always at the ready for such duty, concocted new types of loans to be offered to borrowers as well as new entities that would buy them.

But keeping the mortgage machine humming would also require that investment banks ignore numerous signs of wrongdoing along the way. This meant putting their own interests ahead of their clients' at every turn.

While nobody mistook Wall Street banks for charity organizations, the degree to which these firms embraced and facilitated corrupt mortgage lending was stunning. Their greed and self-interest took the mortgage mania to heights (or depths, depending on your view) it could not possibly have reached without Wall Street's involvement. And in so doing, Wall Street helped propel world financial markets to the brink of collapse.

The voraciousness of these firms would also push the nation's economy into its most serious recession in more than seventy-five years. Their avarice would finally, and forcefully, demonstrate how a noble idea like homeownership could be corrupted into something that so poisoned the global economy it was left in a semi-vegetative state.

⇌

Interest rates were on the upswing in 2004 and adjustable-rate mortgages no longer held the cachet for borrowers that they did when rates were in decline. If they wanted to keep their profits coming, lenders would have to come up with some new and compelling products that would allow borrowers to grab the biggest and best house for the buck.

Interest-only mortgages were just the ticket.

These loans were not exactly new—they had been around for decades as a wealth management tool for well-heeled borrowers. Taking the money they would otherwise use to pay down principal on a mortgage, sophisticated borrowers would invest it in higher-yielding instruments. The borrowers would use the money earned on these investments to pay down loan principal later.

But as often happens in the financial markets, Wall Street

took a product that had worked well for a small group of sophisticates and began hustling it to the unsuspecting masses. Never mind that the complexity of these loans almost guaranteed that they would be misunderstood by first-time homebuyers eager to grab hold of the American dream. To lenders concerned about a decline in their business, and to the equally worried Wall Street firms who financed them, the disasters lurking in these loans were somebody else's problem.

Besides, home affordability was becoming a huge obstacle for first-time borrowers, the very participants who were necessary if homeownership was to keep climbing. After almost a decade of exploding demand for real estate, driven by a combination of demographics, industry avarice, and Washington's lusty support for homeownership, real estate prices were in the stratosphere. New borrowers were once again being shut out of the game.

To their "rescue" came lenders peddling the interest-only mortgage. While a borrower of $100,000 might have had to pay $600 a month on a fixed-rate mortgage, his payments on an interest-only loan, during the early years anyway, would be $500 in interest and $100 in principal. By choosing to pay only the interest, the borrower had an extra $100 to play with.

What many borrowers did not want to understand was that by avoiding paying down any principal on their loans, they were not building up any equity in their homes. By not paying down principal, the size of the mortgage remained the same.

Borrowers who recognized this peril may have dismissed it in the belief that rising home prices would bail them out. It was a fool's game.

But these were not the only mortgages created to keep profits flowing to Wall Street and lenders. An even more toxic loan that allowed borrowers to pay as much or as little interest on their mortgages as they wanted was also being peddled as a solution to the affordability problem. These mortgages were known as negative amortization loans because the amount of interest a borrower chose *not* to pay would be tacked on to the principal owed, increasing his total loan balance. Instead of amortizing or paying down the loan, it grew in size.

Imagine how tempting it was for borrowers facing stagnant incomes to pay a fraction of their loan's interest every month! To make their gambles pay off, they needed home prices to keep surging, or win the lottery with a portion of their deferred payments. As it turned out, winning the lottery would have been easier.

Taken together, these two poisonous products accounted for just 6 percent of loans in 2003. But by the following year, such loans accounted for no less than one quarter of all mortgages originated; in 2005 they represented a staggering 29 percent of the market.

Anyone with a brain could see that borrowers' increased reliance on such loans would come to a disastrous end. But the loans were immensely profitable and so lenders kept pushing them and Wall Street kept funding them. It was the equivalent of spiking the punch bowl long after the party should have been over.

By creating these loans, which piled new consumer debt on top of old, Wall Street's bankers had done something entirely new and nefarious. They had allowed institutions extending credit to consumers in the form of a second mortgage or home equity line of credit to share in the collateral backing all the loans without asking for permission from lenders who were there first and thought they were the sole creditors. This was unheard of among corporate lenders, for example, who required that anyone providing money after an initial loan was made to a company would take a backseat position to the bankers who were there first if the loan went bad.

Recognizing how risky these loans were, Bear Stearns, Lehman Brothers, Goldman, and the rest were careful to bundle them with more traditional mortgages in the securities they were selling to investors. Prior to investing in the pools, prospective buyers were given only broad and generalized information about the loans inside them—details like average borrower credit scores and average loan-to-value ratios. That meant they rarely knew how many tricky loans they wound up owning. Until they started going bad, of course.

Neither did the ratings agencies seem to understand the perils in these loans. This was an important failing—the loans in a pool were not finalized until after the deal closed; therefore the agencies provided a rating based on the *expectation* of the final composition at closing. The rating agencies' analysis was tied to general, not loan-specific, analysis.

But the agencies were comfortable with rating what they didn't see, and in 2005 mortgage securities issuance started to rise again. Only one problem remained: Investors who had previously been willing to buy the lower-rated pieces of these deals were beginning to turn up their noses. These investors had done enough analysis to recognize that the quality of the loans in the pools was deteriorating and their risks, therefore, were rising.

Encountering more objections from its customers put Wall Street salesmen in a bind.

Mortgage securities are built in a vertical stack, with the lowest-rated slices sitting at the bottom of the instrument and higher-rated sections arranged in sequence above. Investors holding the slices at the bottom are the first to absorb losses when borrowers default or stop repaying their mortgages. Those owning the highest-rated pieces are the last to suffer losses and the first in line to receive interest payments from borrowers.

Because most traditional mortgage investors are risk-averse, either because of the restrictions of their investment charters or business practices, they are interested in buying the higher-rated segments of the loan stack; as a result, those slices are easiest to sell.

The more challenging task is finding buyers for the riskier pieces at the bottom of the pile. The way mortgage securities are structured, if you cannot find buyers for the lower-rated slices, the rest of the pool cannot be sold.

As Wall Street poured ever sketchier loans into these securities, some buyers went on strike. Faced with dying interest in the crucial but toxic "foundations" of these securities, Wall Street did what it does best. Through the magic of structured finance, the firms took the low-rated slices, added a little cash to the pile, and sold them as a new pool. A pool that consisted of other pools, actually.

Wall Street has a term for this—it's called putting lipstick on a pig.

In this case the lipsticked pig was the collateralized debt obligation, a pool that contained pieces of other mortgage pools. These instruments turned out to be the perfect dumping ground for the low-rated slices Wall Street couldn't sell on its own. Piling these loans into an even more complex security that the ratings agencies did not understand meant that they could earn higher grades and attract more conservative investors.

It was a classic case of Wall Street's bankers refusing to listen when its investor customers said *no mas*. Rather than accepting the fact that traditional mortgage securities buyers had had their fill after bingeing on these instruments, Wall Street came up with a newfangled investment to keep the profit machinery turning. The creation of collateralized debt obligations as a sort of secret refuse heap for toxic mortgages created even more demand for bad loans from wanton lenders. CDOs prolonged the mania, vastly amplifying the losses that investors would suffer and ballooning the amounts of taxpayer money that would be required to rescue companies like Citigroup and the American International Group.

But for these me-first firms, stuffing questionable loans into CDOs in 2005 and 2006 meant that the mortgage merry-go-round had a few more profitable turns left in it.

⇋

That collateralized debt obligations would play such a crucial role in the financial crisis is another of its many paradoxes. These instruments had been popular just a few years earlier but were abandoned after producing huge losses for investors. Once again, investors' short memories set them up for a repeat performance, only this time around the consequences, and the losses, were far larger.

The first CDO was crafted by none other than Drexel Burnham Lambert, the brassy brokerage firm that became famous, then infamous, for its dominance of the junk bond market and the "greed is good" culture of Wall Street of the late 1980s. Drexel built a CDO in 1987 for Imperial Savings and Loan, a Los Angeles S and L that went belly-up in 1990.

Almost a decade later, CDOs reemerged as instruments containing a wide array of loans that, in theory anyway, promised to perform differently over time. Early on, these CDOs consisted of aircraft lease-equipment debt, manufactured housing loans, and other commercial obligations that were combined and sold to investors based on their risk tolerance. That the risks in these loans were supposed to be noncorrelated or unsynchronized was a good thing in the eyes of investors; if a loan to an aircraft manufacturer failed because of a downturn in that industry, the losses generated in the pool would be offset by loans made to telecom companies that were doing fine.

Given the diversified borrowers whose loans made up the CDOs, the many types of obligations, and the risk models underlying the structures, investors thought they could better estimate the performance of these securities in a variety of economic environments. Investors also liked the yields on these instruments—2 or 3 percentage points higher than those of plain vanilla corporate debt issues.

As is usually the case, though, these higher yields came at a cost.

In July 2001 came American Express's $1 billion loss on CDOs, the instruments whose risks it had not understood. Later, investors learned that many of these securities had exposure to Enron and WorldCom, the most famous corporate flameouts of 2001 and 2002. Investors abandoned the market.

But taking a tainted product off the shelf, dusting it off, and shining it up was a time-honored tradition on Wall Street. All the firms needed to ensure the success of their new CDO sales effort was to garner high ratings for the securities from the ratings agencies, Moody's, Standard & Poor's, and Fitch.

A hallmark of the earlier CDOs had been their makeup: a diversified group of loans. But with thousands of home loans being originated each day across America, the CDOs that characterized 2005 were all mortgages, all the time. All benefits of diversification had vanished; now the portfolios were dangerously concentrated and synchronized.

If Wall Street worried that the ratings agencies would notice this and penalize the securities on their ratings scales, it needn't have. Because grading complex products was so much more lucrative than rating a simple corporate debt issue, the agencies welcomed the business and promptly began assigning improbably high marks to these instruments. Moody's could earn as much as $250,000 to rate a mortgage pool with $350 million in assets, versus the $50,000 in fees generated when rating a municipal bond of a similar size.

As CDO volumes soared, so did the ratings agencies' earnings. Moody's revenues from rating CDOs and other structured finance products totaled almost $900 million in 2006, up 63 percent from the $553 million generated two years earlier. In 2006, Moody's structured finance revenues accounted for fully 44 percent of its $2 billion in sales.

Getting the ratings agencies to assign high grades to complex CDOs was crucial if Wall Street was to persuade conservative investors to buy them. But because most of these instruments contained lower-rated slices of mortgage pools that did not sell the first time around, the ratings agencies' models had to be counted on to transform dross into gold.

Unfortunately for investors, this breathtaking metamorphosis was based on smoke, mirrors, and mind-boggling incompetence. The ratings agencies were wooed by "six-inch hooker heels, and a tramp stamp," as the manager of the world's largest bond fund, Bill Gross, said in 2007.

As usual, the ratings agencies were chronically behind on developments in the financial markets and they could barely keep up with the new instruments springing from the brains of Wall Street's rocket scientists. Fitch, Moody's, and S&P paid their analysts far less than the big brokerage firms did and, not surprisingly, wound up employing people who were often looking to befriend, accommodate, and impress the Wall Street clients in hopes of getting hired by them for a multiple increase in pay.

There were other impediments to good ratings at the agencies. They had a limited history with the newfangled mortgages that were filling these instruments and they had only so much experience with the past performance of the second generation of CDOs. So, even though their models may have seemed impressive enough, their output was only as good as the information their analysts put into them. Their failure to recognize that mortgage underwriting standards had decayed or to account for the possibility that real estate prices could decline completely undermined the ratings agencies' models and undercut their ability to estimate losses that these securities might generate.

While the ratings agencies were snoozing, the CDO issuers were working overtime. In 2004, CDO issuance totaled $157.4 billion; by 2005, the figure had risen to a quarter trillion. Issuance peaked in 2006 when investors bought a staggering $521 billion of this dressed-up dross.

To Wall Streeters, CDOs had several amazing attributes. First, they were often compiled and overseen by veterans of Wall Street and these CDO managers worked hand in glove with the big firms who peddled them to customers. This meant the CDO managers were often in on the con, so instead of scrutinizing closely the loans that Wall Street and their friendly originators delivered, the managers waved dubious loans in by the billions. Given that CDO managers were eager participants in the scheme, there was no quality-control mechanism to ensure that garbage stayed out of these instruments.

With the good performance of the CDOs in a still-hot market, the ratings agencies began to grade the managers and based their ratings on the simple notion that those who managed the most deals must be the best.

But CDOs had another, major allure for the Wall Street firms that peddled them. Because of the way they were structured, they allowed the firms who were selling them to bet against the clients buying them. Among the first to embrace this concept was Goldman Sachs, the most esteemed of the nation's investment banks and often the first mover in any profitable trade.

Goldman was founded in 1869 by Marcus Goldman, a German immigrant. In 1882, his son-in-law, Samuel Sachs, joined the small firm. In the early twentieth century, Goldman specialized in initial public offerings, raising money for companies from public investors.

Over the years, Goldman grew into the preeminent investment bank. For decades it was run with one goal in mind—to do best by its customers. Goldman executives were known as Wall Street's best and brightest and after serving out their time at the company often went into public service. Henry M. Paulson, the Treasury secretary during the early years of the mortgage meltdown, was the last in a long line of federal officials who came to Washington by way of Goldman.

But after Goldman gave up its private partnership structure, raising money from the public in 1999, the tone at the company changed. Profits took priority over customer care and trading desks soon dominated the firm's previous power center—the investment banking arm. Lloyd Blankfein, a commodities trader who joined the firm when it bought J. Aron and Company, a trading house, was a driver of this shift at Goldman. He became its chief executive when Paulson left for Treasury.

Given that traders were in control at Goldman, it is not surprising that the firm's mortgage desk convinced top company officials to make a major bet against the home-loan market. Recognizing that the market was overheated and starting to cool, Goldman quietly began wagering against the very securities it was selling to its clients.

This dubious practice took hold at Goldman in the third quarter of 2006. Later, other CDO managers did the same thing, betting against the instruments they were charged with overseeing for the benefit of their clients.

Investors who relied on the ratings agencies to vet the CDOs never had a chance. The agencies did not see how toxic the loans in them were; in fact the largest ratings firms didn't do loan-level analysis. Moreover, the instruments were far too complex to be analyzed by outsiders—some contained dozens of pieces of other loan pools referencing thousands of mortgages.

With $1.4 trillion in CDOs issued from 2004 through 2007, these instruments represented a huge, new, and exceedingly lenient buyer for mountains of dubious loans. An end to the mortgage boom that had been threatened by rising interest rates in 2004 was averted by lipsticked pigs known as CDOs.

As CDO issuance soared, investment banks increased their cash commitments to small lenders, securing critical loan production. They also bought their own mortgage companies so they could be sure the supply of loans met the demand fueled by CDOs.

With CDO managers lapping up all manner of mortgages, lenders soon found that their production targets were harder and harder to achieve. Countrywide, NovaStar, Fremont, and the rest responded by ramping up the profits generated in each loan. This meant steering borrowers who would otherwise qualify for lower-cost mortgages into highly profitable but much more toxic loans.

Borrowers who could prove that their incomes and assets were ample were pushed into more expensive loans that required no documentation. Mortgage brokers peddled them as easy and hassle-free. These and other tricks hurt borrowers. But they increased the industry's and investment banks' profits.

At the same time, lenders redoubled their efforts to refinance existing borrowers into more exotic mortgage products. The push for production fueled by Wall Street's CDO factories fostered the massive growth in "liar loans," for which borrowers did not have to produce any proof of income or assets. Almost 45 percent of subprime loans made during this period were low-documentation or liar loans and as many as 60 percent overstated their incomes by at least half.

Sure, the lies were the borrowers' ideas in some cases, but the pressure to originate volume caused some lenders to falsify borrowers' mortgage applications routinely. Some sponsored weekend parties where executives would redo borrowers' applications to make them "approvable."

Having invested billions in a lending and mortgage securitization apparatus that had become a key driver of its profits, Wall Street could not allow lenders to slow their production of aggressive new loans to borrowers who would never have qualified for a mortgage before. The face of banking had changed; regulators and lenders now spoke of caveat emptor, let the borrower beware, when it came to lending practices. Why should bankers have to consider which mortgage product was really the best for the customer? It was better to let bankers innovate, creating a variety of products from which borrowers could choose.

Besides, regulators argued, even if they wanted to police these loans, most were made by unregulated mortgage firms. Never mind that they were funded by the institutions that were, in fact, supposed to be regulated.

Behind these creative bankers stood an increasingly powerful participant in the game: mortgage-backed securities traders employed by major investment banks. Generating immense profits to their firms, these traders gained more importance every day. They became drivers of the mortgage securitization process, making decisions that regularly overrode credit risk officers whose job was to prevent the disasters that resulted from trader excess.

Credit risk officers were stick-in-the-muds, naysayers generating only costs, while mortgage traders were central to the firms' profits. To traders, this business was not about homes, borrowers, or the American Dream. Sweet as those notions were, they were secondary to the pieces of paper a trader could move and the gains those transactions generated. Besides, who needed a risk manager when you were operating in a market that only went up?

With Wall Street ever more frantically pushing for more loan production, mortgage quality became gamier and increasingly suspect. While a bank that held a loan cared deeply that it would be repaid, investors in mortgage-backed securities were more interested in avoiding the lost income that resulted when a borrower prepaid his loan. Ongoing cash flows from the payments of mortgage interest were paramount, and to ensure that those flows continued, lenders worked to lock borrowers into their mortgages. They did this by exacting heavy prepayment penalties and by allowing borrowers to carry significantly higher leverage.

Indeed, by the summer of 2005, almost 40 percent of subprime mortgage originations were for amounts exceeding the value of the underlying properties. These borrowers may not have known it, but they were trapped in high-cost and murderous loans. It was only a matter of time before they defaulted.

⇄

In July 2005 the executives at Fremont Investment and Loan got some very good news. Fitch Ratings had announced it was upgrading Fremont's subprime servicer rating on the strength of "notable improvements" in the company's operations.

Like many mortgage originators, Fremont did not just write mortgages, it also serviced them, performing administrative tasks such as taking in borrowers' monthly payments and tracking their escrow accounts and insurance obligations. Servicers also performed these duties for other lenders, for a fee, of course.

In order to attract business, servicers needed to garner high ratings from Fitch, Moody's, and Standard & Poor's. For Fremont, the Fitch upgrade was a shot in the arm.

In its report, Fitch noted a variety of improvements Fremont had made to its servicing unit, including "the refinement of an online central repository for policies and procedures, as well as the addition of a dedicated group of former F.D.I.C. auditors to perform ongoing regulatory assessments and reviews."

While these changes hardly seemed worthy of an upgrade, the volume of loans that Fremont churned out meant big fees for ratings agencies. Perhaps Fitch's upgrade had more to do with the future business Fremont might throw its way; after all, Fremont was servicing more than 100,000 loans totaling $19.1 billion in principal balance at the time and was projecting a servicing portfolio of $24 billion by the end of 2005. That kind of growth in a weakening environment would have made Fremont's servicing business an important relationship for any of the big three ratings firms.

The reed upon which Fitch hung its upgrade of Fremont could not have been thinner—the creation of a central database for the company's procedures and a handful of new auditors was nobody's idea of groundbreaking. Moreover, even as Fitch was rhapsodizing about Fremont's mortgage servicing practices, some sophisticated investors were growing leery of the entire market for home loans.

In May 2005, reports surfaced that the world's largest fixed-income investor, PIMCO, which ran the biggest bond mutual fund, had retreated from the CDO market because of concerns about these instruments' deteriorating credit quality. Only a few months before, Scott Simon, head of PIMCO's mortgage-backed securities unit, had warned that his team was reducing exposure to longer-maturity mortgages and were concentrating their investments in higher-grade pieces of the pools.

Unease about the effects that rising interest rates would have on the market gave investors another reason for caution in mid-2005. In August, the Federal Reserve Board increased its discount rate to 4.5 percent, up from 2 percent the summer before. The Fed was finally trying to tap on the brakes of a runaway real estate market.

Nevertheless, on September 19, 2005, the day before the Fed increased rates by another 0.25 percentage point, Fitch published a new and glowing report on Fremont. This time, the ratings agency was upgrading the lender's corporate debt because of its improved financial condition. Citing "substantial recent increases in regulatory capital levels and ratios and in liquidity," Fitch said Fremont had shielded itself from potential regulatory pressure to bolster its financial footing.

The analysts at Fitch did note two risks to Fremont's business: It was concentrated in commercial real estate lending and subprime mortgage originations, operations that would both be subject to "adverse economic trends over the course of the business cycle." But Fitch said it was satisfied, and recommended that investors should be too, by the current strength in both of Fremont's markets and its current levels of capital and reserves. Both would be there to help the company through "less favorable environments."

What the analysts at Fitch had failed to recognize was the amount of capital that would be required if Fremont's loans were so toxic that they could not be sold to investors. Another possibility that Fitch overlooked: What if the investors who had already purchased Fremont loans or the Wall Street firms that were acting as middlemen began to notice how defective the loans were and forced Fremont to buy them back? Both scenarios would require immense amounts of capital from Fremont, money it simply did not have.

Mortgage-backed securities contain representations and warranty provisions requiring lenders to repurchase loans that are "materially defective" because of a failure to meet certain stated lending standards or borrower characteristics. Among the most likely to fail these tests were the all-popular liar loans that had so dominated the industry's and Fremont's mortgage production.

As the quality of loans across the industry plummeted, the risks skyrocketed that lenders would have to buy back some of the mortgages they had already sold. Even though it was beginning to dawn on Fitch, Moody's, and S&P that a severe slide in loan quality had taken place, none of these agencies warned investors that some firms might not have enough capital to cover buybacks of predatory or liar loans.

In early 2006, Fremont reported earnings for the previous year's fourth quarter. Profits were down 40 percent from the prior year. Although originations had risen 37 percent, Fremont's profitability on sales and securitizations had collapsed by more than half. It was clear that the train was veering off the track.

There was one peculiar bright spot in Fremont's report that should have served as a red flag to regulators and investors.

Amid the bad news, Fremont announced that it had more than tripled its mortgage securitization volume, quarter over quarter and year over year.

With profitability declining, why was the company choosing to securitize more volume? Something was afoot. Were Fremont's bankers, Goldman Sachs and others, beginning to fret about the warehouse lines they had so generously given the company? The big increase in securitizations suggested that Fremont's lenders were pressuring it to get more mortgages out the door to investors so the financiers could get their money back before the roof caved in.

The big banks certainly had the information necessary to determine if loans made by Fremont and other lenders were more likely to default faster than normal. That's because investment banks like Goldman employed independent due-diligence firms to sample the loans they were buying or warehousing from mortgage originators. These due-diligence firms would use on-the-ground inspectors and computer analysis to identify how many loans failed to meet specified underwriting standards. The firms flagged loans that had been made to borrowers who overstated their income, claimed a property to be a primary residence when it actually was a vacation home, or appeared to have used a phony appraisal.

Such due-diligence firms had begun life in the late '80s and '90s when banks were buying other lenders' mortgages to hold in their own portfolios. In those days the due-diligence firms might be asked to sample anywhere from half to all of the mortgages a bank was buying.

As the mortgage mania was gearing up in the early 2000s, bankers continued to sample large portions of the loans destined for mortgage pools. They were protecting themselves from getting stuck with mortgages that went bad between the time they were originated and the moment they were bundled and sold to investors.

But with the time between origination and securitization

shrinking, the risks that those mortgages would lose money for the bank also shrank and the due-diligence process became less important to investment banks. Now the Wall Street firms used the due-diligence outfits more as a "check the box" process than to actually examine the results of the tests.

The existence of the reports did help Wall Street promote its mortgage pools. Selling documents for these securities noted that such analyses had been conducted, providing some assurance to investors that the pools had been reviewed and scrubbed, and were as clean of defects as possible.

Investors who were kicking the tires on a mortgage security would have loved to learn what these due-diligence firms were finding as lax lending took over. But they never saw the reports. They weren't allowed to; investment bankers kept them under lock and key.

Nevertheless, by 2006, even the reduced samples of loans under review were generating alarming results. Huge numbers of loans did not meet the underwriting standards that lenders had claimed. In some cases, as much as 60 percent of an entire mortgage pool was showing material defects in underwriting. Even worse, these defects had no offsetting factors, such as outsized borrower cash reserves.

Historically, when loans were found to have such defects, the investment bank would go to the originators (such as Fremont or NovaStar) and force them to take back the faulty mortgages. But as the loan samples showed that increasing numbers were defective, the investment banks knew there was no way the lenders could afford to repurchase them. Forcing the loans back on the lenders' books, given the lines of credit the bankers had extended, could easily push some of them off the cliff and take the investment banks' money with them.

Faced with the choice of profits or propriety, Wall Street made its decision. Closing their eyes to the problem loans, the banks kept feeding them into the mortgage machinery.

But before they did so, the banks made sure the lenders cut

them enormous discounts on the cost of the loans. These discounts were not passed along to investors; they simply increased the profits earned by the investment banks on the garbage loans.

Former employees at due-diligence firms say that among the banks that used them, almost half of all loans from 2006 on had material defects, with no offsetting factors. And yet these loans were pooled, packaged, and sold to investors. True, there were small warnings buried deep inside these pools' prospectuses; they consisted of the classic lawyerly hedge clause, stating that "the pool may contain underwriting exceptions and these exceptions, at times, may be material."

An investor could easily overlook fourteen little words buried in a several hundred–page prospectus.

⇌

In September 2006, regulators tiptoed into the subprime lending morass, issuing new guidance, not regulations, on so-called non-traditional mortgage products. Once again, the overseers were a day late and many dollars shy with their tepid announcement. The sum total of the guidance was to warn lenders to "consider" the ability of a borrower to make payments over the life of the loan and not just at the introductory or "teaser" rate.

It was like warning an alcoholic not to take a drink.

Weak as it was, the industry greeted the advisory with vitriol. "This guidance seems like regulatory overreach; innovative, non-traditional mortgage products have allowed more people than ever to explore the possibility of homeownership," thundered Regina Lowrie, the head of the Mortgage Bankers Association. And ignoring the symbiotic relationship between mortgage lenders and the major banks he oversaw, John Dugan, the Comptroller of the Currency and one of the four leading bank regulators, falsely claimed that "the most abusive practices have been made outside the banking system."

But it was finally becoming clear to regulators and investors that lenders like Fremont had become reckless beyond words. Investment banks, meanwhile, decided to take the wheel of the listing subprime ship. Desperate to save their reputations and the billions they had committed to build extensive trading platforms, securitization, and origination factories (not to mention warehouse lines), they started becoming much more involved in the operations.

In June 2006, Morgan Stanley announced it had hired two senior executives from Fremont to develop and build a "world-class" wholesale lending platform at the firm. To some it seemed unlikely that Morgan Stanley's move was about building a lending platform; a more credible explanation was that the firm needed to find ways to minimize losses on loans it had bought from Fremont that the lender could not afford to buy back. Who better to set up such operations than recent escapees from Fremont?

By August, investment banks were growing more frantic, pushing their lender partners to slash their originations of risky mortgages. The number of borrowers who were defaulting on loans within months of receiving them was rocketing; this posed severe consequences to both lenders and their enablers. "Early payment defaults," as they were known, allowed investors in the mortgage securities to return the loans to the lender and, in exchange, get their money back. If the lender didn't have enough money to repurchase the defective loans, the investment bank that provided the lines of credit to the lender could be forced to pay.

As early as spring 2006, Fremont's borrowers were reneging on their mortgage obligations in distressing numbers. Investors who had purchased some of the mortgage securities packaged by Goldman Sachs in 2006 learned this the hard way.

One of the worst concoctions ever designed and sold to investors was the GSAMP Trust 2006-s3 (the acronym stood for Goldman Sachs Alternative Mortgage Product). Issued by the firm in April 2006, the pool was swollen with Fremont loans—54 percent of the contents.

Within three months of the trust's issuance, more than 5 percent of the loans in the pool had become severely delinquent. Because borrowers had to have missed three consecutive payments before they were considered "severely delinquent," this meant that 5 percent of this pool's borrowers never made one payment. By August 2007, sixteen months after it was issued, the pool had a 40 percent loss to liquidations.

In a 2007 report from Moody's, Fremont's loans would be deemed worst in class. Never mind that just a year earlier, Moody's had assigned high grades to securitizations stuffed with the very loans the ratings agency now questioned.

So, even as large volumes of fraudulent mortgages continued to flow into Wall Street's securitization warehouses, loans the investment banks had previously pretended were fine and dandy, executives at these firms began to demand that these lenders cough up money to buy back the failing loans. Wall Street used its leverage and inside information about the souring loans to make claims on the lenders' assets before mortgage investors beat them to it.

Paradoxically, even though Fremont's borrowers were defaulting in droves, 2006 was the company's best year yet. Having written almost $28 billion in subprime loans, it ranked as the fifth-largest lender in the category. Goldman had financed a winner all right. Its board members, including Jim Johnson, received an extensive report on its subprime operations on March 26, 2007. The firm reported to the directors that its mortgage business had generated revenues of over $1 billion in 2006.

But executives inside the firm were also hearing horror stories about Fremont loans from clients to whom they had tried to sell Fremont-laced securities. A November 16, 2006, e-mail to her superiors from Melanie Herald-Granoff, a Goldman salesperson, described the pushback she received from a customer she had approached to buy into a Fremont securitization.

"Yesterday when I spoke with Luke and he said they were dropping from the freemont (sic) deal he said he had set up a call with them," Herald-Granoff wrote. "Luke said that he would give me feedback on the call, which is below. After receiving this, I called Luke to thank him, get the verbal version, and just confirm that they still wanted to be out of our deal. That is still the case. They didn't feel like they learned a lot of new information and that the changes fremont is making aren't that major. They are concerned about all the fremont exposure they already have, are going to put Fremont 'in the box' for the time being."

Discussions like these as well as the information Goldman was getting from the due-diligence reports it had commissioned were making the firm's executives nervous. Obviously, the subprime bonanza was peaking or had already.

So in the third quarter of 2006, the firm decided to make a concerted effort not only to rid itself of any mortgage assets it had on its books, it also decided to make a very big wager against the subprime sector as a whole.

Goldman didn't stop selling mortgage securities stuffed with sketchy subprime loans to its clients, mind you. Indeed, in the first three quarters of 2006, Goldman sold $17.8 billion of its own mortgage-backed securities; it also sold $16 billion in CDOs, up from $8 billion in 2005.

The firm seemed to view its customers not so much as people to watch out for, but as trading partners it could take advantage of if they were foolish enough to allow it. Savvy investors knew enough to approach warily any securities Goldman was peddling.

As ever, the ratings agencies did their part to help Goldman sell the Fremont trash it had financed. In January 2007, S&P was rating a mortgage-backed security put together by Goldman Sachs filled with Fremont subprime loans. An e-mail turned over to Congress shows an S&P analyst asking for help on the deal from two senior colleagues.

"I have a Goldman deal with subprime Fremont collateral," the junior analyst wrote. "Since Fremont collateral has been performing not so good, is there anything special I should be aware of?"

One respondent replied, "No, we don't treat their collateral any differently." The other piped up, "Are the FICO scores current?"

"Yup," was the reply. Then, "You are good to go."

In other words, the S&P analyst relied upon one element— borrower credit scores—in assessing whether greater credit risk should be assigned to loans made by an issuer well-known for its questionable loans. In fact, just three weeks earlier, S&P analysts had circulated an article about how Fremont had stopped doing business with eight thousand brokers because their loans had some of the highest delinquency rates in the industry.

Even so, S&P's and Moody's financial engineering justified triple-A ratings on five slices of securities backed by Fremont mortgages in the deal.

⇌

While Goldman's salespeople were busy bundling and selling as many Fremont loans as they could, executives inside the firm were scurrying to off-load mortgages that were still on their books. It was a race against time inside Goldman in early 2007, as internal e-mails produced to Congress show. The paramount goal was to get rid of toxic mortgages.

In early February, Josh Rosner and Joseph Mason presented a lengthy paper* at The Hudson Institute, a Washington think tank, warning of coming losses to holders of mortgage securities, and as a result, the end of credit availability to the housing market. The banks rejected the analysis even as they were quietly jettisoning those very securities from their own books.

A February 2 e-mail written by Dan Sparks, head of Goldman's mortgage department, warned superiors of looming losses on loans the firm had not yet been able to jettison. "We will take a write-down to some retained positions next week as the loan performance data from a few second lien sub-prime deals just came in (comes in monthly) and it is horrible," Sparks wrote. "The team is working on putting loans in the deals back to the originators (New Century, WAMU, and Fremont—all real counterparties) as there seem to be issues potentially including some fraud at origination, but resolution will take months and be contentious."

Less than a week later, another Goldman employee summarized the state of the market for subprime loans in general and

---

*The paper was entitled "How Resilient Are Mortgage Backed Securities to Collateralized Debt Obligation Market Disruptions?"

Fremont's in particular. An e-mail marked "Internal Only" three times, said: "Collateral from all Subprime originators, large and small, has exhibited a notable increase in delinquencies and defaults, however, deals backed by Fremont and Long Beach collateral have generally underperformed the most."

And the minutes of a March 7, 2007, meeting of the Firmwide Risk Committee at Goldman has Sparks declaring "game over" in mortgages. His talking points also noted an "accelerating meltdown for subprime lenders such as Fremont and New Century."

Nevertheless, by the end of that month, Goldman had packaged and sold to investors more than $1 billion in mortgage securities backed by Fremont loans. It had also placed internal bets against the same Fremont loans it was selling to its customers.

⇌

Sparks was certainly right about the game being over in March 2007. Investment banks were furiously pulling in warehouse lines, cutting off oxygen to the lenders once lauded as the driving force behind Wall Street's earnings. Borrowers who had been given risky loans and who had grown accustomed to refinancing their mortgages to take cash out of their homes suddenly found no replacement loans available to them, even at higher initial interest rates. Early payment defaults roared higher.

The machine that Wall Street had built was faltering, lenders that still had cash were receiving calls for it from investors. Option One Mortgage, H&R Block's captive lender, was getting buyback requests for hundreds of millions of dollars in loans. If the rate of early payment defaults kept rising, it would be only a matter of time before the firms collapsed under the crushing capital calls.

The problems were becoming clear enough, but few regulators seemed to notice the calamity in the making. Capitol Hill, for its part, was asleep. As the housing market rotted from the core, Ben Bernanke expressed his concern about inflationary pressures and Tim Geithner, president of the powerful New York Fed, sounded warnings on unregulated hedge funds.

Testifying before the Congressional Joint Economic Committee in March 2007, Bernanke, considered a scholar on central banking, said, "The impact on the broader economy and financial markets of the problems in the subprime market seems likely to be contained." And later that month, Paulson, the secretary of the Treasury who had recently run Goldman Sachs, echoed Bernanke's view that the mortgage crisis would not infect the overall economy or world financial markets.

"It looks to me like this housing issue is going to be contained," Paulson told members of Congress on March 28. Never mind that many of the most disastrous securities had been created by Goldman during the Paulson years.

Things were decidedly not contained at Fremont Investment and Loan, however. That month the company noted in a regulatory filing that the California Court of Appeals had ruled against it in a lawsuit that had been brought by the California insurance commissioner, the same regulator that had liquidated Fremont Indemnity just four years earlier. The commissioner had found that Fremont was selling adjustable-rate mortgages to subprime borrowers "in an unsafe and unsound manner that greatly increases the risk that borrowers will default on the loans or otherwise cause losses."

At the same time, Fremont was visited with a cease and desist order from the FDIC, a regulatory action that was the kiss of death for a financial institution. The FDIC enumerated fourteen problematic practices at Fremont, including operating without effective risk-management policies and with a large volume of poor-quality loans, and conducting business without sufficient capital or liquidity.

The laundry list of ills was so voluminous that it suggested that Fremont's bank examiners had, like Rip Van Winkle, been asleep for years. But the biggest blow to Fremont came in the FDIC's requirement that it shore up its capital and reserves to cover possible losses on its loans.

Fremont was in a bind. Investors knew the company could not

cut originations and generate enough capital to meet the FDIC's demands. Neither could Fremont raise money in the stock market since it was still battling with its auditor over its 2006 financial results.

Fremont began selling to investors loans that were languishing on its books.

In early April, New Century, another huge subprime lender, filed for bankruptcy. That same day, Fremont informed investors that its auditor, Grant Thornton, had resigned, the second accounting firm to reject Fremont in less than a year. Grant Thornton had found items that may have "materially affected the reliability" of the information they were given by Fremont management. The auditors also noted that the executives had failed to provide necessary information on a timely basis.

By the end of April it appeared only a matter of time before Fremont would sink beneath the waves. The company had, with little fanfare, sold nearly all of its subprime operations. Its employees sued Fremont, claiming that it had improperly filled employee retirement accounts with Fremont stock, which had cratered in value. In their suits, employees noted that James McIntyre, Fremont's chairman and the founder's son, had astutely sold $11 million of his stock during the summer of 2006. Fremont directors had sold $5.5 million in 2007. If Fremont was really a sound and suitable investment for the little people, why was management running for the hills?*

Fremont was certainly dying; its condition was terminal. Just as its mortgages had become a cancer on the communities it had supposedly served, the company itself was riddled with cancerous loans it was being forced to buy back. The patient would linger on life support for another year.

In April 2008, Fremont announced that it received default notices on over $3 billion of subprime mortgages it had originated in March 2007 and that it did not have the cash to buy back the

---

*The suit was the subject of settlement discussions in late 2010.

loans as promised. In fact, Fremont Investment and Loan did not even have the minimum of $250 million in net tangible book value it had agreed to maintain.

That month, with Fremont's stock in the cellar and its operations all but shuttered, the ratings agencies finally downgraded Fremont. They assigned the company's debt the ignominious status of junk.

Fremont filed for bankruptcy in 2008. As part of the proceedings, the California insurance commissioner sued to take control of the Ansel Adams photographs that had graced the company's headquarters for more than thirty years. When Christie's sold the prints at auction, they fetched $3.8 million. After an investigation determined that the photographs had belonged to Fremont's defunct insurance unit, the California commissioner moved to recover the auction proceeds. An investigation showed that the amazing Adams collection had been quietly transferred from the insurer to its parent in 1989 when James McIntyre fired his brother David and took over the company.

"We had no idea the prints existed until they were sold," Scott Pearce, a senior officer with the insurance commissioner's office, told the *San Fernando Valley Business Journal* in 2008.

After the bankruptcy was wrapped up, some vestiges of Fremont—mostly the rights to tax benefits generated by the company's massive losses—were taken over by a company called Signature Holdings.

James McIntyre is no longer involved in the company his father had founded forty-five years earlier.

EPILOGUE

I am extremely proud of my service to Fannie Mae and in other important dimensions of public service. I believe Barack Obama's candidacy for president of the United States is the most exciting and important of my lifetime. I would not dream of being a party to distracting attention from that historic effort.

—JAMES A. JOHNSON, resigning from the Obama advisory team, June 11, 2008

When Fremont and other subprime lenders began hurtling off the cliff in 2007, Jim Johnson, the former chief executive of Fannie Mae and architect of the public-private homeownership push, still enjoyed the respect of many in Washington and the business community.

After leaving Fannie Mae in 1999, Johnson had run the Kennedy Center for the Performing Arts in Washington and the prestigious Brookings Institution, a liberal think tank. Both positions gave him immense credibility in Washington's policy and cultural circles.

Meanwhile, Johnson's membership on the boards of Target Corp., the retailer, Goldman Sachs, and United Healthcare lent him prestige among corporate leaders. In 2001, he joined the Washington-based private equity firm, Perseus Partners, as vice chairman.

Under the terms of his exit from Fannie Mae, Johnson had

also secured a high-paying consulting gig with an annual pay of almost $400,000 in 2002. He also got a car and driver for himself and his wife, office space, and two employees at the expense of the company.

In 2006, however, Johnson was brushed by the accounting scandal that had erupted a year earlier at Fannie Mae. The OFHEO investigation into the company's bookkeeping tricks was published in May; among its conclusions—the improprieties had begun when Johnson was chief executive. The report did not name him as a perpetrator, however.

In the aftermath of the accounting scandal, Johnson reached out to his former company and offered to cut his consulting fees. By then they amounted to $600,000 a year, according to a report in the *Washington Post*. He also offered up his support staff and driver. "I should do my part to assist Fannie Mae's efforts to reduce expenditures at this difficult time," he had told one of the company's directors.

Unfortunately for Johnson, his goal of becoming Treasury secretary kept eluding him. He had played a major role in John Kerry's ill-fated presidential campaign in 2004, advising the candidate on cabinet members. This earned him support from prominent Democrats, as the *New York Times* reported in July. "Jim Johnson is entitled to anything he wants," one high-level official told the *Times*, "maybe the embassy in London or maybe Treasury secretary."

But the Kerry campaign faltered, as Mondale's had twenty years earlier, and Johnson's power base once again fell to Brookings, his corporate directorships, and his prodigious Rolodex, augmented by his membership in such exclusive policy clubs as American Friends of Bilderberg, the Hamilton Project, the Business Council, the Council on Foreign Relations, and the Trilateral Commission.

In 2007, with the economy headed toward disaster, the former chief executive of Fannie Mae could still pick up the phone and reach the nation's most powerful people. In January 2007, Johnson met with Timothy Geithner, the president of the New York Fed, and in June of that year, he spoke twice with Henry Paulson, the Treasury secretary, whose pay Johnson had set in his capacity as chairman of Goldman Sachs's compensation committee of the board. It is unclear what these discussions involved, but the subprime mess was already well under way when they took place.

Of course, Johnson's board duties at Goldman Sachs placed him at the pinnacle of Wall Street. But the position would also leave him dangerously close to the center of the subprime mortgage storm that was brewing even then.

In the fall of 2007, Johnson returned to his old playbook. It was time for another partnership, he said, in which the public sector and private industry would join hands for the greater good. A Blueprint for American Prosperity, designed to bolster America's cities, was put forward by Brookings in November 2007. Promotional materials surrounding the launch of the Blueprint sounded remarkably like the homeownership push made a dozen years earlier.

The Blueprint was "a multi-year initiative aimed at creating a new Federal partnership with state and local leaders and with the private sector to advance American prosperity," Johnson announced at its launch in Washington. "The ability of the United States to compete globally and to meet the great environmental and social challenges of the 21st century rests largely on the health, vitality and prosperity of the nation's major cities and metropolitan areas."

Many of the same figures were on hand for this launch who had been standing alongside Johnson twelve years earlier. Henry Cisneros, the former HUD director who had sat on the board of KB Home with Johnson and had overseen Clinton's National Partners in Homeownership a little more than a decade before, delivered the keynote address at the Blueprint's launch. Brookings created a Metropolitan Leadership Council to help promote the agenda; its members included Johnson, of course, but also executives from Goldman Sachs and Target.

But unlike the public-private partnership to promote homeownership, which gained traction quickly, the effort by the Brookings

crowd has been moribund. It ran smack into the economic meltdown.

⇔

The economic crisis of 2008 actually created the ultimate public-
private partnership. With the collapse in mid-March 2008 of Bear
Stearns, the scrappy but venerable investment bank, the government stepped in to help resolve a private failure. The Federal
Reserve Bank of New York, led by Geithner and joined by Paulson at Treasury, brokered a shotgun marriage of Bear Stearns to
JPMorgan Chase.

It was a sweetheart deal for JPMorgan Chase, but with the
taxpayer taking on $30 billion of toxic assets from Bear, the trans-
action was the ultimate collaboration with the taxpayer. It was
the first major demonstration that the government would not allow
a brokerage firm, whose reckless lending and leverage had sown
the seeds of its own destruction, to go bankrupt. Bear Stearns
executives had taken in all the profits of their disastrous practices
but when the due bill arrived for these activities, it was the taxpayers' obligation.

After Bear Stearns, six months of quiet ensued. Then came
the rapid-fire failures of Fannie Mae and Freddie Mac, Lehman
Brothers, and the American International Group. It is not yet
known how much these debacles will cost the American taxpayer,
but conservative estimates put the total in the hundreds of billions of dollars.

A dozen years after the Congressional Budget Office's Marvin
Phaup and June O'Neill had suggested that privatizing Fannie
Mae and Freddie Mac could reduce the risk of a costly taxpayer
bailout, that costly bailout occurred. And on Christmas Eve 2009,
Geithner, now the Treasury secretary of the United States, qui-
etly removed the $400 billion bailout caps on Fannie and Freddie.
It was clear that the taxpayers' bill for the mortgage finance com-
panies could soon exceed that amount.

In addition to beggaring the American people, the twin rescues of Fannie and Freddie made liars out of many people. First among them was Johnson, who had claimed that Fannie would never cost the taxpayers a dime. Barney Frank, Fannie's ardent supporter, was also proven wrong in his assessment that the company posed no threat to the public.

It wasn't until 2010, when Frank found himself in a relatively spirited contest for his congressional seat, that he spoke out with regret about his support for Fannie Mae. In August, Frank conceded that not every American should be a homeowner. The government should abolish Fannie and Freddie, he said.

⇌

Even as Fannie and Freddie sped toward insolvency in 2008, Jim Johnson held sway in Washington. No one seemed to connect him and his years at Fannie's helm with any of the problems that doomed the company. His ballooning of Fannie's balance sheet and mortgage portfolio, his successful battle to keep the company's capital cushion razor thin—all was forgotten.

It was a prime example of the short memories on Wall Street and the revolving door in Washington.

Paradoxically, it took the collapse of Countrywide Financial and the subsequent scrutiny brought to the company's practices for Johnson's reputation to be tarnished. His long and profitable relationship with Angelo Mozilo, the founder of the mortgage lender that became synonymous with subprime, became just too close for comfort during the election of 2008. Asked by Barack Obama to vet vice presidential candidates (always a bridesmaid, never a bride), Johnson was forced to resign from his advisory position when his cut-rate loans from Countrywide were disclosed. Once again, his hopes for running the Treasury Department were dashed.

But like any able teacher, Johnson's legacy lies in the people whose careers he touched and whose success he launched during his years at Fannie Mae. As head of Fannie Mae during the glory years, he taught many up-and-comers how to play the game and ensure the survival of their culture of self-interest. Many Johnson minions are deeply embedded in the nation's capital, proving once again that in Washington, failing at a job only serves to prepare for an even bigger post in the years to come.

It is indeed one of the most frustrating aspects of this story—the rise of subprime, the dereliction of duty by so many who participated in the mortgage mess. The cast of characters that helped create the mess continues to hold high positions or are holding jobs of even greater power.

Some examples: William Daley, White House chief of staff, served on the Fannie Mae board during the 1990s. Timothy Geithner, the relaxed regulator at the New York Federal Reserve Bank, became Treasury Secretary. Others include Tom Donilon, Fannie's longtime head of government affairs and a key political operative, who is now national security advisor to Obama. Thomas R. Nides, the Fannie Mae human resources executive who figured in the OFHEO investigation into earnings manipulations at the company, was nominated to the position of deputy secretary of state for management and resources in fall 2010. When the White House publicized both appointments, neither Donilon's nor Nides's years at Fannie Mae were mentioned.

⇌

Will a debacle like the credit crisis of 2008 ever happen again? Most certainly, because Congress decided against fixing the problem of too-big-to-fail institutions when it had its chance.

The law that Congress devised in response to the crisis was called the Dodd-Frank Wall Street Reform and Consumer Protection Act of 2010. It spanned more than fifteen hundred pages; Glass-Steagall, a law that protected consumers ably for sixty-six years, consisted of only thirty-four.

The irony of having two of the nation's most strident defenders of Fannie Mae sponsoring the new reform act was lost on few of those who knew the entire sordid Fannie story. And yet the law failed the most basic test—it did not insist that large and unmanageable institutions be cut down to size to alleviate their threats to taxpayers in the future. Nor did it increase the accountability of those running institutions that will need government assistance in the future.

The law was also silent on how to resolve the insolvent Freddie Mac and Fannie Mae.

At the end of 2010, as policymakers began to consider what to do with the beleaguered Fannie and Freddie, Barney Frank had this to say: "I think blaming Fannie and Freddie as a primary cause of the crisis is a mistake. Fannie and Freddie helped it get going, but there would have been people doing it without them."

⇌

Some of the key players in the years leading up to the financial crisis have left the scene but many are still in positions of power. Here is a list of where they are as of late 2010.

W. LANCE ANDERSON—cofounder of NovaStar, subprime lender that collapsed in 2008; now operating a property appraiser and providing banking services to low-income consumers.

RICHARD BAKER—former Louisiana Republican congressman and sometime antagonist of Fannie Mae; president of the Managed Funds Association, a lobbying group for hedge funds.

ROY BARNES—former governor of Georgia whose aggressive predatory lending law in 2002 was beaten back by the credit-rating agencies; lawyer in private practice.

LELAND BRENDSEL—former chairman of Freddie Mac; retired.

WILLIAM BRENNAN JR.—Atlanta Legal Aid official who helped Roy Barnes craft the best predatory lending law in the nation only to have it eviscerated by the credit-ratings agencies; retired in fall 2010.

MARC COHODES—short seller who targeted NovaStar; managing his own money and farming.

ANDREW CUOMO—director of HUD who urged Fannie and Freddie to finance more low-income mortgages; governor of the state of New York.

EDWARD DEMARCO—former Treasury staffer whose report on privatization of Fannie Mae had to be rewritten; acting director of Federal Housing Finance Authority, Fannie's and Freddie's regulator.

ARMANDO FALCON—head, Office of Federal Housing Enterprise, Fannie's beleaguered regulator from 1999 through 2005; chairman, Falcon Capital Advisors, an investment firm.

ROGER FERGUSON—former vice-chairman of the Federal Reserve Board of Governors who worked behind the scenes to water down bank capital requirements; chief executive of TIAA-CREF, the huge pension fund.

PETER FISHER—former Treasury official; head of fixed-income at BlackRock, Inc.

BARNEY FRANK—Democratic congressman from Massachusetts.

STEPHEN FRIEDMAN—former chairman of Goldman Sachs and former director of Fannie Mae; former chairman of the Federal Reserve Bank of New York; chairman of the President's Intelligence Oversight Board.

TIMOTHY GEITHNER—former president of New York Federal Reserve Bank and friend to banks and brokerage firms; U.S. Treasury secretary.

GARY GENSLER—former assistant secretary of the Treasury who came out against Fannie and Freddie in 2000; chairman of Commodity Futures Trading Commission.

ALAN GREENSPAN—former chairman of the Federal Reserve Board; economist and consultant.

SCOTT F. HARTMAN—cofounder of NovaStar, subprime lender that collapsed in 2008; founder of Credentia Group, a money management firm.

JIM JOHNSON—trustee emeritus at the Brookings Institution, director of Target, Goldman Sachs.

ANGELO MOZILO—founder of Countrywide Financial; settled SEC insider trading case without admitting or denying allegations. Paid $67.5 million but most was funded by Countrywide.

ALICIA MUNNELL—member of the Boston Fed team that wrote the 1992 study alleging racial bias in lending; Peter F. Drucker

Professor in Management Sciences at Boston College's Carroll School of Management.

PETER NICULESCU—Fannie Mae executive who worked with Goldman Sachs on Project Libra, a mortgage instrument designed to manipulate Fannie Mae's earnings; partner at CMRA, a risk-management firm providing consulting and litigation support services to financial institutions.

JUNE O'NEILL—former director, Congressional Budget Office; professor of economics at Baruch College, New York City.

PETER ORSZAG—author of flawed paper minimizing Fannie Mae's potential costs to the taxpayers; resigned as director of Office of Management and Budget in the Obama administration in July 2010. Joined Citigroup as vice-chairman.

ROBERT PEACH AND JOHN MCCARTHY—New York Federal Reserve Bank economists who wrote disastrous 2006 study concluding that there was no housing bubble; still there.

MARVIN PHAUP—former Congressional Budget Office researcher who was attacked for writing the 1996 study quantifying the cost of Fannie's and Freddie's government subsidies for the first time; professorial lecturer, George Washington University.

FRANKLIN D. RAINES—former chief executive of Fannie Mae; retired.

DAVID ROSENBLUM—Goldman Sachs executive who helped Fannie Mae manipulate its earnings through a mortgage instrument called Project Libra; still at the firm.

ROBERT RUBIN—former U.S. Treasury secretary who helped kill off Glass-Steagall and then became vice-chairman of Citigroup during its reckless lending years; Brookings Institution trustee and counselor to Centerview Partners, a hedge fund.

LARRY SUMMERS—former Treasury official who, at the suggestion of Fannie Mae, watered down the 1996 Treasury report on privatizing the company; resigned as director of the National Economic Council under Obama in September 2010.

DICK SYRON—former head of Boston Federal Reserve Bank when problematic guidelines regarding racial bias in lending were produced; terminated as chief executive of Freddie Mac when the government took over the company in 2008.

WALKER TODD—former researcher at Cleveland Fed who identified Senator Chris Dodd's role expanding the federal safety net to include brokerage firms and insurance companies; research fellow at American Institute for Economic Research.

ROBERT ZOELLICK—former Fannie Mae enforcer; president of the World Bank since July 2007.

AFTERWORD

When plunder becomes a way of life for a group of men living together in society, they create for themselves in the course of time a legal system that authorizes it and a moral code that glorifies it.

—FRÉDÉRIC BASTIAT,
nineteenth-century French economist
and writer

In the months since we finished writing *Reckless Endangerment,* policymakers have attempted to repair the damage to the nation's economy and financial system. The Dodd-Frank Wall Street Reform and Consumer Protection Act, passed in July 2010, called for hundreds of regulations that were designed to prevent another financial maelstrom. In addition, multiple homeowner-assistance programs have been launched to try to stem the foreclosure crisis.

And yet, these efforts, together with so many others, accomplished little. As 2011 drew to a close, foreclosures were rising as home prices continued to fall—values were down 31.2 percent from the April 2006 peak—banks were still on shaky financial footing, and unemployment was alarmingly high.

For most on Main Street, the government's response to the crisis added up to a whole lot of nothing.

Wall Street and the big financial institutions did better, of course. But the various rescues devised to save the nation's banks—at the peak, the Federal Reserve had committed almost $8 trillion to a series of programs, according to an analysis by Bloomberg News—contributed to a growing sense among many Americans that the institutions that perpetrated the crisis received massive amounts of relief while innocent investors and consumers, harmed by their deplorable practices, got stiffed.

This double standard was voiced most effectively by the widespread "Occupy Wall Street" movement that took hold in the fall of 2011 in a small park in lower Manhattan. It quickly spread to cities across the nation, and the Occupiers' message that banks should be held accountable for wrecking the economy reaped supportive commentary from both liberals and conservatives.

The failure by federal and state prosecutors to bring successful cases against major bank executives who played significant roles in the mortgage boom only fueled the view that there were two sets of rules in America: one for rich, powerful, and politically connected institutions and individuals, and one for the rest of us. By the end of 2011, only one senior-level mortgage official at a relatively large firm had been convicted and sentenced to prison: Lee Farkas, former chief executive of Taylor, Bean & Whitaker. Neither Farkas nor his company was a household name, however, and his conviction and thirty-year prison term were anomalies.

Angelo Mozilo, for example, the former head of Countrywide—itself one of a handful of companies most responsible for underwriting the poisonous loans that begat the foreclosure crisis—was cleared of wrongdoing by the Department of Justice in mid-2011. Federal prosecutors in Los Angeles announced that they were closing the investigation into Mozilo without bringing charges.

Mozilo also walked away from civil liability by paying a $22.5 million penalty in an insider trading case. Settling the matter with the Securities and Exchange Commission, Mozilo neither admitted nor denied the commission's allegations that he had sold almost $500 million worth of Countrywide shares during a period when he knew his company's business had grown increasingly toxic and unsustainable. When he sold his company to Bank of America in January 2008, Mozilo saddled the banking giant with a home-loan albatross, dragging it into a morass of litigation over improper underwriting, securitization, and foreclosure practices.

Although the Countrywide brand name was retired when its operations were subsumed into Bank of America, the infamy of Mozilo's company lived on during the burgeoning foreclosure crisis. Of all the major banks dealing with troubled borrowers, Bank of America gained the worst reputation among consumers, their advocates, and the Treasury Department because of its lackluster efforts to help modify delinquent loans.

One former employee at a loan workout unit at the bank described its practices when deposed by lawyers for Nevada's attorney general. He testified that employees working on Bank of America's consumer help lines were warned by superiors to conclude discussions with troubled borrowers within seven minutes or receive a reprimand. It's no wonder borrowers couldn't get any help.

Banks trying to foreclose on troubled borrowers were also found to have routinely broken the law by filing improper papers with the courts. Such documents were often obvious forgeries, or they misrepresented that the foreclosing institution had the right to seize a home because it held the security interest or note on the underlying property. By 2011 it had become clear that thousands of foreclosures had been commenced and completed based on phony documentation or hastily drawn legal papers. A loan-administration manager in the default document group of Wells Fargo Mortgage testified that he typically signed between 50 and 150 foreclosure documents a day; he also stated that he did not independently verify the information that he legally attested to.

Still, when state attorneys general cited these and other foreclosure abuses and asked the banks for restitution for borrowers, the nation's largest institutions worked overtime to ensure that any penalties against them would be nominal. In March 2012, state and federal officials struck a settlement with five large banks over their foreclosure abuses. The deal called for $26 billion in reparations, but only $5 billion of this was cash. The rest came in the form of monetary credits given to the banks in exchange for principal reductions and other help to troubled borrowers. Homeowners who were improperly foreclosed upon received $1.5 billion, amounting to less than $2,000 per person.

For many on Main Street, it was stunning that the same institutions that had brought the economy to the brink refused to own up to the damage their practices had done. Even more brazen were the attempts by these banks and their lobbyists to stymie many of the government's moves to reform lending practices. Contending that such reforms were preventing a recovery in the housing market or the economy, Wall Street banks, the Mortgage Bankers Association, major lenders, and other business groups rallied to prevent new rules that would protect against the kind of reckless lending and trading that almost felled our financial system.

One example is a rule required under the Dodd-Frank Act and put forward by the primary federal regulators. Designed to ensure that problematic home loans would not be placed into mortgage securities and sold off to unsuspecting investors, regulators proposed that banks issuing securities holding loans that did not meet certain quality requirements would have to keep 5 percent of the issue on their own books. This requirement, it was hoped, would remove the incentive for banks to issue securities filled with dubious loans because they'd be somebody else's problem as soon as they were sold.

Congress, under Dodd-Frank, had directed regulators to define high-quality loans that would be exempt from such risk-retention requirements, known as Qualified Residential Mortgages. But defining the characteristics of these loans became a battleground. Regulators proposed that only those loans for which borrowers had contributed 20 percent of the property's purchase price could be considered high quality and therefore sold off entirely to investors. Private mortgage insurers, who typically were required to insure any portion of a loan backed by Fannie or Freddie above an 80 percent loan-to-value ratio, were no longer thought to reduce default risk effectively enough to be included in the rule. After all, they had failed to provide independent reviews of the loans they had insured in the years leading up to the crisis and, in fact, had not paid out on many mortgages that subsequently failed.

After the risk-retention rule was proposed, mortgage insurers, banks, and their lobbyists fought back, saying that such a requirement was far too stringent and would hurt homeownership by shutting out those who could not cobble together a 20 percent down payment. The unholy alliances that drove the nation to crisis returned when more than forty consumer groups—lenders, realtors, and civil rights organizations—banded together and demanded a loosening of these rules. Once again regulators were being pressed to undermine the very law that Congress directed them to create and enforce. After rule makers at the FDIC and other regulators received letters signed by 44 senators and 282 members of the House of Representatives, and a group called the "Coalition for Sensible Housing Policy," the rule was sent back to the drawing board to be weakened.

It was déjà vu all over again. The industry was rolling out the tired homeownership bromides that Fannie Mae had perfected throughout the 1990s and 2000s: By enforcing reasonable lending standards, regulators would prevent minorities, first-time homebuyers, and low-income individuals from experiencing the dream of homeownership. They preferred to go back to the good old days of anything-goes lending when all you needed to get a mortgage was a pulse.

An equally concerted push against reform came from Wall Street. To reduce the risk that losses made by traders at big banks would require taxpayer bailouts, regulators proposed that these institutions spin off the units that make bets for the firm—known as proprietary trading. The Volcker Rule, as it was called, was an attempt to guarantee that insured deposits would not be used as gambling chits by firms that would then have to be rescued by the government if their bets went wrong. When the rule was finally written, after much backroom battling, it was far weaker than it had been at the outset. Even Paul Volcker, the esteemed former chairman of the Federal Reserve Board for whom the rule was named, called it a disappointment.

Both these efforts to water down reform showed that bankers viewed their profits—and the rich bonuses they would generate—as more important than the safety and soundness of the financial system. Moreover, these and other attempts to undermine commonsense rules demonstrated these institutions' profound arrogance as well as their refusal to learn from their mistakes.

For the most part, the Washington and regulatory response to these efforts was further coddling. The fact is, there had never been any appetite to pursue the bad actors in this drama with anything resembling a vengeance. Indeed, questionable bank practices were allowed to continue under the guise of protecting the financial system. Regulators seemed to equate hefty bank profits with a safe system; anything that pinched bank earnings was viewed with suspicion or as tough medicine to be administered only after the institutions had fully recovered from the disaster.

The extent of the regulators' kid-glove approach became clear in the so-called stress tests applied to banks in 2009 to assess their financial soundness. By no means rigorous, these tests seemed designed to let all but the weakest institutions pass as solvent. The tests analyzed banks' positions under two scenarios, best-case and adverse, but even when some banks blew through the worst-case figures, regulators did not force them to shore up their balance sheets. Even these banks were, according to regulators, just fine.

Rather than accept significantly higher capital for domestic institutions, Secretary of the Treasury Timothy F. Geithner argued that such rules were better left to the international capital standard setters that always met in Basel, Switzerland. That gave the banks another chance to meddle with the regulatory process to achieve their aims.

And so the largest banks were never forced to properly mark down their portfolios of imperiled second mortgages or home equity lines of credit. In 2012, well after these loans had fallen in value to either zero or pennies on the dollar, several of the big banks were still valuing them on their books at eighty cents on the dollar or more.

The institutions that had received hundreds of billions of dollars in support from the Federal Reserve throughout the crisis also did not report to investors on these inflows and the impact they had on the banks' operations. The SEC requires such disclosures to be included in the management discussion and analysis section of a company's financial reports, according to rules written after the savings and loan failures of the 1980s. The rules state that if any type of federal financial assistance has "materially affected or are reasonably likely to have a future material effect upon financial condition or results of operations, the management discussion and analysis should provide disclosure of the nature, amounts and effects of such assistance."

In the summer of 2011, this routine failure by regulators to hold banks accountable for accurate and honest financial statements wrought havoc again when the European sovereign debt debacle took hold. Once more, U.S. banks claimed that their exposures to the woes of these indebted nations were immaterial, just as many had done in the midst of the subprime debacle.

But in spite of the fact that these institutions' disclosures had not proven reliable in the years leading up to or following the credit crisis, regulators did nothing to make the banks produce a more comprehensive or detailed analysis of their exposures to the burgeoning disaster in Europe. Investors were asked to rely on the banks' reassurances, the old "trust me" response. Unwilling to do so, they abandoned bank stocks in droves, pushing them to historically low valuations by the end of 2011.

For investors, selling the shares of firms whose accounting

they didn't trust was about the only way to hold these institutions accountable in the aftermath of the crisis. But such actions did not satisfy those who recognized that the punishment did not even come close to matching the crime.

Given the U.S. government's central role in the crisis, it is perhaps no coincidence that there were so few investigations and prosecutions of wrongdoers by the end of 2011. Since so many high-powered players involved in the questionable practices that led to the crisis hailed from Washington, digging too deeply into the mess would have touched some mighty participants. Regulatory participation in the practices that led to the crisis—allowing poisonous lending and freeing up balance sheets to greater risk taking—meant hard-nosed government investigators could very easily have wound up probing themselves, their friends, or those in their communities. As a result, many wondered whether the government really wanted to identify who did what during this episode.

The situation stands in stark contrast to what happened after hundreds of banks failed in the savings and loan debacle in the late 1980s and early 1990s. Back then, the FBI opened 5,500 investigations into bank fraud and wrongdoing, based on regulatory referrals. These investigations generated 1,100 prosecutions, resulting in convictions and jail time for 839 bank officials and executives.

Fast-forward to recent times. In the spring of 2008, just as the credit storm was gathering, the FBI decided to scale back a plan to assign more field agents to mortgage-fraud investigations. That summer, just weeks before the collapse of Fannie Mae, Freddie Mac, Lehman Brothers, and AIG, the Department of Justice also rejected calls to create a task force devoted to mortgage-related cases, leaving these complex matters understaffed and poorly funded.

Two years into the crisis, Congress passed the Fraud Enforcement and Recovery Act, allocating $165 million to the Justice Department and the FBI for new financial crisis cases. Later on, lawmakers quietly rescinded all but $30 million of that allocation.

Accountability was also AWOL for the massive damage done to investors by the credit ratings agencies. Four years after the crisis erupted, the ratings agencies were still operating under the same conflicted business models, and yet their debt grades continued to hold sway among investors. While the SEC had been directed to reduce investor reliance on ratings, and thereby cut the influence these companies had, the regulatory agency did nothing on that front.

For those interested in keeping the ratings agencies honest, the only hope was that private litigation would hold them accountable. At the end of 2011, three lawsuits had survived the ratings agencies' legal attempts to shut them down. For years, the agencies had defended themselves against legal attacks by maintaining that they were journalists issuing opinions, entitled to the same First Amendment protections relied upon by *The New York Times* and other news outlets. Never mind that their access to insider data disqualified them as external observers. Many hoped that the lawsuits wending their way through the courts after the mortgage meltdown would overcome this specious argument once and for all.

Among the more disappointing aspects of the regulatory response to the financial crisis was its absolute denial on the topic of Fannie Mae and Freddie Mac. Since the fall of 2008, when both companies were placed into conservatorship and became the taxpayers' responsibility, they once again became central to an inflamed political debate. On one side were those desiring a safe and sound mortgage financing system; on the other were those who would use the companies' size and reach to drive social policy—even if doing so would violate the legal obligations of the government overseer charged with protecting taxpayers from excessive losses. The conservator, as this overseer is known, must take necessary actions to limit losses at Fannie and Freddie, conserve the value of their assets, and try to restore them to strong financial footing.

In February 2011, two years after his inauguration and months after promising to provide a road map to restructure Fannie Mae and Freddie Mac, President Barack Obama announced his proposals for the GSEs. They were not prescriptive; rather, they were suggestions of three possible approaches to resolving the mortgage finance system that the GSEs had dominated for so long. There were no explicit demands for regulations or legislation to create meaningful disclosure rules that would allow investors to properly price the riskiest mortgages, no standards directing mortgage loan servicers to treat borrowers or investors fairly. Instead, the Treasury Department offered a list of options. The first would create a fully private mortgage finance system in which the only guaranteed loans would be offered by the Federal Housing Administration, the Department of Agriculture, and the Department of Veterans Affairs. The second option would augment the government's role by creating a taxpayer backstop for private mortgages in case of a future credit crisis. The final option would largely privatize the mortgage market but would also reinsure some mortgage securities.

None of the options was explicitly endorsed by the White House. "We are going to start the process of reform now, but we are going to do it responsibly and carefully so that we support the recovery and the process of repair of the housing market," said Secretary Geithner. It would take three more years, he argued, for the housing market to recover and another two to three years for the government to agree on the future of the government's role in mortgage financing.

Washington had again demonstrated its lack of interest in leading the market toward any real resolution, citing the risks of further harming the housing market. After the release of the Obama administration's proposals, Representative Barney Frank told Bloomberg News that Republicans and Democrats would strike a deal by the end of the year. As 2011 drew to a close, it was clear that Washington would rather put off any leadership decisions regarding Fannie and Freddie until some unknown date in the future, presumably after the 2012 presidential election.

Some in Washington have expressed an interest in weaning markets away from the dominance of Fannie and Freddie by increasing the insurance fees the GSEs charge to guarantee mortgages, requiring borrowers to increase their down payments to at least 10 percent and increasing the amount of private mortgage insurance borrowers purchase to reduce the size of the loans that Fannie and Freddie could guarantee. Only eight months after the GSE loan limits of $729,500 expired and were reduced to $625,500, realtors, mortgage bankers, and others began to press Congress to raise those limits again, lest more borrowers be shut out of homeownership.

With the ongoing damage to the economy exacted by the housing crisis, Fannie and Freddie, already the recipients of more than $180 billion of taxpayer support since being taken over, have once again become political tools. Congress defined the rules of the conservator, intended to limit taxpayer losses and prevent the companies from becoming the vehicle for further social engineering in housing policy. Still, with neither Democratic nor Republican legislators willing to make hard decisions that could conceivably be used as election issues, there was no legislation put forward to redefine the role of the GSEs.

As a result, the Obama administration had few choices to effect reductions of mortgage principal by banks that might stanch the bleeding in the housing market. Rather than the executive or legislative branch taking responsibility for its inaction, the convenient approach was to press the GSE conservator to allow Fannie and Freddie to write down principal amounts owed on the mortgages they insure, thus increasing the potential cost to the taxpayers and violating the law that directs the conservator's actions.

With little accomplished to repair the mortgage finance system and with collusion among regulators, legislators, and the financial industry having returned in full force, it appears likely, barring another mess in the immediate future, that Washington will follow a "path of least resistance." As a result, the financial system of tomorrow will be only marginally changed from the system which led us to the precipice. Once again, consumers and the public interest will come in a distant second place to the greed and desires of a handful of self-appointed financial elites.

Nowhere was this more evident than in legislators' refusal to address the problems raised by too-big-to-fail institutions. While Dodd-Frank created a way for regulators to resolve big and politically interconnected institutions, it did nothing to cut these banks down to a manageable size. Before the crisis there were two such institutions—Fannie Mae and Freddie Mac. Afterward, there were many more, including all the large banks that investors knew would be bailed out if they got into trouble.

The 1933 Glass-Steagall Act, the Depression-era law that had protected consumers from rapacious bankers for almost seven decades, was just thirty-four pages long. Dodd-Frank and its thousands of pages would probably not protect consumers for even ten years.

⇌

While many of those involved in creating the crisis remained in powerful positions, one central player decided to bow out in late November 2011. Barney Frank, the bombastic and unceasing supporter of Fannie Mae, announced that he would not seek reelection in 2012. After thirty years in Congress, he said he hoped to teach and write in retirement. "It's been a privilege to fight for the quality of people's lives, but I'm ready to put a little more quality into my own life," Frank told reporters.

As for Jim Johnson, the former Fannie Mae chief executive and architect of the homeownership push, we still haven't heard from him. But according to those who know him, he remains a man-about-town in Washington and on Wall Street. Livin' large and livin' the dream.

NOTES ON SOURCES

This book is based on interviews and conversations conducted by Josh and me over more than a decade.

Josh's conversations took place to inform his ongoing analysis of the GSEs, the structured finance market, the subprime mortgage industry, and national housing policy, which he provided to institutional clients and policymakers. My interviews occurred over the same period, when I was a reporter at *Forbes* magazine and then the *New York Times*.

Most of *Reckless Endangerment* relies upon original reporting conducted by Josh and me on parallel paths beginning in the mid-1990s and continuing into 2010. Josh's notes from meetings and conversations with participants in Washington, Basel, and Wall Street and my own files, which I created in January 2007 and kept adding to, now consist of well over a thousand pages of interviews on the subject.

Missing from our mountain of notes, alas, is any commentary

from James A. Johnson, the former chief executive of Fannie Mae. We requested interviews with Johnson in e-mails and phone calls over a period of five months; we never received a response.

We have identified as many of our sources as we could whenever we could. But some sources with firsthand knowledge of these events were fearful of being named, given that many of the participants remain in positions of power. We granted these individuals anonymity but were careful to verify their comments and recollections with others who were also on hand.

Josh and I made extensive use of the *Congressional Record*, the Report of the Special Examination of Fannie Mae published in May 2006 by the Office of Federal Housing Enterprise Oversight, corporate financial filings, documents produced under the Freedom of Information Act, civil lawsuits, and public records of regulatory actions. Thanks to the wonderful folks at The Center for Responsive Politics, we were also able to dig into lobbying records that they have aggregated online. The records filed by the Fannie Mae Foundation revealed a great deal about how the company used its financial muscle to burnish its image and expand its influence.

We also delved into the trove of documents produced to Congress as it pursued inquiries into the financial crisis, including materials made public during hearings before the Permanent Subcommittee on Investigations, the Committee on Oversight and Government Reform, and the Financial Crisis Inquiry Commission.

Where we have relied upon the work of other fine reporters, such as those at the *New York Times*, Bloomberg, the *Wall Street Journal*, the *Washington Post*, the *Washingtonian*, the *American Banker*, *Inside Mortgage Finance*, and *Mortgage Finance Daily* we have credited them in the text.

We are especially grateful for the time our sources devoted to helping us with our project. Any errors in this text are ours entirely.

ACKNOWLEDGMENTS

Because this book is the product of decades of experience for both Josh and me, there are many people to thank. But before we do, we would like to express our gratitude to the people who supported our efforts to produce an honest history of the financial panic of 2008. They are our agents, Lynn Chu and Glen Hartley of Writers Representatives, Steve Rubin, president and publisher of Henry Holt and Company, Paul Golob, the editorial director of Times Books, Alex Ward, editorial director of book development at the *New York Times*, and Ellis Levine, the lawyer who vetted our work. A special thanks goes to our editor, Serena Jones, who provided crucial guidance and perspective as our manuscript progressed.

As a reporter at the *New York Times*, my acknowledgments must begin with my colleagues there—the best news-gathering organization on the planet. I am especially grateful to those who have given me a front row seat for thirteen of the most extraordinary years in financial history. Joe Lelyveld, Bill Keller, and Glenn Kramon brought me to the paper but I have also received immense support over the years from Jill Abramson, John Geddes, Winnie O'Kelley, and David McCraw. Larry Ingrassia, the editor of the Business section, has also been an ally. Colleagues that I have had special fun collaborating with are Louise Story, Geraldine Fabrikant, Andrew Martin, and Don Van Natta. I am also grateful to current and former researchers at the *Times*, Donna Anderson, Alain Delaqueriere, Jack Begg, and Jack Styczynski.

Arthur O. Sulzberger Jr.'s commitment to tough and fearless journalism has been instrumental to my work.

Among my editors at the *Times*, none was more supportive than Tim O'Brien, one of the great defenders of the journalistic faith. Tim never let me down and took up my battles with an alacrity and determination that are characteristic of . . . a fighting Irishman.

Nobody taught me more about how to commit journalism than the late James Walker Michaels, the brilliant editor of *Forbes* magazine during its heyday. Thank you, Jim, for everything.

The people who have helped me to understand the origins and depths of this crisis are legion. Some are mentioned in these pages. Those who are not: Edward Kane, professor of economics at Boston College; my old friend and money manager Bill Fleckenstein; Sylvain Raines and Ann Rutledge, resident geniuses at R & R Consulting; and April Charney, Jacksonville (Fla.) Legal Aid's queen of the foreclosure defense practice. Others who helped me see the role banks played during and after the crisis are Mike Kratzer, Kevin Byers, O. Max Gardner III, Howard Rothbloom, Chris Whalen, Robert Arvanitis, Janet Tavakoli, Harry Fath, and the inimitable Joan McCullough.

A special thanks to Steve Eisman for being even more skeptical than I am and for sharing his insights and outrage.

Two fellow journalists who illuminated the dark corners of this mess are Bob Ivry and the late Mark Pittman, both from Bloomberg. Thank you for your amazing work.

There is no greater blessing than the friends who are always there for you. Ann Wengler, Mara Covell, Laurel Cutler, Susan

Armenti, Caroline Frank, Mary Beth Sullivan, Charlotte Lipson, Lew and Fern Lowenfels, Judy Resnick, Ina Saltz, Shad Rowe, Manjeet Kripalani, Judy Dobrzynski—thanks for years of wonderful and nourishing friendships.

My mother, who died before this book was finished, gets a big hug. Do they have bookstores in heaven? Thanks to my dad for helping me see that I could do whatever I set my mind to. Jack and Gretta, Mimi and Fritz—you believed in me all those years ago. Thank you for that.

Finally, special appreciation and recognition are due to my treasured sister.

—GCM

This book is, at its core, about the roots and underpinnings of a financial crisis we continue to live through. Below that surface, and underlying the text, are the values and ideals of the many friends, family, and other civically minded people I've been blessed to have known and been inspired by. Many I have had the good fortune to know, work with, and learn from directly; others have taught me by example from afar. Given the nature of this work, many of those who continue to serve in government and public policy have asked not to be named. Still, I am obliged to acknowledge those, many of them career government employees and others as current and former Hill staffers, who have offered their best years in service of the public trust. It is these, often career public servants, who best represent the ideals of good government and most clearly demonstrate that service is a virtuous calling, divorced from partisan politics.

I also owe a debt of gratitude to the numerous friends, colleagues, and clients who have offered me guidance, shared their knowledge, given professional, personal, and emotional support in following my beliefs, digging for the facts, and tying the pieces together. The list is long and, again, many would choose not to be named. I would be remiss were I not to thank the partners of

Oppenheimer & Co., where I spent the 1990s, for teaching me the business and demonstrating an example of what a partnership and integrity on Wall Street can and should look like. I also thank my former partners and friends Vincent Daniel, Jeff Spetalnick, and Michael Corasaniti for their friendship, camaraderie, and support.

Over the many years that I have been raising warnings, I have come into contact with many wonderful people. While some of them are identifiable as Democrats or Republicans, all of them have demonstrated a love for this country that supersedes partisan politics. I thank Alex Pollock for his historical insights, and David Kotok for his abiding friendship and for introducing me to a wonderful group of fishing buddies, including Barry Ritholtz and Chris Whalen, all of whom live their professional lives with the same values as they do their personal lives. Thank you Ann Rutledge and Sylvain Raynes for your ongoing friendship and assistance. I want to thank Rob Johnson who, through his intelligence and personal integrity, has demonstrated a valuable vision of a post-partisan world. To that end I must also thank Rich Sokolow for his friendship and for introducing me to two organizations, The All-Stars Project and IndependentVoting.org, which promote a better vision of our future.

I must also thank the many fine journalists I have met over the years. There is no group of people more vital to protecting the public interest. I especially thank the fine professionals I have had the privilege to work with at Bloomberg, CNBC, the *New York Times*, the *Wall Street Journal*, the *American Banker*, MSNBC, the Huffington Post, and New Deal 2.0. Among those I thank are Bob Ivry, Kathleen Hays, Jody Shenn, Matt Miller, Brian Sullivan, Dawn Kopecki, Bethany McLean, Charles Gasparino, Susan Webber, and Shahien Nasiripour. I must also honor the memory of Mark Pittman, a journalist without peer, whose friendship, unyielding sense of justice, and belief in the power of the pen pushed me forward when, like Sisyphus, I grew weary.

I also offer a great debt of gratitude to the Hon. Stanley Sporkin, whose patriotism, unflinching integrity, and belief in the value of independent research have been of great comfort and support for almost a decade. Thanks are due to the late Charles Kindleberger for the time he shared with me and his encouragement to continue to pursue "what could be the last chapter in the revised edition of *Manias, Panics, and Crashes*." His foresight, at a time when few could recognize the dangers of the reckless path our policymakers were treading, provided the greatest motivation to pursue this story.

Lastly and perhaps most importantly, I want to thank the many friends and family members who offered advice, support, and encouragement during the process of writing this book. While there are too many friends and family to name, I do want to thank my mother, my late father, and also Beth, Marianne, Garth, and Jodi; your advice and support have been invaluable and I love you all for putting up with me.

—J.R.

INDEX

GRETCHEN MORGENSON is a business reporter and columnist at the *New York Times*, where she also serves as assistant business and financial editor. She was awarded the Pulitzer Prize in 2002 for her "trenchant and incisive" coverage of Wall Street. Prior to joining the *Times* in 1998, she worked as a broker at Dean Witter in the 1980s, and as a reporter at *Forbes*, *Worth*, and *Money* magazines. She lives with her husband and son in New York City.

JOSHUA ROSNER is a managing director at the independent research consultancy Graham Fisher and Company and advises regulators and institutional investors on housing and mortgage-finance–related issues.